OXFORD READINGS IN PHILOSOPHY

CONSEQUENTIALISM AND ITS CRITICS

D1254920

CONSEQUENTIALISM AND ITS CRITICS

EDITED BY
SAMUEL SCHEFFLER

OXFORD UNIVERSITY PRESS

*This book has been printed digitally and produced in a standard specification
in order to ensure its continuing availability*

OXFORD
UNIVERSITY PRESS

Great Clarendon Street, Oxford OX2 6DP

Oxford University Press is a department of the University of Oxford.
It furthers the University's objective of excellence in research, scholarship,
and education by publishing worldwide in

Oxford New York

Auckland Cape Town Dar es Salaam Hong Kong Karachi
Kuala Lumpur Madrid Melbourne Mexico City Nairobi
New Delhi Shanghai Taipei Toronto
With offices in
Argentina Austria Brazil Chile Czech Republic France Greece
Guatemala Hungary Italy Japan South Korea Poland Portugal
Singapore Switzerland Thailand Turkey Ukraine Vietnam

Oxford is a registered trade mark of Oxford University Press
in the UK and in certain other countries

Published in the United States
by Oxford University Press Inc., New York

Introduction and selection © Oxford University Press 1988

ISBN 978-0-19-875073-4

Printed and bound in Great Britain by
CPI Antony Rowe, Chippenham and Eastbourne

CONTENTS

CONTENTS

INTRODUCTION

THE dispute between consequentialism and its opponents grows out of a deep puzzle about our moral ideas. The puzzle that fuels the dispute concerns an apparent conflict between the canons of rationality that we most naturally apply and the moral values we most confidently affirm.

Consequentialism in its purest and simplest form is a moral doctrine which says that the right act in any given situation is the one that will produce the best overall outcome, as judged from an impersonal standpoint which gives equal weight to the interests of everyone. Somewhat more precisely, we may think of a consequentialist theory of this kind as coming in two parts. First, it gives some principle for ranking overall states of affairs from best to worst from an impersonal standpoint, and then it says that the right act in any given situation is the one that will produce the highest-ranked state of affairs that the agent is in a position to produce. Obviously, there can be as many different theories of this type as there are criteria for ranking overall outcomes. One thing they all share, however, is a very simple and seductive idea: namely, that so far as morality is concerned, what people ought to do is to minimize evil and maximize good, to try, in other words, to make the world as good a place as possible.

On the face of it, this idea, which lies at the heart of consequentialism, seems hard to resist. For given only the innocent-sounding assumption that good is morally preferable to evil, it seems to embody the principle that we should maximize the desirable and minimize the undesirable, and that principle seems to be one of the main elements of our conception of practical rationality. Anyone who resists consequentialism seems committed to the claim that morality tells us to do less good than we are in a position to do, and to prevent less evil than we are in a position to prevent. And this does not sound nearly as plausible.

Nevertheless, consequentialism has implications that appear to conflict sharply with some of our most firmly held moral convictions, and the dispute between consequentialism and its opponents concerns the appropriate response to this fact. Consequentialists typically argue that, appearances to the contrary notwithstanding, our common-sense moral values can, in one way or another, be reconciled with consequentialist principles, up to a point at least. And to the extent that such reconciliation is impossible, the appropriate conclusion is that common-sense morality is irrational and needs revision. Non-consequentialists, by contrast, typically argue that consequentialism can at best be reconciled not with our actual values, but only with their simulacra. To reflect our actual values, they claim, a moral view must include what have recently come to be called *agent-relative* elements, which are incompatible with consequentialism. And, they add, since our actual values have a more secure place in human thought and practice than any abstract conception of moral rationality that conflicts with them, the appropriate conclusion is that a moral view with agent-relative elements is to be preferred to a consequentialist view. Over the years, various refinements have been offered on behalf of each of these positions, and the debate has become increasingly sophisticated. But the basic underlying disagreement remains substantially unchanged.

The most familiar version of consequentialism is utilitarianism, which in its classical form says that the best state of affairs from among any set is the one that contains the greatest net balance of aggregate human pleasure or happiness or satisfaction. This view has been subject to three particularly influential objections. The first, which is represented within this volume by the selection from John Rawls's book *A Theory of Justice*, is that utilitarianism gives no direct weight to considerations of justice or fairness in the distribution of goods. Provided that net aggregate satisfaction is maximized, in other words, utilitarianism is indifferent as to how satisfactions and dissatisfactions are distributed among distinct individuals. So if overall satisfaction will be maximized under an arrangement in which goods and resources are channelled to people whose circumstances are already comfortable, while other people are allowed to languish in abject poverty, then that arrangement is precisely the one that utilitarianism will recommend. Or if the total happiness can be maximally increased by denying freedom to a few, then that again is what utilitarianism will require. Utilitarians standardly reply to these charges by pointing out that, given certain plausible empirical assumptions, it will almost never in fact be the case that a radically inegalitarian distribution of resources or liberties will produce the greatest attainable sum of satisfaction. However, this reply leaves critics unpersuaded. For since it makes the importance of distributive considerations entirely dependent on their efficacy in promoting maximum satisfaction, it both denies their intrinsic moral significance and requires them to be set aside if ever and whenever their efficacy lapses.

The second objection that has been very influential is that utilitarianism requires people to do *whatever* act will, in a given situation, produce the best available outcome overall, and, as Nagel emphasizes in 'War and Massacre', this may mean doing something quite horrible. If the only way to prevent ten murders is to commit one yourself, then utilitarianism would appear to require that you do just that. Or suppose that your country is waging a just war, and that an enemy agent you have captured tells you that he has planted a bomb in an area crowded with civilians and that, unless defused, it will soon go off, killing many people. Suppose that there is not enough time to conduct a general search for the bomb, and that all of your attempts to get the agent to reveal its location are unsuccessful. Suppose, however, that you have captured him with his family, and that by torturing his small child in front of him you could eventually destroy his resolve and get him to give you the information. Utilitarianism seems to imply not only that you may but that you *must* torture the child. These implications and others like them strike many people as entirely unacceptable.

The third objection to utilitarianism claims that it is an excessively demanding moral theory, because it seems to require that one neglect or abandon one's own pursuits whenever one could produce even slightly more good in some other way. Nor, it seems, is this an empty demand, for in a world as full of human suffering and misery as this one, only those with an extraordinary degree of moral self-confidence will be prepared to claim that there is no possible way they could do any more good for the world than by doing exactly what they are already doing. So utilitarianism seems very demanding, and while most people would agree that morality may sometimes require great sacrifices, many regard as excessive the idea that one may never devote time and energy to one's own pursuits unless there is no other way in which one could produce more good overall. Indeed, in the selection by Bernard Williams that is included in this book, he argues with great force that the demands of utilitarianism are so extreme as to undermine the *integrity* of the individual agent.

These are powerful objections, and many of the people who find them compelling also find themselves drawn away from utilitarianism and toward a non-consequentialist view. Non-consequentialist views may or may not agree with consequentialist theories in holding that there is some legitimate way of ranking overall states of affairs from best to worst. Even if they do, however, and even if they think that the impersonal evaluation of outcomes often affects the rightness or wrongness of actions, they nevertheless typically deviate in two important ways from the second part of the simple consequentialist account, which holds that the right act in any given situation is the one that will produce the best outcome overall. First, they maintain that there are occasions on which one may be forbidden to do something, even if doing that thing would have the best overall outcome. Perhaps the prohibited act would involve doing something horrible to someone. Or perhaps it wouldn't, but there is nevertheless some other act that one is under an obligation to perform. Second, they maintain that even on those occasions when one is not positively forbidden to do the thing that would have the best outcome overall, one is not always required to do it either. *Sometimes* one may be so required, but quite often it is up to the individual. Morality, they say, leaves people some freedom of choice, and this means that there are times when one may do what would produce the best results overall if one wants to, but one may also do something else instead.

These two points may be summed up by saying that even when non-consequentialists believe that it makes sense to rank overall outcomes from best to worst, they also typically believe both in *agent-relative constraints* (or *deontological* constraints, as they are often called), which sometimes prohibit the performance of acts that would have optimal results, and in *agent-relative permissions*, which sometimes make the performance of such acts optional.[1] The agent relativity of these constraints and permissions consists in the fact that their application to individual agents is not based on or supported by any appeal to what would be best from an impersonal standpoint. Of course, to those non-consequentialists who do not accept the impersonal evaluation of overall outcomes at all, the moral principles governing human action are exclusively agent-relative.

For the sake of simplicity, I will from now on use the term 'agent-relative moralities' to refer to non-consequentialist views that include both agent-relative constraints and agent-relative permissions. However, as I will later emphasize, this should not be taken to exclude the possibility of a moral view that includes one of these two agent-relative elements but not the other. Agent-relative moralities seem attractive to people who find the three objections to utilitarianism compelling. For since such moralities include agent-relative constraints, they do not insist that one must always perform that act, however horrible, that will produce the best overall results. Since they include agent-relative permissions, they do not insist that one may devote time and energy to one's own projects and commitments only when there is no other way in which one could do more good overall. And although their conceptions of distributive justice vary, depending on their detailed content, none of them is committed to sacrificing a person's welfare or liberty whenever doing so would maximize net aggregate satisfaction.

Consequentialists, however, argue that, in order to avoid the difficulties encountered by simple utilitarianism, it is not necessary to accept a version of agent-relative morality. Those objections, they say, can also be accommodated within a broadly consequentialist framework. Although there is disagreement among

---

[1] In my book *The Rejection of Consequentialism*, and in my paper 'Agent-Centred Restrictions, Rationality, and the Virtues', which is included in this volume, I refer to agent-relative constraints as *agent-centred restrictions*. And instead of agent-relative permissions I speak of an *agent-centred prerogative*.

consequentialists about how best to do this, the following suggestions are representative.

To a large extent, utilitarianism's vulnerability on the issue of distributive justice can be attributed to the specific way in which it evaluates outcomes. Given any two outcomes with different totals of aggregate satisfaction, in other words, utilitarianism will always say that the outcome with the higher total is better, even if satisfaction is distributed very unequally in that outcome and much more equally in the other, and even if the difference in total satisfaction between the two outcomes is small. Many consequentialists would agree that this is an implausible way of evaluating outcomes, but would insist that the natural solution is to substitute a principle of evaluation that is more sensitive to distributive concerns, rather than abandoning consequentialism altogether. As Scanlon points out in 'Rights, Goals, and Fairness', there are at least two ways to accommodate distributive concerns in the evaluation of outcomes. One is by giving extra weight to the interests of those who are worst off, so that the satisfaction of their interests counts disproportionately in determining what the best outcome would be in any given situation. The other is by treating distributive equality as a good in itself, which must be considered along with factors like net aggregate satisfaction in determining the value of an overall outcome.

The more egalitarian variants of consequentialism suggested by these criteria of evaluation could avoid much of the criticism that has been directed at utilitarianism under the heading of 'distributive justice'. However, they would still require that one must do whatever is necessary to produce the best overall outcome in any situation, and even to produce an egalitarian outcome it may be necessary to harm someone. To the extent that this willingness to harm people in order to produce the best overall results is part of what has prompted the traditional objection about distributive justice, that objection merges with the second of our three criticisms of utilitarianism, which is that the view may sometimes require doing horrible things to people.

In the case of that objection and the third one, which claims that utilitarianism is excessively demanding, it cannot be said that they arise in response to a feature of utilitarianism that is not shared by consequentialist theories more generally. For what in fact prompts both of them is the requirement always to promote the best overall outcome, and that requirement is a feature of all simple consequentialist theories. Thus these two objections raise fundamental questions for consequentialists, and there is a deep division within consequentialist thought about how best to respond to them. All consequentialists agree that, despite initial appearances, consequentialism itself supports presumptions against trying to promote the overall good either by doing horrible things to people, or by abandoning the projects and commitments one cares most about. For such things are almost always counter-productive in consequentialist terms. Indeed, most sophisticated consequentialists would say that one ought to cultivate in oneself, and to encourage in others, strong motivational aversions both to inflicting harms and to abandoning the people and projects one cares most about. However, it is hard to deny that there may be *some* occasions when inflicting a harm or abandoning one's projects really would have the best results in consequentialist terms. In these situations, one will produce less than optimal results if one is guided by the consequentialist presumption or motivated by the consequentialist aversion. It is in the discussion of these situations that the division in consequentialist thought emerges most clearly.

Some consequentialists say, as Peter Railton does in 'Alienation, Consequentialism, and the Demands of Morality', that the right thing to do in these cases is, as always, to perform the act that will produce the best overall outcome. Of course, they add, one may not be able to bring oneself to do this if one's aversion to the relevant type of act is strong. So one may in fact do the wrong thing in these situations. But this need not be grounds for blame or regret, since it may still be desirable from a consequentialist point of view that one should have such an aversion. For if one did not, one might do even less good overall in the long run. Without a strong general aversion to harming others, for example, one might be tempted to inflict harms not only when that would produce optimal results, but also when it would merely secure some personal advantage. And while the ideal arrangement might be to have an aversion to harming that was felt in all and only those cases where harming was non-optimal, this may not be a psychologically realistic possibility for human beings. In other words, even the best motivations that human beings can realistically have—the motivations that will lead them to produce the most net good in the long run—may also cause them to do the wrong thing in consequentialist terms on at least some occasions. If so, we should still encourage the development of the best possible motivations, and we should not blame well-motivated people when they cannot bring themselves to do the right thing. Neither, however, should we flinch from that description of the situation: the thing they cannot bring themselves to do is the *right* thing.

Other consequentialists, including those traditionally called 'rule utilitarians', take a different view of these situations. They say that, unless perhaps the result would be very bad indeed, the right thing to do is to continue to act in accordance with the relevant presumptions and aversions, even though this means doing less good than one could in these cases. For, they argue, while consequentialist reasoning determines what presumptions are justified and what motivations should be encouraged, these presumptions and motivations then take priority over case-by-case consequential calculation in situations where they apply. Scanlon argues in his paper that *rights* can best be understood on a 'two-tier' model of this general kind.

Each of these responses represents a development within consequentialist thought that goes beyond the simplest formulations of the view. Each narrows the gap between consequentialism and our everyday moral intuitions. Neither one, however, is without its critics. Some people feel that the first response treats the inability to harm others or to abandon one's commitments, whenever doing so would produce impersonally optimal results, as a human weakness to which, unfortunately, certain concessions must be made. And this they regard as morally perverse. The second response, meanwhile, is thought by some to constitute an intrinsically unstable compromise, which tries to occupy a non-existent middle ground between the first response on the one hand and an explicitly agent-relative morality on the other.

Nevertheless, the appeal of consequentialism persists, largely because the simple idea that animates it continues to seem so plausible, and because the air of paradox surrounding agent-relative moralities remains so difficult to dispel convincingly. As is evident from our discussion of the three objections to utilitarianism, agent-relative moralities have great intuitive appeal when applied to particular cases. Indeed, most would agree that they mirror everyday moral thought much more closely than consequentialism does. However, it also remains true that there are times when such moralities forbid us to do as much good as we could, or to prevent as much evil. Most starkly, they insist that there are occasions when one must not violate an agent-relative constraint even if that is the only way to prevent more widespread violation of the very same constraint by others. And while these prohibitions may seem intuitively appropriate when applied to individual cases, there is nevertheless, as Robert Nozick emphasizes in the selection from *Anarchy, State, and Utopia* that is reprinted here, a distinct appearance of irrationality about them. For if the violation of agent-relative constraints is morally so objectionable, it seems extremely odd, on the surface at least, for morality to tell us that we *must not* act in such a way as to minimize their occurrence. The seeming conflict between our moral intuitions and a very natural and familiar conception of rationality seems here to be exhibited in its purest and most extreme form.

This apparent conflict has led many philosophers to conclude that the most defensible moral view is probably some form of consequentialism. Many others, however, are not so sure. Although the more sophisticated forms of consequentialism do narrow the gap between it and common-sense morality, even they do not accept common-sense morality's understanding of itself. They agree with our everyday moral intuitions only to the extent that those intuitions can be reconstrued or reinterpreted in conse-quentialist terms. Since many philosophers have greater faith in our agent-relative intuitions than in the more abstract considera-tions that favour consequentialism, many hope that it will prove possible to explain those intuitions in a way that eliminates any appearance of irrationality.

As far as agent-relative or deontological constraints are con-cerned, it is natural to suppose that such an explanation would proceed by identifying something about people that makes it inappropriate to victimize them in the ways that the constraints prohibit. For when we think about a case in which, say, we would have to harm one person in order to prevent five comparable harms to others, it seems intuitively that there is something about our potential victim that makes it wrong to go ahead. Nozick develops this line of thought by suggesting that to harm the one person would be to overlook the fact that he is a separate person who has just one life to lead, and who would receive no compensating benefit for being harmed. This sounds initially quite plausible, but upon reflection it is puzzling. For it is presumably true of the five other people that each of them is also a separate person with just one life to lead, who would receive no compensating benefit for being harmed. So why should we be forbidden to inflict one uncompensated harm in order to prevent even more such harms? This is a general puzzle about *victim-based* explanations of agent-relative constraints. Any appeal to the victim's possession of some morally significant property seems unable to explain why we may not victimize one person who has that property in order to prevent the victimization of an even larger number of people, each of whom has the very same property. Such appeals simply make all violations of the constraints look equally objectionable, and thus seem to count in favour of allowing, rather than prohibiting, the minimization of total overall violations. They therefore seem to provide no support for agent-relative constraints, whose function is precisely to forbid minimization.

The most obvious alternative to a victim-based explanation of deontological constraints is an *agent-based* explanation. Such an explanation would point to something about the agent that makes it wrong for him to victimize one person even in order to minimize the total overall number of comparable victimizations. The advantages and the limits of an agent-based approach are examined by Nagel in the selection from his book *The View from Nowhere*.

Despite the attempts that have been made to explain deontological constraints, strong doubts about the rationality of agent-relative morality continue to be expressed, as the papers in this volume by Derek Parfit and by me indicate.[2] Yet there also continue to be many philosophers who are not willing either to abandon our deeply felt agent-relative convictions, or to submit them to consequentialist reinterpretation, whatever the difficulties of providing them with a satisfactory rationale may be. At this point, the debate can appear to have reached an impasse, with some people insisting that agent relativity is irrational, and others insisting that our agent-relative intuitions are so strong and so securely entrenched that it would be a mistake to abandon them. When a discussion reaches an apparent stand-off of this kind, it is natural to wonder whether a different approach to the issues might help to break the deadlock.

One idea, which I have developed elsewhere,[3] takes as its starting-point the observation that the sharpest apparent conflicts between agent-relative morality and our conception of rationality are generated by agent-relative *constraints*: by the claim that one is morally forbidden to minimize morally objectionable activity. Accordingly, the suggestion is, we should examine the possibility of a moral view that departs from consequentialism to the extent of incorporating agent-relative permissions, but not to the extent of accepting agent-relative constraints. On a view of this kind, one would be always permitted but not always required to perform the act that would produce the best available outcome overall.

The possibility of breaking the impasse between consequentialism and agent-relative moralities by introducing moral views with alternative structures is also investigated by Amartya Sen in 'Rights and Agency'. Sen first proposes for consideration three conceptual innovations. The first is to construe rights as features of states of affairs which must be taken into account in consequential evaluation. The second involves making certain finer-grained distinctions among different types of agent relativity. And the third consists in allowing rankings of overall outcomes to vary from person to person. If we take these ideas seriously, he suggests, we will see that the range of possible moral views widens

---

[2] Parfit discusses the issues raised in his paper at greater length in *Reasons and Persons*. Further relevant discussion appears in the July 1986 issue of *Ethics*, which is devoted to papers about Parfit's book and to replies by him.

[3] In *The Rejection of Consequentialism*.

considerably. In particular, there are some previously neglected views that may plausibly combine elements of consequentialism with elements of traditional agent-relative moralities.

The introduction of new moral structures does not represent the only way of trying to break the apparent deadlock between consequentialism and agent-relative morality. An alternative is to argue, as Philippa Foot does in 'Utilitarianism and the Virtues'. that there is something wrong with the terms in which the issue is usually posed. Foot's idea is that any difficulty there may appear to be in resolving the disagreement results from the acceptance of an illicit assumption, without which consequentialism loses all of its appeal. The assumption she identifies as the source of the trouble is the assumption that it always makes sense to talk about the goodness or badness of the state of affairs produced by an action. Without this assumption, she argues, consequentialists could not even succeed in formulating the charge that agent-relative moralities sometimes tell us, irrationally, to choose a worse state of affairs over a better. And, she claims, the assumption is false: expressions like 'best state of affairs' make sense only in certain limited contexts where the virtue of benevolence provides them with a sense. As against this, I argue in my paper that the seeming irrationality of agent-relative morality does not depend on the assumption that it always makes sense to talk about better and worse states of affairs. The difficulty goes deeper than that, I claim; it is not so easy to dispel the appearance of a conflict between agent-relative constraints, on the one hand, and a very powerful and familiar conception of rationality on the other.

There is, finally, a third strategy for trying to break the impasse between consequentialism and agent-relative moralities. Rather than proposing a moral theory with a different structure or attempting to show that the appearance of deadlock rests on a mistake, one may instead attempt a reconciliation between the two views. Sophisticated forms of consequentialism often claim to have achieved just such a reconciliation, but those sympathetic to agent-relative moralities have rarely been convinced that the claim was warranted. In 'The Authority of the Moral Agent', Conrad Johnson tries to exploit a legal analogy suggested by the work of

Rawls and Joseph Raz to arrive at a more fully satisfying reconciliation.

CONCLUSION

The dispute between consequentialism and agent-relative morality has been fierce and persistent because each side can claim, with apparent justice, that the other clashes with an aspect of our thought that seems very difficult to give up. Consequentialism appears willing to discard or reinterpret intuitive moral judgements in which we have great confidence. Agent-relative moralities vindicate those judgements; however, they also seem to clash with a conception of rationality that was not invented by consequentialists, but rather occupies a secure place in practical deliberation more generally. In the end, each reader must decide whether any of the ideas discussed in this volume represents a satisfactory solution to the problem.

S.S.

1

CLASSICAL UTILITARIANISM

JOHN RAWLS

THERE are many forms of utilitarianism, and the development of the theory has continued in recent years. I shall not survey these forms here, nor take account of the numerous refinements found in contemporary discussions. My aim is to work out a theory of justice that represents an alternative to utilitarian thought generally and so to all of these different versions of it. I believe that the contrast between the contract view and utilitarianism remains essentially the same in all these cases. Therefore I shall compare justice as fairness with familiar variants of intuitionism, per-fectionism, and utilitarianism in order to bring out the underlying differences in the simplest way.[1] With this end in mind, the kind of utilitarianism I shall describe here is the strict classical doctrine which receives perhaps its clearest and most accessible formulation in Sidgwick. The main idea is that society is rightly ordered, and therefore just, when its major institutions are arranged so as to achieve the greatest net balance of satisfaction summed over all the individuals belonging to it.[2]

We may note first that there is, indeed, a way of thinking of society which makes it easy to suppose that the most rational

John Rawls: 'Classical Utilitarianism', from *A Theory of Justice* (Harvard University Press, 1971/Oxford University Press 1972), pp. 22–7. Copyright © 1971 by the President and Fellows of Harvard College. Reprinted by permission of the publishers.

[1] ['Justice as fairness' is Rawls's name for his own theory of justice, which is presented as a version of social contract theory—Ed.]

[2] I shall take H. Sidgwick's *The Methods of Ethics* as summarizing the development of utilitarian moral theory. Book III of his *Principles of Political Economy* (London, 1883) applies this doctrine to questions of economic and social justice, and is a precursor of A. C. Pigou, *The Economics of Welfare* (London: Macmillan, 1920).

conception of justice is utilitarian. For consider: each man in realizing his own interests is certainly free to balance his own losses against his own gains. We may impose a sacrifice on ourselves now for the sake of a greater advantage later. A person quite properly acts, at least when others are not affected, to achieve his own greatest good, to advance his rational ends as far as possible. Now why should not a society act on precisely the same principle applied to the group and therefore regard that which is rational for one man as right for an association of men? Just as the well-being of a person is constructed from the series of satisfactions that are experienced at different moments in the course of his life, so in very much the same way the well-being of society is to be constructed from the fulfilment of the systems of desires of the many individuals who belong to it. Since the principle for an individual is to advance as far as possible his own welfare, his own system of desires, the principle for society is to advance as far as possible the welfare of the group, to realize to the greatest extent the comprehensive system of desire arrived at from the desires of its members. Just as an individual balances present and future gains against present and future losses, so a society may balance satisfactions and dissatisfactions between different individuals. And so by these reflections one reaches the principle of utility in a natural way: a society is properly arranged when its institutions maximize the net balance of satisfaction. The principle of choice for an association of men is interpreted as an extension of the principle of choice for one man. Social justice is the principle of rational prudence applied to an aggregative conception of the welfare of the group.[3]

This idea is made all the more attractive by a further consideration. The two main concepts of ethics are those of the right and the good; the concept of a morally worthy person is, I believe, derived from them. The structure of an ethical theory is, then, largely determined by how it defines and connects these two basic notions. Now it seems that the simplest way of relating them is taken by teleological theories: the good is defined independently

---

[3] On this point see also D. P. Gauthier, *Practical Reasoning* (Oxford: Clarendon Press, 1963), pp. 126 f.

from the right, and then the right is defined as that which maximizes the good.[4] More precisely, those institutions and acts are right which of the available alternatives produce the most good, or at least as much good as any of the other institutions and acts open as real possibilities (a rider needed when the maximal class is not a singleton). Teleological theories have a deep intuitive appeal since they seem to embody the idea of rationality. It is natural to think that rationality is maximizing something and that in morals it must be maximizing the good. Indeed, it is tempting to suppose that it is self-evident that things should be arranged so as to lead to the most good.

It is essential to keep in mind that in a teleological theory the good is defined independently from the right. This means two things. First, the theory accounts for our considered judgements as to which things are good (our judgements of value) as a separate class of judgements intuitively distinguishable by common sense, and then proposes the hypothesis that the right is maximizing the good as already specified. Second, the theory enables one to judge the goodness of things without referring to what is right. For example, if pleasure is said to be the sole good, then presumably pleasures can be recognized and ranked in value by criteria that do not presuppose any standards of right, or what we would normally think of as such. Whereas if the distribution of goods is also counted as a good, perhaps a higher-order one, and the theory directs us to produce the most good (including the good of distribution among others), we no longer have a teleological view in the classical sense. The problem of distribution falls under the concept of right as one intuitively understands it, and so the theory lacks an independent definition of the good. The clarity and simplicity of classical teleological theories derives largely from the fact that they factor our moral judgements into two classes, the one being characterized separately while the other is then connected with it by a maximizing principle.

Teleological doctrines differ, pretty clearly, according to how the conception of the good is specified. If it is taken as the realization of human excellence in the various forms of culture, we

---

[4] Here I adopt W. K. Frankena's definition of teleological theories in *Ethics* (Englewood Cliffs, NJ: Prentice Hall, Inc., 1963). p. 13.

have what may be called perfectionism. This notion is found in Aristotle and Nietzsche, among others. If the good is defined as pleasure, we have hedonism; if as happiness, eudaimonism, and so on. I shall understand the principle of utility in its classical form as defining the good at the satisfaction of desire, or perhaps better, as the satisfaction of rational desire. This accords with the view in all essentials and provides, I believe, a fair interpretation of it. The appropriate terms of social co-operation are settled by whatever in the circumstances will achieve the greatest sum of satisfaction of the rational desires of individuals. It is impossible to deny the initial plausibility and attractiveness of this conception.

The striking feature of the utilitarian view of justice is that it does not matter, except indirectly, how this sum of satisfactions is distributed among individuals any more than it matters, except indirectly, how one man distributes his satisfactions over time. The correct distribution in either case is that which yields the maximum fulfilment. Society must allocate its means of satisfaction whatever these are, rights and duties, opportunities and privileges, and various forms of wealth, so as to achieve this maximum if it can. But in itself no distribution of satisfaction is better than another except that the more equal distribution is to be preferred to break ties.[5] It is true that certain common-sense precepts of justice, particularly those which concern the protection of liberties and rights, or which express the claims of desert, seem to contradict this contention. But from a utilitarian standpoint the explanation of these precepts and of their seemingly stringent character is that they are those precepts which experience shows should be strictly respected and departed from only under exceptional circumstances if the sum of advantages is to be maximized.[6] Yet, as with all other precepts, those of justice are derivative from the one end of attaining the greatest balance of satisfaction. Thus there is no reason in principle why the greater gains of some should not compensate for the lesser losses of others; or, more importantly, why the violation of the liberty of a few might not be made right by the greater good shared by many. It simply happens that under

[5] On this point see Sidgwick, *The Methods of Ethics*, pp. 416 f.
[6] See J. S. Mill, *Utilitarianism*, ch. 5, last two pars.

most conditions, at least in a reasonably advanced stage of civilization, the greatest sum of advantages is not attained in this way. No doubt the strictness of common-sense precepts of justice has a certain usefulness in limiting men's propensities to injustice and to socially injurious actions, but the utilitarian believes that to affirm this strictness as a first principle of morals is a mistake. For just as it is rational for one man to maximize the fulfilment of his system of desires, it is right for a society to maximize the net balance of satisfaction taken over all of its members.

The most natural way, then, of arriving at utilitarianism (although not, of course, the only way of doing so) is to adopt for society as a whole the principle of rational choice for one man. Once this is recognized, the place of the impartial spectator and the emphasis on sympathy in the history of utilitarian thought is readily understood. For it is by the conception of the impartial spectator and the use of sympathetic identification in guiding our imagination that the principle for one man is applied to society. It is this spectator who is conceived as carrying out the required organization of the desires of all persons into one coherent system of desire; it is by this construction that many persons are fused into one. Endowed with ideal powers of sympathy and imagination, the impartial spectator is the perfectly rational individual who identifies with and experiences the desires of others as if these desires were his own. In this way he ascertains the intensity of these desires and assigns them their appropriate weight in the one system of desire the satisfaction of which the ideal legislator then tries to maximize by adjusting the rules of the social system. On this conception of society separate individuals are thought of as so many different lines along which rights and duties are to be assigned and scarce means of satisfaction allocated in accordance with rules so as to give the greatest fulfilment of wants. The nature of the decision made by the ideal legislator is not, therefore, materially different from that of an entrepreneur deciding how to maximize his profit by producing this or that commodity, or that of a consumer deciding how to maximize his satisfaction by the purchase of this or that collection of goods. In each case there is a single person whose system of desires determines the best allocation of limited means. The correct decision is essentially a question of efficient administration. This view of social co-operation is the consequence of extending to society the principle of choice for one man, and then, to make this extension work, conflating all persons into one through the imaginative acts of the impartial sympathetic spectator. Utilitarianism does not take seriously the distinction between persons.

2

CONSEQUENTIALISM AND INTEGRITY*

BERNARD WILLIAMS

1. THE STRUCTURE OF CONSEQUENTIALISM

NO one can hold that everything, of whatever category, that has value, has it in virtue of its consequences. If that were so, one would just go on for ever, and there would be an obviously hopeless regress. That regress would be hopeless even if one takes the view, which is not an absurd view, that although men set themselves ends and work towards them, it is very often not really the supposed end, but the effort towards it on which they set value—that they travel, not really in order to arrive (for as soon as they have arrived they set out for somewhere else), but rather they choose somewhere to arrive, in order to travel. Even on that view, not everything would have consequential value; what would have non-consequential value would in fact be travelling, even though people had to think of travelling as having the consequential value, and something else—the destination—the non-consequential value.

If not everything that has value has it in virtue of consequences, then presumably there are some types of thing which have non-consequential value, and also some particular things that have such value because they are instances of those types. Let us say, using a traditional term, that anything that has that sort of value, has *intrinsic* value.[1] I take it to be the central idea of consequen-

Bernard Williams, from *Utilitarianism: For and Against*, ed. Smart and Williams (Cambridge University Press, 1973), pp. 82–118. Reprinted by permission of the publisher.

* This is not the title of the original printing.

[1] The terminology of things 'being valuable', 'having intrinsic value', etc., is not meant to beg any questions in general value-theory. Non-cognitive theories, such as Smart's, should be able to recognize the distinctions made here.

tialism that the only kind of thing that has intrinsic value is states of affairs, and that anything else that has value has it because it conduces to some intrinsically valuable state of affairs.

How much, however, does this say? Does it succeed in distinguishing consequentialism from anything else? The trouble is that the term 'state of affairs' seems altogether too permissive to exclude anything: may not the obtaining of absolutely anything be represented formally as a state of affairs? A Kantian view of morality, for instance, is usually thought to be opposed to consequentialism, if any is; at the very least, if someone were going to show that Kantianism collapsed into consequentialism, it should be the product of a long and unobvious argument, and not just happen at the drop of a definition. But on the present account it looks as though Kantianism can be made instantly into a kind of consequentialism—a kind which identifies the states of affairs that have intrinsic value (or at least intrinsic moral value) as those that consist of actions being performed for duty's sake.[2] We need something more to our specification if it is to be the specification of anything distinctly consequentialist.

The point of saying that consequentialism ascribes intrinsic value to states of affairs is rather to *contrast* states of affairs with other candidates for having such value: in particular, perhaps, actions. A distinctive mark of consequentialism might rather be this, that it regards the value of actions as always consequential (or, as we may more generally say, derivative), and not intrinsic. The value of actions would then lie in their causal properties, of producing valuable states of affairs; or if they did not derive their value in this simple way, they would derive it in some more roundabout way, as for instance by being expressive of some motive, or in accordance with some rule, whose operation in society conduced to desirable states of affairs. (The lengths to which such indirect derivations can be taken without wrecking the point of consequentialism is something we shall be considering later.[3])

[2] A point noted by Smart, p. 13. [All of Williams's references to J. J. C. Smart are to Smart's essay 'An Outline of a System of Utilitarian Ethics', in *Utilitarianism: For and Against*, pp. 3–74—Ed.]

[3] [Williams is referring here to a section of his essay that is not reprinted in this volume—Ed.]

To insist that what has intrinsic value is states of affairs and not actions seems to come near an important feature of consequentialism. Yet it may be that we have still not hit exactly what we want, and that the restriction is now too severe. Surely *some* actions, compatibly with consequentialism, might have intrinsic value? This is a question which has a special interest for utilitarianism, that is to say, the form of consquentialism concerned particularly with happiness. Traditionally utilitarians have tended to regard happiness or, again, pleasure, as experiences or sensations which were related to actions and activity as effect to cause; and, granted that view, utilitarianism will indeed see the value of all action as derivative, intrinsic value being reserved for the experiences of happiness. But that view of the relations between action and either pleasure or happiness is widely recognized to be inadequate. To say that a man finds certain actions or activity pleasant, or that they make him happy, or that he finds his happiness in them, is certainly not always to say that they induce certain sensations in him, and in the case of happiness, it is doubtful whether that is ever what is meant. Rather it means such things (among others) as that he enjoys doing these things for their own sake. It would trivialize the discussion of utilitarianism to tie it by definition to inadequate conceptions of happiness or pleasure, and we must be able to recognize as versions of utilitarianism those which, as most modern versions do, take as central some notion such as *satisfaction*, and connect that criterially with such matters as the activities which a man will freely choose to engage in. But the activities which a man engages in for their own sake are activities in which he finds intrinsic value. So any specification of consequentialism which logically debars action or activity from having intrinsic value will be too restrictive even to admit the central case, utilitarianism, so soon as that takes on a more sophisticated and adequate conception of its basic value of happiness.

So far then, we seem to have one specification of consequentialism which is too generous to exclude anything, and another one which is too restrictive to admit even the central case. These difficulties arise from either admitting without question actions among desirable states of affairs, or blankly excluding all actions from the state of affairs category. This suggests that we shall do better by looking at the interrelations between states of affairs and actions.

It will be helpful, in doing this, to introduce the notion of the *right* action for an agent in given circumstances. I take it that in any form of direct consequentialism, and certainly in act-utilitarianism, the notion of the right action in given circumstances is a maximizing notion:[4] the right action is that which out of the actions available to the agent brings about or represents the highest degree of whatever it is the system in question regards as intrinsically valuable—in the central case, utilitarianism, this is of course happiness. In·this argument, I shall confine myself to direct consequentialism, for which 'right action' is unqualifiedly a maximizing notion.

The notion of the right action as that which, of the possible alternatives, maximizes the good (where this embraces, in unfavourable circumstances, minimizing the bad), is an objective notion in this sense, that it is perfectly possible for an agent to be ignorant or mistaken, and non-culpably ignorant or mistaken, about what is the right action in the circumstances. Thus the assessment by others of whether the agent did, in this sense, do the right thing, is not bounded by the agent's state of knowledge at the time, and the claim that he did the wrong thing is compatible with recognizing that he did as well as anyone in his state of knowledge could have done.[5] It might be suggested that, contrary to this, we have already imported the subjective conditions of action in speaking of the best of the actions *available to him*: if he is ignorant or misinformed, then the actions which might seem to us available to him were not in any real sense available. But this would be an exaggeration; the notion of availability imports some, but not all, kinds of subjective condition. Over and above the question of actions which, granted his situation and powers, were physically not available to him, we might perhaps add that a course of action was not really available to an agent if his historical, cultural, or psychological situation was such that it could not possibly occur to him. But it is scarcely reasonable to extend the notion of

---

[4] Cf. Smart's definition, p. 45.
[5] In Smart's terminology, the 'rational thing': pp. 46–7.

unavailability to actions which merely did not occur to him; and surely absurd to extend it to actions which did occur to him, but where he was misinformed about their consequences.

If then an agent does the right thing, he does the best of the alternatives available to him (where that, again, embraces the least bad: we shall omit this rider from now on). Standardly, the action will be right in virtue of its causal properties, of maximally conducing to good states of affairs. Sometimes, however, the relation of the action to the good state of affairs may not be that of cause to effect—the good state of affairs may be constituted, or partly constituted, by the agent's doing that act (as when under utilitarianism he just enjoys doing it, and there is no project available to him more productive of happiness for him or anyone else).

Although this may be so under consequentialism, there seems to be an important difference between this situation and a situation of an action's being right for some non-consequentialist reason, as for instance under a Kantian morality. This difference might be brought out intuitively by saying that for the consequentialist, even a situation of this kind in which the action itself possesses intrinsic value is one in which the rightness of the act is derived from the goodness of a certain state of affairs—the act is right *because* the state of affairs which consists in its being done is better than any other state of affairs accessible to the agent; whereas for the non-consequentialist it is sometimes, at least, the other way round, and a state of affairs which is better than the alternatives is so because it consists of the right act being done. This intuitive description of the difference has something in it, but it needs to be made more precise.

We can take a step towards making it more precise, perhaps, in the following way. Suppose S is some particular concrete situation. Consider the statement, made about some particular agent

In S, he did the right thing in doing A.   (1)

For consequentialists, (1) implies a statement of the form

The state of affairs P is better than any other state of affairs accessible to him.   (2)

Here a state of affairs being 'accessible' to an agent means that it is a state of affairs which is the consequence of, or is constituted by, his doing an act available to him (for that, see above); and P is a state of affairs accessible to him only in virtue of his doing A.[6]

Now in the exceptional case where it is just his doing A which carries the intrinsic value, we get for (2)

> The state of affairs which consists in his doing A is better than any other state of affairs accessible to him.   (3)

It was just the possibility of this sort of case which raised the difficulty of not being able to distinguish between a sophisticated consequentialism and non-consequentialism. The question thus is: if (3) is what we get for consequentialism in this sort of case, is it what a non-consequentialist would regard as implied by (1)? If so, we still cannot tell the difference between them. But the answer in fact seems to be 'no'.

There are two reasons for this. One reason is that a non-consequentialist, though he must inevitably be able to attach a sense to (1), does not have to be able to attach a sense to (3) at all, while the consequentialist, of course, attaches a sense to (1) only because he attaches a sense to (3). Although the non-consequentialist is concerned with right actions—such as the carrying out of promises—he may have no general way of comparing states of affairs from a moral point of view at all. Indeed, we shall see later, and in greater depth than these schematic arguments allow, that the emphasis on the necessary comparability of situations is a peculiar feature of consequentialism in general, and of utilitarianism in particular.

A different kind of reason emerges if we suppose that the non-consequentialist does admit, in general, comparison between states of affairs. Thus, we might suppose that some non-consequentialist would consider it a better state of things in which more, rather than fewer, people kept their promises, and kept them for non-consequentialist reasons. Yet consistently with that he could accept, in a particular case, all of the following: that X

---

[6] 'Only' here may seem a bit strong: but I take it that it is not an unreasonable demand on an account of his doing *the* right thing in S that his action is uniquely singled out from the alternatives. A further detail: one should strictly say, not that (1) implies a statement of the form (2), but that (1) implies *that there is* a true statement of that form.

would do the right thing only if he kept his promise; that keeping his promise involve (or consist in) doing A; that several other people would, as a matter of fact, keep their promises (and for the right reasons) if and only if X did not do A. There are all sorts of situations in which this sort of thing would be true: thus it might be the case that an effect of X's doing A would be to provide some inducement to these others which would lead them to break promises which otherwise they would have kept. Thus a non-consequentialist can hold both that it is a better state of affairs in which more people keep their promises, and that the right thing for X to do is something which brings it about that fewer promises are kept. Moreover, it is very obvious what view of things goes with holding that. It is one in which, even though from some abstract point of view one state of affairs is better than another, it does not follow that a given agent should regard it as his business to bring it about, even though it is open to him to do so. More than that, it might be that he could not properly regard it as his business. If the goodness of the world were to consist in people's fulfilling their obligations, it would by no means follow that a given agent should regard it as his business to bring it about, even though it is open to him to do so. More than that, it might be that he could not properly regard it as his business. If the goodness of the world were to consist in people's fulfilling their obligations, it would by no means follow that one of my obligations was to bring it about that other people kept their obligations.

Of course, no sane person could really believe that the goodness of the world just consisted in people keeping their obligations. But that is just an example, to illustrate the point that under non-consequentialism (3) does not, as one might expect, follow from (1). Thus even allowing some actions to have intrinsic value, we can still distinguish consequentialism. A consequentialist view, then, is one in which a statement of the form (2) follows from a statement of the form (1). A non-consequentialist view is one in which this is not so—not even when the (2)-statement takes the special form of (3).

This is not at all to say that the alternative to consequentialism is that one has to accept that there are some actions which one should always do, or again some which one should never do, *whatever the consequences*: this is a much stronger position than any involved, as I have defined the issues, in the denial of consequentialism. All that is involved, on the present account, in the denial of consequentialism, is that with respect to some type of action, there are some situations in which that would be the right thing to do, even though the state of affairs produced by one's doing that would be worse than some other state of affairs accessible to one. The claim that there is a type of action which is right *whatever the consequences* can be put by saying that with respect to some type of action, assumed as being adequately specified, then *whatever* the situation may (otherwise) be, that will be the right thing to do, *whatever* other state of affairs might be accessible to one, however much better it might be than the state of affairs produced by one's doing this action.

If that somewhat Moorean formulation has not hopelessly concealed the point, it will be seen that this second position—the *whatever the consequences* position—is very much stronger than the first, the mere rejection of consequentialism. It is perfectly consistent, and it might be thought a mark of sense, to believe, while not being a consequentialist, that there was no type of action which satisfied this second condition: that if an adequate (and non-question-begging) specification of a type of action has been given in advance, it is always possible to think of some situation in which the consequences of doing the action so specified would be so awful that it would be right to do something else.

Of course, one might think that there just *were* some types of action which satisfied this condition; though it seems to me obscure how one could have much faith in a list of such actions unless one supposed that it had supernatural warrant. Alternatively, one might think that while logically there was a difference between the two positions, in social and psychological fact they came to much the same thing, since so soon (it might be claimed) as people give up thinking in terms of certain things being right or wrong whatever the consequences, they turn to thinking in purely consequential terms. This might be offered as a very general proposition about human thought, or (more plausibly) as a sociological proposition about certain situations of social change, in which utilitarianism (in particular) looks the only coherent alternative to a dilapidated set of values. At the level of language, it is worth noting that the use of the word '*absolute*' mirrors, and perhaps also assists, this association: the claim that no type of action is 'absolutely right'—leaving aside the sense in which it means that the rightness of anything depends on the value-system of a society (the confused doctrine of relativism)—can mean either that no type of action is right-whatever-its-consequences, or, alternatively, that 'it all depends on the consequences', that is, in each case the decision whether an action is right is determined by its consequences.

A particular sort of psychological connection—or, in an old-fashioned use of the term, a 'moral' connection—between the two positions might be found in this. If people do not regard certain things as 'absolutely out', then they are prepared to start thinking about extreme situations in which what would otherwise be out might, exceptionally, be justified. They will, if they are to get clear about what they believe, be prepared to compare different extreme situations and ask what action would be justified in them. But once they have got used to that, their inhibitions about thinking of everything in consequential terms disappear: the difference between the extreme situations and the less extreme presents itself no longer as a difference between the exceptional and the usual, but between the greater and the less—and the consequential thoughts one was prepared to deploy in the greater it may seem quite irrational not to deploy in the less. *A fortiori*, someone might say: but he would have already had to complete this process to see it as a case of *a fortiori*.

One could regard this process of adaptation to consequentialism, moreover, not merely as a blank piece of psychological association, but as concealing a more elaborate structure of thought. One might have the idea that the *unthinkable* was itself a moral category; and in more than one way. It could be a feature of a man's moral outlook that he regarded certain courses of action as unthinkable, in the sense that he would not entertain the idea of doing them: and the witness to that might, in many cases, be that they simply would not come into his head. Entertaining certain alternatives, regarding them indeed as *alternatives*, is itself something that he regards as dishonourable or morally absurd.

But, further, he might equally find it unacceptable to consider what to do in certain conceivable situations. Logically, or indeed empirically conceivable they may be, but they are not to him morally conceivable, meaning by that that their occurrence as situations presenting him with a choice would represent not a special problem in his moral world, but something that lay beyond its limits. For him, there are certain situations so monstrous that the idea that the processes of moral rationality could yield an answer in them is insane: they are situations which so transcend in enormity the human business of moral deliberation that from a moral point of view it cannot matter any more what happens. Equally, for him, to spend time thinking what one would decide if one were in such a situation is also insane, if not merely frivolous.

For such a man, and indeed for anyone who is prepared to take him seriously, the demand, in Herman Kahn's words, to *think the unthinkable* is not an unquestionable demand of rationality, set against a cowardly or inert refusal to follow out one's moral thoughts. Rationality he sees as a demand not merely on him, but on the situations in, and about, which he has to think; unless the environment reveals minimum sanity, it is insanity to carry the decorum of sanity into it. Consequentialist rationality, however, and in particular utilitarian rationality, has no such limitations: making the best of a bad job is one of its maxims, and it will have something to say even on the difference between massacring seven million, and massacring seven million and one.

There are other important questions about the idea of the morally unthinkable which we cannot pursue here. Here we have been concerned with the role it might play in someone's connecting, by more than a mistake, the idea that there was nothing which was right whatever the consequences, and the different idea that everything depends on consequences. While someone might, in this way or another, move from one of those ideas to the other, it is very important that the two ideas are different: especially important in a world where we have lost traditional reasons for resisting the first idea, but have more than enough reasons for fearing the second.

2. NEGATIVE RESPONSIBILITY: AND TWO EXAMPLES

Although I have defined a state of affairs being *accessible* to an agent in terms of the actions which are *available* to him,[7] nevertheless it is the former notion which is really more important for consequentialism. Consequentialism is basically indifferent to whether a state of affairs consists in what I do, or is produced by what I do, where that notion is itself wide enough to include, for instance, situations in which other people do things which I have made them do, or allowed them to do, or encouraged them to do, or given them a chance to do. All that consequentialism is interested in is the idea of these doings being *consequences* of what I do, and that is a relation broad enough to include the relations just mentioned, and many others.

Just what the relation is, is a different question, and at least as obscure as the nature of its relative, cause and effect. It is not a question I shall try to pursue; I will rely on cases where I suppose that any consequentialist would be bound to regard the situations in question as consequences of what the agent does. There are cases where the supposed consequences stand in a rather remote relation to the action, which are sometimes difficult to assess from a practical point of view, but which raise no very interesting question for the present enquiry. The more interesting points about consequentialism lie rather elsewhere. There are certain situations in which the causation of the situation, the relation it has to what I do, is in no way remote or problematic in itself, and entirely justifies the claim that the situation is a consequence of what I do: for instance, it is quite clear, or reasonably clear, that if I do a certain thing, this situation will come about, and if I do not, it will not. So from a consequentialist point of view it goes into the calculation of consequences along with any other state of affairs accessible to me. Yet from some, at least, non-consequentialist points of view, there is a vital difference between some such situations and others: namely, that in some a vital link in the production of the eventual outcome is provided by *someone else's* doing something. But for consequentialism, all causal connections

---

[7] See last section, pp. 24–5.

are on the same level, and it makes no difference, so far as that goes, whether the causation of a given state of affairs lies through another agent, or not.

Correspondingly, there is no relevant difference which consists *just* in one state of affairs being brought about by me, without intervention of other agents, and another being brought about through the intervention of other agents; although some genuinely causal differences involving a difference of value may correspond to that (as when, for instance, the other agents derive pleasure or pain from the transaction), that kind of difference will already be included in the specification of the state of affairs to be produced. Granted that the states of affairs have been adequately described in causally and evaluatively relevant terms, it makes no further comprehensible difference who produces them. It is because consequentialism attaches value ultimately to states of affairs, and its concern is with what states of affairs the world contains, that it essentially involves the notion of *negative responsibility*: that if I am ever responsible for anything, then I must be just as much responsible for things that I allow or fail to prevent, as I am for things that I myself, in the more everyday restricted sense, bring about.[8] Those things also must enter my deliberations, as a responsible moral agent, on the same footing. What matters is what states of affairs the world contains, and so what matters with respect to a given action is what comes about if it is done, and what comes about if it is not done, and those are questions not intrinsically affected by the nature of the causal linkage, in particular by whether the outcome is partly produced by other agents.

The strong doctrine of negative responsibility flows directly from consequentialism's assignment of ultimate value to states of affairs. Looked at from another point of view, it can be seen also as a special application of something that is favoured in many moral outlooks not themselves consequentialist—something which,

---

[8] This is a fairly modest sense of 'responsibility', introduced merely by one's ability to reflect on, and decide, what one ought to do. This presumably escapes Smart's ban (p. 54) on the notion of 'the responsibility' as 'a piece of metaphysical nonsense'—his remarks seem to be concerned solely with situations of interpersonal blame.

indeed, some thinkers have been disposed to regard as the essence of morality itself: a principle of impartiality. Such a principle will claim that there can be no relevant difference from a moral point of view which consists just in the fact, not further explicable in general terms, that benefits or harms accrue to one person rather than to another—'it's me' can never in itself be a morally comprehensible reason.[9] This principle, familiar with regard to the reception of harms and benefits, we can see consequentialism as extending to their production: from the moral point of view, there is no comprehensible difference which consists just in my bringing about a certain outcome rather than someone else's producing it. That the doctrine of negative responsibility represents in this way the extreme of impartiality, and abstracts from the identity of the agent, leaving just a locus of causal intervention in the world—that fact is not merely a surface paradox. It helps to explain why consequentialism can seem to some to express a more serious attitude than non-consequentialist views, why part of its appeal is to a certain kind of high-mindedness. Indeed, that is part of what is wrong with it.

For a lot of the time so far we have been operating at an exceedingly abstract level. This has been necessary in order to get clearer in general terms about the differences between consequentialist and other outlooks, an aim which is important if we want to know what features of them lead to what results for our thought. Now, however, let us look more concretely at two examples, to see what utilitarianism might say about them, what we might say about utilitarianism and, most importantly of all, what would be implied by certain ways of thinking about the situations. The examples are inevitably schematized, and they are open to the objection that they beg as many questions as they illuminate. There are two ways in particular in which examples in moral philosophy tend to beg important questions. One is that, as presented, they arbitrarily cut off and restrict the range of alternative courses of action—this objection might particularly be made against the first of my two examples. The second is that they

---

[9] There is a tendency in some writers to suggest that it is not a comprehensible reason at all. But this, I suspect, is due to the overwhelming importance those writers ascribe to the moral point of view.

inevitably present one with the situation as a going concern, and cut off questions about how the agent got into it, and correspondingly about moral considerations which might flow from that: this objection might perhaps specially arise with regard to the second of my two situations. These difficulties, however, just have to be accepted, and if anyone finds these examples cripplingly defective in this sort of respect, then he must in his own thought rework them in richer and less question-begging form. If he feels that no presentation of any imagined situation can ever be other than misleading in morality, and that there can never be any substitute for the concrete experienced complexity of actual moral situations, then this discussion, with him, must certainly grind to a halt: but then one may legitimately wonder whether every discussion with him about conduct will not grind to a halt, including any discussion about the actual sitautions, since discussion about how one would think and feel about situations somewhat different from the actual (that is to say, situations to that extent imaginary) plays an important role in discussion of the actual.

(1) George, who has just taken his Ph.D. in chemistry, finds it extremely difficult to get a job. He is not very robust in health, which cuts down the number of jobs he might be able to do satisfactorily. His wife has to go out to work to keep them, which itself causes a great deal of strain, since they have small children and there are severe problems about looking after them. The results of all this, especially on the children, are damaging. An older chemist, who knows about this situation, says that he can get George a decently paid job in a certain laboratory, which pursues research into chemical and biological warfare. George says that he cannot accept this, since he is opposed to chemical and biological warfare. The older man replies that he is not too keen on it himself, come to that, but after all George's refusal is not going to make the job or the laboratory go away; what is more, he happens to know that if George refuses the job, it will certainly go to a contemporary of George's who is not inhibited by any such scruples and is likely if appointed to push along the research with greater zeal than George would. Indeed, it is not merely concern for George and his family, but (to speak frankly and in confidence) some alarm about this other man's excess of zeal, which has led the

older man to offer to use his influence to get George the job . . . George's wife, to whom he is deeply attached, has views (the details of which need not concern us) from which it follows that at least there is nothing particularly wrong with research into CBW. What should he do?

(2) Jim finds himself in the central square of a small South American town. Tied up against the wall are a row of twenty Indians, most terrified, a few defiant, in front of them several armed men in uniform. A heavy man in a sweat-stained khaki shirt turns out to be the captain in charge and, after a good deal of questioning of Jim which establishes that he got there by accident while on a botanical expedition, explains that the Indians are a random group of the inhabitants who, after recent acts of protest against the government, are just about to be killed to remind other possible protestors of the advantages of not protesting. However, since Jim is an honoured visitor from another land, the captain is happy to offer him a guest's privilege of killing one of the Indians himself. If Jim accepts, then as a special mark of the occasion, the other Indians will be let off. Of course, if Jim refuses, then there is no special occasion, and Pedro here will do what he was about to do when Jim arrived, and kill them all. Jim, with some desperate recollection of schoolboy fiction, wonders whether, if he got hold of a gun, he could hold the captain, Pedro, and the rest of the soldiers to threat, but it is quite clear from the set-up that nothing of that kind is going to work: any attempt at that sort of thing will mean that all the Indians will be killed, and himself. The men against the wall, and the other villagers, understand the situation, and are obviously begging him to accept. What should he do?

To these dilemmas, it seems to me that utilitarianism replies, in the first case, that George should accept the job, and in the second, that Jim should kill the Indian. Not only does utilitarianism give these answers but, if the situations are essentially as described and there are no further special factors, it regards them, it seems to me, as *obviously* the right answers. But many of us would certainly wonder whether, in (1), that could possibly be the right answer at all; and in the case of (2), even one who came to think that perhaps that was the answer, might well wonder whether it was obviously the answer. Nor is it just a question of the rightness or obviousness of these answers. It is also a question of what sort of considerations come into finding the answer. A feature of utilitarianism is that it cuts out a kind of consideration which for some others makes a difference to what they feel about such cases: a consideration involving the idea, as we might first and very simply put it, that each of us is specially responsible for what *he* does, rather than for what other people do. This is an idea closely connected with the value of integrity. It is often suspected that utilitarianism, at least in its direct forms, makes integrity as a value more or less unintelligible. I shall try to show that this suspicion is correct. Of course, even if that is correct, it would not necessarily follow that we should reject utilitarianism; perhaps, as utilitarians sometimes suggest, we should just forget about integrity, in favour of such things as a concern for the general good. However, if I am right, we cannot merely do that, since the reason why utilitarianism cannot understand integrity is that it cannot coherently describe the relations between a man's projects and his actions.

3. TWO KINDS OF REMOTER EFFECT

A lot of what we have to say about this question will be about the relations between my projects and other people's projects. But before we get on to that, we should first ask whether we are assuming too hastily what the utilitarian answers to the dilemmas will be. In terms of more direct effects of the possible decisions, there does not indeed seem much doubt about the answer in either case; but it might be said that in terms of more remote or less evident effects counterweights might be found to enter the utilitarian scales. Thus the effect on George of a decision to take the job might be invoked, or its effect on others who might know of his decision. The possibility of there being more beneficent labours in the future from which he might be barred or disqualified, might be mentioned; and so forth. Such effects—in particular, possible effects on the agent's character, and effects on the public at large—are often invoked by utilitarian writers dealing with problems about lying or promise-breaking, and some similar considerations might be invoked here.

There is one very general remark that is worth making about

arguments of this sort. The certainty that attaches to these hypotheses about possible effects is usually pretty low; in some cases, indeed, the hypothesis invoked is so implausible that it would scarcely pass if it were not being used to deliver the respectable moral answer, as in the standard fantasy that one of the effects of one's telling a particular lie is to weaken the disposition of the world at large to tell the truth. The demands on the certainty or probability of these beliefs as beliefs about particular actions are much milder than they would be on beliefs favouring the unconventional course. It may be said that this is as it should be, since the presumption must be in favour of the conventional course: but that scarcely seems a *utilitarian* answer, unless utilitarianism has already taken off in the direction of not applying the consequences to the particular act at all.

Leaving aside that very general point, I want to consider now two types of effect that are often invoked by utilitarians, and which might be invoked in connection with these imaginary cases. The attitude or tone involved in invoking these effects may sometimes seem peculiar; but that sort of peculiarity soon becomes familiar in utilitarian discussions, and indeed it can be something of an achievement to retain a sense of it.

First, there is the psychological effect on the agent. Our descriptions of these situations have not so far taken account of how George or Jim will be after they have taken the one course or the other; and it might be said that if they take the course which seemed at first the utilitarian one, the effects on them will be in fact bad enough and extensive enough to cancel out the initial utilitarian advantages of that course. Now there is one version of this effect in which, for a utilitarian, some confusion must be involved, namely that in which the agent feels bad, his subsequent conduct and relations are crippled, and so on, *because he thinks that he has done the wrong thing*—for if the balance of outcomes was as it appeared to be *before* invoking this effect, then he has not (from the utilitarian point of view) done the wrong thing. So that version of the effect, for a rational and utilitarian agent, could not possibly make any difference to the assessment of right and wrong. However, perhaps he is not a thoroughly rational agent, and is disposed to have bad feelings, whichever he decided to do. Now such feelings, which are from a strictly utilitarian point of view irrational—nothing, a utilitarian can point out, is advanced by having them—cannot, consistently, have any great weight in a utilitarian calculation. I shall consider in a moment an argument to suggest that they should have no weight at all in it. But short of that, the utilitarian could reasonably say that such feelings should not be encouraged, even if we accept their existence, and that to give them a lot of weight is to encourage them. Or, at the very best, even if they are straightforwardly and without any discount to be put into the calculation, their weight must be small: they are after all (and at best) one man's feelings.

That consideration might seem to have particular force in Jim's case. In George's case, his feelings represent a larger proportion of what is to be weighed, and are more commensurate in character with other items in the calculation. In Jim's case, however, his feelings might seem to be of very little weight compared with other things that are at stake. There is a powerful and recognizable appeal that can be made on this point: as that a refusal by Jim to do what he has been invited to do would be a kind of self-indulgent squeamishness. That is an appeal which can be made by other than utilitarians—indeed, there are some uses of it which cannot be consistently made by utilitarians, as when it essentially involves the idea that there is something dishonourable about such self-indulgence. But in some versions it is a familiar, and it must be said a powerful, weapon of utilitarianism. One must be clear, though, about what it can and cannot accomplish. The most it can do, so far as I can see, is to invite one to consider how seriously, and for what reasons, one feels that what one is invited to do is (in these circumstances) wrong, and, in particular, to consider that question from the utilitarian point of view. When the agent is not seeing the situation from a utilitarian point of view, the appeal cannot force him to do so; and if he does come round to seeing it from a utilitarian point of view, there is virtually nothing left for the appeal to do. If he does not see it from a utilitarian point of view, he will not see his resistance to the invitation, and the unpleasant feelings he associates with accepting it, *just* as disagreeable experiences of his; they figure rather as emotional expressions of a thought that to accept would be wrong. He may be asked, as by the appeal, to consider whether he is right, and indeed whether he is fully serious, in thinking that. But the assertion of the appeal, that he is being self-indulgently squeamish, will not itself answer that question, or even help to answer it, since it essentially tells him to regard his feelings just as unpleasant experiences of his, and he cannot, by doing that, answer the question they pose when they are precisely not so regarded, but are regarded as indications[10] of what he thinks is right and wrong. If he does come round fully to the utilitarian point of view then of course he will regard these feelings just as unpleasant experiences of his. And once Jim—at least—has come to see them in that light, there is nothing left for the appeal to do, since *of course* his feelings, so regarded, are of virtually no weight at all in relation to the other things at stake. The 'squeamishness' appeal is not an argument which adds in a hitherto neglected consideration. Rather, it is an invitation to consider the situation, and one's own feelings, from a utilitarian point of view.

The reason why the squeamishness appeal can be very unsettling, and one can be unnerved by the suggestion of self-indulgence in going against utilitarian considerations, is not that we are utilitarians who are uncertain what utilitarian value to attach to our moral feelings, but that we are partially at least not utilitarians, and cannot regard our moral feelings merely as objects of utilitarian value. Because our moral relation to the world is partly given by such feelings, and by a sense of what we can or cannot 'live with', to come to regard those feelings from a purely utilitarian point of view, that is to say, as happenings outside one's moral self, is to lose a sense of one's moral identity; to lose, in the most literal way, one's integrity. At this point utilitarianism alienates one from one's moral feelings; we shall see a little later how, more basically, it alienates one from one's actions as well.

If, then, one is really going to regard one's feelings from a strictly utilitarian point of view, Jim should give very little weight at all to his; it seems almost indecent, in fact, once one has taken

---

[10] On the non-cognitivist meta-ethic in terms of which Smart presents his utilitarianism, the term 'indications' here would represent an understatement.

that point of view, to suppose that he should give any at all. In George's case one might feel that things were slightly different. It is interesting, though, that one reason why one might think that—namely that one person principally affected is his wife—is very dubiously available to a utilitarian. George's wife has some reason to be interested in George's integrity and his sense of it; the Indians, quite properly, have no interest in Jim's. But it is not at all clear how utilitarianism would describe that difference.

There is an argument, and a strong one, that a strict utilitarian should give not merely small extra weight, in calculations of right and wrong, to feelings of this kind, but that he should give absolutely no weight to them at all. This is based on the point, which we have already seen, that if a course of action is, before taking these sorts of feelings into account, utilitarianly preferable, then bad feelings about that kind of action will be from a utilitarian point of view irrational. Now it might be thought that even if that is so, it would not mean that in a utilitarian calculation such feelings should not be taken into account; it is after all a well-known boast of utilitarianism that it is a realistic outlook which seeks the best in the world as it is, and takes any form of happiness or unhappiness into account. While a utilitarian will no doubt seek to diminish the incidence of feelings which are utilitarianly irrational—or at least of disagreeable feelings which are so—he might be expected to take them into account while they exist. This is without doubt classical utilitarian doctrine, but there is good reason to think that utilitarianism cannot stick to it without embracing results which are startlingly unacceptable and perhaps self-defeating.

Suppose that there is in a certain society a racial minority. Considering merely the ordinary interests of the other citizens, as opposed to their sentiments, this minority does no particular harm; we may suppose that it does not confer any very great benefits either. Its presence is in those terms neutral or mildly beneficial. However, the other citizens have such prejudices that they find the sight of this group, even the knowledge of its presence, very disagreeable. Proposals are made for removing in some way this minority. If we assume various quite plausible things (as that programmes to change the majority sentiment are likely to be protracted and ineffective) then even if the removal would be unpleasant for the minority, a utilitarian calculation might well end up favouring this step, especially if the minority were a rather small minority and the majority were very severely prejudiced, that is to say, were made very severely uncomfortable by the presence of the minority.

A utilitarian might find that conclusion embarrassing; and not merely because of its nature, but because of the grounds on which it is reached. While a utilitarian might be expected to take into account certain other sorts of consequences of the prejudice, as that a majority prejudice is likely to be displayed in conduct disagreeable to the minority, and so forth, he might be made to wonder whether the unpleasant experiences of the prejudiced people should be allowed, *merely as such*, to count. If he does count them, merely as such, then he has once more separated himself from a body of ordinary moral thought which he might have hoped to accommodate; he may also have started on the path of defeating his own view of things. For one feature of these sentiments is that they are from the utilitarian point of view itself irrational, and a thoroughly utilitarian person would either not have them, or if he found that he did tend to have them, would himself seek to discount them. Since the sentiments in question are such that a rational utilitarian would discount them in himself, it is reasonable to suppose that he should discount them in his calculations about society; it does seem quite unreasonable for him to give just as much weight to feelings—considered just in themselves, one must recall, as experiences of those that have them—which are essentially based on views which are from a utilitarian point of view irrational, as to those which accord with utilitarian principles. Granted this idea, it seems reasonable for him to rejoin a body of moral thought in other respects congenial to him, and discount those sentiments, just considered in themselves, totally, on the principle that no pains or discomforts are to count in the utilitarian sum which their subjects have just because they hold views which are by utilitarian standards irrational. But if he accepts that, then in the cases we are at present considering no extra weight at all can be put in for bad feelings of George or Jim about their choices, if those choices are, leaving out those feelings, on the first round utilitarianly rational.

The psychological effect on the agent was the first of two general effects considered by utilitarians, which had to be discussed. The second is in general a more substantial item, but it need not take so long, since it is both clearer and has little application to the present cases. This is the *precedent effect*. As Burke rightly emphasized, this effect can be important: that one morally *can* do what someone has actually done, is a psychologically effective principle, if not a deontically valid one. For the effect to operate, obviously some conditions must hold on the publicity of the act and on such things as the status of the agent (such considerations weighed importantly with Sir Thomas More); what these may be will vary evidently with circumstances.

In order for the precedent effect to make a difference to a utilitarian calcualtion, it must be based upon a confusion. For suppose that there is an act which would be the best in the circumstances, except that doing it will encourage by precedent other people to do things which will not be the best things to do. Then the situation of those other people must be relevantly different from that of the original agent; if it were not, then in doing the same as what would be the best course for the original agent, they would necessarily do the best thing themselves. But if the situations are in this way relevantly different, it must be a confused perception which takes the first situation, and the agent's course in it, as an adequate precedent for the second.

However, the fact that the precedent effect, if it really makes a difference, is in this sense based on a confusion, does not mean that it is not perfectly real, nor that it is to be discounted: social effects are by their nature confused in this sort of way. What it does emphasize is that calculations of the precedent effect have got to be realistic, involving considerations of how people are actually likely to be influenced. In the present examples, however, it is very implausible to think that the precedent effect could be invoked to make any difference to the calculation. Jim's case is extraordinary enough, and it is hard to imagine who the recipients of the effect might be supposed to be; while George is not in a sufficiently public situation or role for the question to arise in that form, and in any case one might suppose that the motivations of others on such an issue were quite likely to be fixed one way or another already.

No appeal, then, to these other effects is going to make a difference to what the utilitarian will decide about our examples. Let us now look more closely at the structure of those decisions.

4. INTEGRITY

The situations have in common that if the agent does not do a certain disagreeable thing, someone else will, and in Jim's situation at least the result, the state of affairs after the other man has acted, if he does, will be worse than after Jim has acted, if Jim does. The same, on a smaller scale, is true of George's case. I have already suggested that it is inherent in consequentialism that it offers a strong doctrine of negative responsibility: if I know that if I do X, O_1 will eventuate, and if I refrain from doing X, O_2 will, and that O_2 is worse than O_1, then I am responsible for O_2 if I refrain voluntarily from doing X. 'You could have prevented it', as will be said, and truly, to Jim, if he refuses, by the relatives of the other Indians. (I shall leave the important question, which is to the side of the present issue, of the obligations, if any, that nest round the word 'know': how far does one, under utilitarianism, have to research into the possibilities of maximally beneficent action, including prevention?)

In the present cases, the situation of O_2 includes another agent bringing about results worse than O_1. So far as O_2 has been identified up to this point—merely as the worse outcome which will eventuate if I refrain from doing X—we might equally have said that what that other brings about is O_2; but that would be to underdescribe the situation. For what occurs if Jim refrains from action is not solely twenty Indians dead, but *Pedro's killing twenty Indians*, and that is not a result which Pedro brings about, though the death of the Indians is. We can say: what one does is not included in the outcome of what one does, while what another does can be included in the outcome of what one does. For that to be so, as the terms are now being used, only a very weak condition has to be satisfied: for Pedro's killing the Indians to be the outcome of Jim's refusal, it only has to be causally true that if Jim had not refused, Pedro would not have done it.

That may be enough for us to speak, in some sense, of Jim's responsibility for that outcome, if it occurs; but it is certainly not enough, it is worth noticing, for us to speak of Jim's *making* those things happen. For granted this way of their coming about, he could have made them happen only by making Pedro shoot, and there is no acceptable sense in which his refusal makes Pedro shoot. If the captain had said on Jim's refusal, 'you leave me with no alternative', he would have been lying, like most who use that phrase. While the deaths, and the killing, may be the outcome of Jim's refusal, it is misleading to think, in such a case, of Jim having an *effect* on the world through the medium (as it happens) of Pedro's acts; for this is to leave Pedro out of the picture in his essential role of one who has intentions and projects, projects for realizing which Jim's refusal would leave an opportunity. Instead of thinking in terms of supposed effects of Jim's projects on Pedro, it is more revealing to think in terms of the effects of Pedro's projects on Jim's decision. This is the direction from which I want to cricitize the notion of negative responsibility.

There are of course other ways in which this notion can be criticized. Many have hoped to discredit it by insisting on the basic moral relevance of the distinction between action and inaction, between intervening and letting things take their course. The distinction is certainly of great moral significance, and indeed it is not easy to think of any moral outlook which could get along without making some use of it. But it is unclear, both in itself and in its moral applications, and the unclarities are of a kind which precisely cause it to give way when, in very difficult cases, weight has to be put on it. There is much to be said in this area, but I doubt whether the sort of dilemma we are considering is going to be resolved by a simple use of this distinction. Again, the issue of negative responsibility can be pressed on the question of how limits are to be placed on one's apparently boundless obligation, implied by utilitarianism, to improve the world. Some answers are needed to that, too—and answers which stop short of relapsing into the bad faith of supposing that one's responsibilities could be adequately characterized just by appeal to one's role.[11] But, once again, while that is a real question, it cannot be brought to bear directly on the present kind of case, since it is hard to think of anyone supposing that in Jim's case it would be an adequate response for him to say that it was none of his business.

What projects does a utilitarian agent have? As a utilitarian, he has the general project of bringing about maximally desirable outcomes; how he is to do this at any given moment is a question of what causal levers, so to speak, are at that moment within reach. The desirable outcomes, however, do not just consist of agents carrying out *that* project; there must be other more basic or lower-order projects which he and other agents have, and the desirable outcomes are going to consist, in part, of the maximally harmonious realization of those projects ('in part', because one component of a utilitarianly desirable outcome may be the occurrence of agreeable experiences which are not the satisfaction of anybody's projects). Unless there were first-order projects, the general utilitarian project would have nothing to work on, and would be vacuous. What do the more basic or lower-order projects comprise? Many will be the obvious kinds of desires for things for oneself, one's family, one's friends, including basic necessities of life and, in more relaxed circumstances, objects of taste. Or there may be pursuits and interests of an intellectual, cultural, or creative character. I introduce those as a separate class not because the objects of them lie in a separate class and provide—as some utilitarians, in their churchy way, are fond of saying— 'higher' pleasures. I introduce them separately because the agent's identification with them may be of a different order. It does not have to be: cultural and aesthetic interests just belong, for many, along with any other taste; but some people's commitment to these kinds of interests just is at once more thoroughgoing and serious than their pursuit of various objects of taste, while it is more individual and permeated with character than the desire for the necessities of life.

Beyond these, someone may have projects connected with his

<hr>

[11] For some remarks bearing on this, see *Morality*, the section on 'Goodness and roles', and Cohen's article there cited. [Williams's book *Morality* was published by Harper & Row in 1972—Ed.]

support of some cause: Zionism, for instance, or the abolition of chemical and biological warfare. Or there may be projects which flow from some more general disposition towards human conduct and character, such as a hatred of injustice, or of cruelty, or of killing.

It may be said that this last sort of disposition and its associated project do not count as (logically) 'lower-order' relative to the higher-order project of maximizing desirable outcomes; rather, it may be said, it is itself a 'higher-order' project. The vital question is not, however, how it is to be classified, but whether it and similar projects are to count among the projects whose satisfaction is to be included in the maximizing sum and, correspondingly, as contributing to the agent's happiness. If the utilitarian says 'no' to that, then he is almost certainly committed to a version of utilitarianism as absurdly superficial and shallow as Benthamite versions have often been accused of being. For this project will be discounted, presumably, on the ground that it involves, in the specification of its object, the mention of other people's happiness or interests: thus it is the kind of project which (unlike the pursuit of food for myself) presupposes a reference to other people's projects. But that criterion would eliminate any desire at all which was not blankly and in the most straightforward sense egoistic.[12] Thus we should be reduced to frankly egoistic first-order projects and—for all essential purposes—the one second-order utilitarian project of maximally satisfying first-order projects. Utilitarianism has a tendency to slide in this direction, and to leave a vast hole in the range of human desires, between egoistic inclinations and necessities at one end, and impersonally benevolent happiness-management at the other. But the utilitarianism which has to leave this hole is the most primitive form, which offers a quite rudimentary account of desire. Modern versions of the theory are supposed to be neutral with regard to what sorts of things make people happy or what their projects are. Utilitarianism would do well then to acknowledge the evident fact that among the things that make people happy is not only making other people happy,

---

[12] On the subject of egoistic and non-egoistic desires, see 'Egoism and Altruism', in *Problems of the Self* (London: Cambridge University Press, 1973).

but being taken up or involved in any of a vast range of projects, or—if we waive the evangelical and moralizing associations of the word—commitments. One can be committed to such things as a person, a cause, an institution, a career, one's own genius, or the pursuit of danger.

Now none of these is itself the *pursuit of happiness*: by an exceedingly ancient platitude, it is not at all clear that there could be anything which was just that, or at least anything that had the slightest chance of being successful. Happiness, rather, requires being involved in, or at least content with, something else.[13] It is not impossible for utilitarianism to accept that point: it does not have to be saddled with a naive and absurd philosophy of mind about the relation between desire and happiness. What it does have to say is that if such commitments are worth while, then pursuing the projects that flow from them, and realizing some of those projects, will make the person for whom they are worth while, happy. It may be that to claim that is still wrong: it may well be that a commitment can make sense to a man (can make sense of his life) without his supposing that it will make him *happy*.[14] But that is not the present point; let us grant to utilitarianism that all worthwhile human projects must conduce, one way or another, to happiness. The point is that even if that is true, it does not follow, nor could it possibly be true, that those projects are themselves projects of pursuing happiness. One has to believe in, or at least want, or, quite minimally, be content with, other things, for there to be anywhere that happiness can come from.

Utilitarianism, then, should be willing to agree that its general aim of maximizing happiness does not imply that what everyone is doing is just pursuing happiness. On the contrary, people have to be pursuing other things. What those other things may be,

---

[13] This does not imply that there is no such thing as the project of pursuing pleasure. Some writers who have correctly resisted the view that all desires are desires for pleasure, have given an account of pleasure so thoroughly adverbial as to leave it quite unclear how there could be a distinctively hedonist way of life at all. Some room has to be left for that, though there are important difficulties both in defining it and living it. Thus (particularly in the case of the very rich) it often has highly ritual aspects, apparently part of a strategy to counter boredom.

[14] For some remarks on this possibility, see *Morality*, section on 'What is morality about?'

uilitarianism, sticking to its professed empirical stance, should be prepared just to find out. No doubt some possible projects it will want to discourage, on the grounds that their being pursued involves a negative balance of happiness to others: though even there, the unblinking accountant's eye of the strict utilitarian will have something to put in the positive column, the satisfactions of the destructive agent. Beyond that, there will be a vast variety of generally beneficent or at least harmless projects; and some, no doubt, will take the form not just of tastes or fancies, but of what I have called 'commitments'. It may even be that the utilitarian researcher will find that many of those with commitments, who have really identified themselves with objects outside themselves, who are thoroughly involved with other persons, or institutions, or activities or causes, are actually happier than those whose projects and wants are not like that. If so, that is an important piece of utilitarian empirical lore.

When I say 'happier' here, I have in mind the sort of consideration which any utilitarian would be committed to accepting: as for instance that such people are less likely to have a breakdown or commit suicide. Of course that is not all that is actually involved, but the point in this argument is to use to the maximum degree utilitarian notions, in order to locate a breaking-point in utilitarian thought. In appealing to this strictly utilitarian notion, I am being more consistent with utilitarianism than Smart is. In his struggles with the problem of the brain-electrode man, Smart (p. 22) commends the idea that 'happy' is a partly evaluative term, in the sense that we call 'happiness' those kinds of satisfaction which, as things are, we approve of. But *by what standard* is this surplus element of approval supposed, from a utilitarian point of view, to be allocated? There is no source for it, on a strictly utilitarian view, except further degrees of satisfaction, but there are none of those available, or the problem would not arise. Nor does it help to appeal to the fact that we dislike in prospect things which we like when we get there, for from a utilitarian point of view it would seem that the original dislike was merely irrational or based on an error. Smart's argument at this point seems to be embarrassed by a well-known utilitarian uneasiness, which comes from a feeling that it is not respectable to

48 BERNARD WILLIAMS

ignore the 'deep', while not having anywhere left in human life to
locate it.[15]

Let us now go back to the agent as utilitarian, and his higher-
order project of maximizing desirable outcomes. At this level, he
is committed only to that: what the outcome will actually consist of
will depend entirely on the facts, on what persons with what
projects and what potential satisfactions there are within calculable
reach of the causal levers near which he finds himself. His own
substantial projects and commitments come into it, but only as one
lot among others—they potentially provide one set of satisfactions
among those which he may be able to assist from where he
happens to be. He is the agent of the satisfaction system who
happens to be at a particular point at a particular time: in Jim's
case, our man in South America. His own decisions as a utilitarian
agent are a function of all the satisfactions which he can affect
from where he is: and this means that the projects of others, to an
indeterminately great extent, determine his decision.

This may be so either positively or negatively. It will be so
positively if agents within the causal field of his decision have
projects which are at any rate harmless, and so should be assisted.
It will equally be so, but negatively, if there is an agent within the
causal field whose projects are harmful, and have to be frustrated
to maximize desirable outcomes. So it is with Jim and the soldier
Pedro. On the utilitarian view, the undesirable projects of other
people as much determine, in this negative way, one's decisions as
the desirable ones do positively: if those people were not there, or
had different projects, the causal nexus would be different, and it
is the actual state of the causal nexus which determines the
decision. The determination to an indefinite degree of my
decisions by other people's projects is just another aspect of my
unlimited responsibility to act for the best in a causal framework
formed to a considerable extent by their projects.

The decision so determined is, for utilitarianism, the right
decision. But what if it conflicts with some project of mine? This,
the utilitarian will say, has already been dealt with: the satisfaction

[15] One of many resemblances in spirit between utilitarianism and high-minded
evangelical Christianity.

to you of fulfilling your project, and any satisfactions to others of your so doing, have already been through the calculating device and have been found inadequate. Now in the case of many sorts of projects, that is a perfectly reasonable sort of answer. But in the case of projects of the sort I have called 'commitments', those with which one is more deeply and extensively involved and identified, this cannot just by itself be an adequate answer, and there may be no adequate answer at all. For, to take the extreme sort of case, how can a man, a utilitarian agent, come to regard as one satisfaction among others, and a dispensable one, a project or attitude round which he has built his life, just because someone else's projects have so structured the causal scene that that is how the utilitarian sum comes out?

The point here is not, as utilitarians may hasten to say, that if the project or attitude is that central to his life, then to abandon it will be very disagreeable to him and great loss of utility will be involved. I have already argued in Section 3 that it is not like that; on the contrary, once he is prepared to look at it like that, the argument in any serious case is over anyway. The point is that he is identified with his actions as flowing from projects and attitudes which in some cases he takes seriously at the deepest level, as what his life is about (or, in some cases, this section of his life— seriousness is not necessarily the same as persistence). It is absurd to demand of such a man, when the sums come in from the utility network which the projects of others have in part determined, that he should just step aside from his own project and decision and acknowledge the decision which utilitarian calculation requires. It is to alienate him in a real sense from his actions and the source of his action in his own convictions. It is to make him into a channel between the input of everyone's projects, including his own, and an output of optimific decision; but this is to neglect the extent to which *his* actions and *his* decisions have to be seen as the actions and decisions which flow from the projects and attitudes with which he is most closely identified. It is thus, in the most literal sense, an attack on his integrity.[16]

---

[16] Interestingly related to these notions is the Socratic idea that courage is a virtue particularly connected with keeping a clear sense of what one regards as most important. They also centrally raise questions about the value of pride. Humility,

These sorts of considerations do not in themselves give solutions to practical dilemmas such as those provided by our examples; but I hope they help to provide other ways of thinking about them. In fact, it is not hard to see that in George's case, viewed from this perspective, the utilitarian solution would be wrong. Jim's case is different, and harder. But if (as I suppose) the utilitarian is probably right in this case, that is not to be found out just by asking the utilitarian's questions. Discussions of it—and I am not going to try to carry it further here—will have to take seriously the distinction between my killing someone, and its coming about because of what I do that someone else kills them: a distinction based, not so much on the distinction between action and inaction, as on the distinction between my projects and someone else's projects. At least it will have to start by taking that seriously, as utilitarianism does not; but then it will have to build out from there by asking why that distinction seems to have less, or a different, force in this case than it has in George's. One question here would be how far one's powerful objection to killing people just is, in fact, an application of a powerful objection to their being killed. Another dimension of that is the issue of how much it matters that the people at risk are actual, and there, as opposed to hypothetical, or future, or merely elsewhere.[17]

There are many other considerations that could come into such a question, but the immediate point of all this is to draw one particular contrast with utilitarianism: that to reach a grounded decision in such a case should not be regarded as a matter of just discounting one's reactions, impulses, and deeply held projects in the face of the pattern of utilities, nor yet merely adding them in—but in the first instance of trying to understand them.

as something beyond the real demand of correct self-appraisal, was specially a Christian virtue because it involved subservience to God. In a secular context it can only represent subservience to other men and their projects.

[17] For a more general discussion of this issue see C. Fried, *An Anatomy of Values* (Cambridge, Mass.: Harvard University Press, 1970), Part Three.

3

WAR AND MASSACRE

THOMAS NAGEL

FROM the apathetic reaction to atrocities committed in Vietnam
by the United States and its allies, one may conclude that moral
restrictions on the conduct of war command almost as little
sympathy among the general public as they do among those
charged with the formation of US military policy.[1] Even when
restrictions on the conduct of warfare are defended, it is usually on
legal grounds alone: their moral basis is often poorly understood. I
wish to argue that certain restrictions are neither arbitrary nor
merely conventional, and that their validity does not depend
simply on their usefulness. There is, in other words, a moral basis
for the rules of war, even though the conventions now officially in
force are far from giving it perfect expression.

I

No elaborate moral theory is required to account for what is wrong
in cases like the Mylai massacre, since it did not serve, and was not
intended to serve, any strategic purpose. Moreover, if the
participation of the United States in the Indo–Chinese war is
entirely wrong to begin with, then that engagement is incapable of
providing a justification for *any* measures taken in its pursuit—not
only for the measures which are atrocities in every war, however
just its aims.

But this war has revealed attitudes of a more general kind,
which influenced the conduct of earlier wars as well. After it has

---

Thomas Nagel, 'War and Massacre', from *Mortal Questions* (Cambridge University
Press, 1979), pp. 53–74. Reprinted by permission of the publisher.

[1] This essay was completed in 1971. Direct US military involvement in the
Vietnam War lasted from 1961 to 1973. Hence the present tense.

ended, we shall still be faced with the problem of how warfare may be conducted, and the attitudes that have resulted in the specific conduct of this war will not have disappeared. Moreover, similar problems can arise in wars or rebellions fought for very different reasons, and against very different opponents. It is not easy to keep a firm grip on the idea of what is not permissible in warfare, because while some military actions are obvious atrocities, other cases are more difficult to assess, and the general principles underlying these judgements remain obscure. Such obscurity can lead to the abandonment of sound intuitions in favour of criteria whose rationale may be more obvious. If such a tendency is to be resisted, it will require a better understanding of the restrictions than we now have.

I propose to discuss the most general moral problem raised by the conduct of warfare: the problem of means and ends. In one view, there are limits on what may be done even in the service of an end worth pursuing—and even when adherence to the restriction may be very costly. A person who acknowledges the force of such restrictions can find himself in acute moral dilemmas. He may believe, for example, that by torturing a prisoner he can obtain information necessary to prevent a disaster, or that by obliterating one village with bombs he can halt a campaign of terrorism. If he believes that the gains from a certain measure will clearly outweigh its costs, yet still suspects that he ought not to adopt it, then he is in a dilemma produced by the conflict between two disparate categories of moral reason: categories that may be called *utilitarian* and *absolutist*.

Utilitarianism gives primacy to a concern with what will *happen*. Absolutism gives primacy to a concern with what one is *doing*. The conflict between them arises because the alternatives we face are rarely just choices between *total outcomes*: they are also choices between alternative pathways or measures to be taken. When one of the choices is to do terrible things to another person, the problem is altered fundamentally; it is no longer merely a question of which outcome would be worse.

Few of us are completely immune to either of these types of moral intuition, though in some people, either naturally or for doctrinal reasons, one type will be dominant and the other suppressed or weak. But it is perfectly possible to feel the force of both types of reason very strongly; in that case the moral dilemma in certain situations of crisis will be acute, and it may appear that every possible course of action or inaction is unacceptable for one reason or another.

II

Although it is this dilemma that I propose to explore, most of the discussion will be devoted to its absolutist component. The utilitarian component is straightforward by comparison, and has a natural appeal to anyone who is not a complete sceptic about ethics. Utilitarianism says that one should try, either individually or through institutions, to maximize good and minimize evil (the definition of these categories need not enter into the schematic formulation of the view), and that if faced with the possibility of preventing a great evil by producing a lesser, one should choose the lesser evil. There are certainly problems about the formulation of utilitarianism, and much has been written about it, but its intent is morally transparent. Nevertheless, despite the additions and refinements, it continues to leave large portions of ethics unaccounted for. I do not suggest that some form of absolutism can account for them all, only that an examination of absolutism will lead us to see the complexity, and perhaps the incoherence, of our moral ideas.

Utilitarianism certainly justifies *some* restrictions on the conduct of warfare. There are strong utilitarian reasons for adhering to any limitation which seems natural to most people—particularly if the limitation is widely accepted already. An exceptional measure which seems to be justified by its results in a particular conflict may create a precedent with disastrous long-term effects.[2] It may even be argued that war involves violence on such a scale that it is never justified on utilitarian grounds—the consequences of refusing to go to war will never be as bad as the war itself would be, even if atrocities were not committed. Or in a more sophisticated vein it

---

[2] Straightforward considerations of national interest often tend in the same direction: the inadvisability of using nuclear weapons seems to be overdetermined in this way.

might be claimed that a uniform policy of never resorting to military force would do less harm in the long run, if followed consistently, than a policy of deciding each case on utilitarian grounds (even though on occasion particular applications of the pacifist policy might have worse results than a specific utilitarian decision). But I shall not consider these arguments, for my concern is with reasons of a different kind, which may remain when reasons of utility and interest fail.[3]

In the final analysis, I believe that the dilemma cannot always be resolved. While not every conflict between absolutism and utilitarianism creates an insoluble dilemma, and while it seems to me certainly right to adhere to absolutist restrictions unless the utilitarian considerations favouring violation are overpoweringly weighty and extremely certain—nevertheless, when that special condition is met, it may become impossible to adhere to an absolutist position. What I shall offer, therefore, is a somewhat qualified defence of absolutism. I believe it underlies a valid and fundamental type of moral judgement—which cannot be reduced to or overridden by other principles. And while there may be other principles just as fundamental, it is particularly important not to lose confidence in our absolutist intuitions, for they are often the only barrier before the abyss of utilitarian apologetics for large-scale murder.

III

One absolutist position that creates no problems of interpretation is pacifism: the view that one may not kill another person under any circumstances, no matter what good would be achieved or evil averted thereby. The type of absolutist position that I am going to discuss is different. Pacifism draws the conflict with utilitarian considerations very starkly. But there are other views according to which violence may be undertaken, even on a large scale, in a

[3] These reasons, moreover, have special importance in that they are available even to one who denies the appropriateness of utilitarian considerations in international matters. He may acknowledge limitations on what may be done to the soldiers and civilians of other countries in pursuit of his nation's military objectives, while denying that one country should in general consider the interests of nationals of other countries in determining its policies.

clearly just cause, so long as certain absolute restrictio
character and direction of that violence are observed. The
drawn somewhat closer to the bone, but it exists.

The philosopher who has done most to advance contemporary
philosophical discussion of such a view, and to explain it to those
unfamiliar with its extensive treatment in Roman Catholic moral
theology, is G. E. M. Anscombe. In 1958 Miss Anscombe
published a pamphlet entitled *Mr Truman's Degree*,[4] on the
occasion of the award by Oxford University of an honorary
doctorate to Harry Truman. The pamphlet explained why she had
opposed the decision to award that degree, recounted the story of
her unsuccessful opposition, and offered some reflections on the
history of Truman's decision to drop atom bombs on Hiroshima
and Nagasaki, and on the difference between murder and
allowable killing in warfare. She pointed out that the policy of
deliberately killing large numbers of civilians either as a means or
as an end in itself did not originate with Truman, and was common
practice among all parties during World War II for some time
before Hiroshima. The Allied area bombings of German cities by
conventional explosives included raids which killed more civilians
than did the atomic attacks; the same is true of certain fire-bomb
raids on Japan.

The policy of attacking the civilian population in order to induce
an enemy to surrender, or to damage his morale, seems to have
been widely accepted in the civilized world, and seems to be
accepted still, at least if the stakes are high enough. It gives
evidence of a moral conviction that the deliberate killing of non-
combatants—women, children, old people—is permissible if
enough can be gained by it. This follows from the more general
position that any means can in principle be justified if it leads to a

---

[4] (Privately printed.) See also her essay 'War and Murder', in *Nuclear Weapons and Christian Conscience*, ed. W. Stein (London: The Merlin Press, 1961). The present paper is much indebted to these two essays throughout. These and related subjects are extensively treated by P. Ramsey in *The Just War* (New York: Scribners, 1968). Among recent writings that bear on the moral problem are J. Bennett, 'Whatever the Consequences', and P. Foot, 'The Problem of Abortion and the Doctrine of the Double Effect'. Miss Anscombe's replies are 'A Note on Mr. Bennett', *Analysis* 25, no. 3 (1966), 208 and 'Who is Wronged?', *Oxford Review* 5 (1967), 16–17.

Such an attitude is evident not only in the
⸻t weapons systems but also in the day-to-
global war in Indo-China: the indiscriminate
-personnel weapons, napalm, and aerial
to prisoners; massive relocation of civilians;
nd so forth. An absolutist position opposes
rtain acts cannot be justified no matter what
nong those acts is murder—the deliberate
killing of the harmless: civilians, prisoners of war, and medical
personnel.

In the present war such measures are sometimes said to be
regrettable, but they are generally defended by reference to
military necessity and the importance of the long-term consequences of success or failure in the war. I shall pass over the
inadequacy of this consequentialist defence in its own terms. (That
is the dominant form of moral criticism of the war, for it is part of
what people mean when they ask, 'Is it worth it?') I am concerned
rather to account for the inappropriateness of offering any defence
of that kind for such actions.

Many people feel, without being able to say much more about it,
that something has gone seriously wrong when certain measures
are admitted into consideration in the first place. The fundamental
mistake is made there, rather than at the point where the overall
benefit of some monstrous measure is judged to outweigh its
disadvantages, and it is adopted. An account of absolutism might
help us to understand this. If it is not allowable to *do* certain
things, such as killing unarmed prisoners or civilians, then no
argument about what will happen if one does not do them can
show that doing them would be all right.

Absolutism does not, of course, require one to ignore the
consequences of one's acts. It operates as a limitation on utilitarian
reasoning, not as a substitute for it. An absolutist can be expected
to try to maximize good and minimize evil, so long as this does not
require him to transgress an absolute prohibition like that against
murder. But when such a conflict occurs, the prohibition takes
complete precedence over any consideration of consequences.
Some of the results of this view are clear enough. It requires us to
forgo certain potentially useful military measures, such as the

slaughter of hostages and prisoners or indiscriminate attempts to reduce the enemy civilian population by starvation, epidemic infectious diseases like anthrax and bubonic plague, or mass incineration. It means that we cannot deliberate on whether such measures are justified by the fact that they will avert still greater evils, for as intentional measures they cannot be justified in terms of any consequences whatever.

Someone unfamiliar with the events of this century might imagine that utilitarian arguments, or arguments of national interest, would suffice to deter measures of this sort. But it has become evident that such considerations are insufficient to prevent the adoption and employment of enormous anti-population weapons once their use is considered a serious moral possibility. The same is true of the piecemeal wiping out of rural civilian populations in airborne anti-guerrilla warfare. Once the door is opened to calculation of utility and national interest, the usual speculations about the future of freedom, peace, and economic prosperity can be brought to bear to ease the consciences of those responsible for a certain number of charred babies.

For this reason alone it is important to decide what is wrong with the frame of mind which allows such arguments to begin. But it is also important to understand absolutism in the cases where it genuinely conflicts with utility. Despite its appeal, it is a paradoxical position, for it can require that one refrain from choosing the lesser of two evils when that is the only choice one has. And it is additionally paradoxical because, unlike pacifism, it permits one to do horrible things to people in some circumstances but not in others.

IV

Before going on to say what, if anything, lies behind the position, there remain a few relatively technical matters which are best discussed at this point.

First, it is important to specify as clearly as possible the kind of thing to which absolutist prohibitions can apply. We must take seriously the proviso that they concern what we deliberately do to people. There could not, for example, without incoherence, be an absolute prohibition against *bringing about* the death of an innocent person. For one may find oneself in a situation in which, no matter what one does, some innocent people will die as a result. I do not mean just that there are cases in which someone will die no matter what one does, because one is not in a position to affect the outcome one way or other. That, it is to be hoped, is one's relation to the deaths of most innocent people. I have in mind, rather, a case in which someone is bound to die, but who it is will depend on what one does. Sometimes these situations have natural causes, as when too few resources (medicine, lifeboats) are available to rescue everyone threatened with a certain catastrophe. Sometimes the situations are man-made, as when the only way to control a campaign of terrorism is to employ terrorist tactics against the community from which it has arisen. Whatever one does in cases such as these, some innocent people will die as a result. If the absolutist prohibition forbade doing what would result in the deaths of innocent people, it would have the consequence that in such cases nothing one could do would be morally permissible.

This problem is avoided, however, because what absolutism forbids is *doing* certain things to people, rather than bringing about certain *results*. Not everything that happens to others as a result of what one does is something that one has *done* to them. Catholic moral theology seeks to make this distinction precise in a doctrine known as the law of double effect, which asserts that there is a morally relevant distinction between bringing about or permitting the death of an innocent person deliberately, either as an end in itself or as a means, and bringing it about or permitting it as a side-effect of something else one does deliberately. In the latter case, even if the outcome is foreseen, it is not murder, and does not fall under the absolute prohibition, though of course it may still be wrong for other reasons (reasons of utility, for example). Briefly, the principle states that one is sometimes permitted knowingly to bring about or permit as a side-effect of one's actions something which it would be absolutely impermissible to bring about or permit deliberately as an end or as a means. In application to war or revolution, the law of double effect permits a certain amount of civilian carnage as a side-effect of bombing munitions plants or attacking enemy soldiers. And even this is permissible only if the cost is not too great to be justified by one's objectives.

However, despite its importance and its usefulness in accounting for certain plausible moral judgements, I do not believe that the law of double effect is a generally applicable test for the consequences of an absolutist position. Its own application is not always clear, so that it introduces uncertainty where there need not be uncertainty.

In Indo-China, for example, there is a great deal of aerial bombardment, strafing, spraying of napalm, and employment of pellet- or needle-spraying anti-personnel weapons against rural villages in which guerrillas are suspected to be hiding, or from which small-arms fire has been received. The majority of those killed and wounded in these aerial attacks are reported to be women and children, even when some combatants are caught as well. However, the government regards these civilian casualties as a regrettable side-effect of what is a legitimate attack against an armed enemy.

It might be thought easy to dismiss this as sophistry: if one bombs, burns, or strafes a village containing a hundred people, twenty of whom one believes to be guerrillas, so that by killing most of them one will be statistically likely to kill most of the guerrillas, then is not one's attack on the group of one hundred a *means* of destroying the guerrillas, pure and simple? If one makes no attempt to discriminate between guerrillas and civilians, as is impossible in an aerial attack on a small village, then one cannot regard as a mere side-effect the deaths of those in the group that one would not have bothered to kill if more selective means had been available.

The difficulty is that this argument depends on one particular description of the act, and the reply might be that the means used against the guerrillas is not: killing everybody in the village—but rather: obliteration bombing of the *area* in which the twenty guerrillas are known to be located. If there are civilians in the area as well, they will be killed as a side-effect of such action.[5]

---

[5] This counter-argument was suggested by Rogers Albritton.

Because of casuistical problems like this, I prefer to stay with
the original, unanalysed distinction between what one does to
people and what merely happens to them as a result of what one
does. The law of double effect provides an approximation to that
distinction in many cases, and perhaps it can be sharpened to the
point where it does better than that. Certainly the original
distinction itself needs clarification, particularly since some of the
things we do to people involve things happening to them as a result
of other things we do. In a case like the one discussed, however, it
is clear that by bombing the village one slaughters and maims the
civilians in it. Whereas by giving the only available medicine to
one of two sufferers from a disease, one does not kill the other or
deliberately allow him to die, even if he dies as a result.

The second technical point is this. The absolutist focus on
actions rather than outcomes does not merely introduce a new,
outstanding item into the catalogue of evils. That is, it does not say
that the worst thing in the world is the deliberate murder of an
innocent person. For if that were all, then one could presumably
justify one such murder on the ground that it would prevent
several others, or ten thousand on the ground that they would
prevent a hundred thousand more. That is a familiar argument.
But if this is allowable, then there is no absolute prohibition
against murder after all. Absolutism requires that we *avoid*
murder at all costs, not that we *prevent* it at all costs.

It would also be possible to adopt a deontological position less
stringent than absolutism, without falling into utilitarianism.
There are two ways in which someone might acknowledge the
moral relevance of the distinction between deliberate and non-
deliberate killing, without being an absolutist. One would be to
count murder as a specially bad item in the catalogue of evils,
much worse than accidental death or non-deliberate killing. But
the other would be to say that deliberately killing an innocent is
impermissible unless it is the only way to prevent some very large
evil (say the deaths of fifty innocent people). Call this the
threshold at which the prohibition against murder is overridden.
The position is not absolutist, obviously, but it is also not
equivalent to an assignment of utilitarian disvalue to murder equal
to the disvalue of the threshold. This is easily seen. If a murder had

the disvalue of fifty accidental deaths, it would still be permissible on utilitarian grounds to commit a murder to prevent one other murder, plus some lesser evil like a broken arm. Worse still, we would be required on utilitarian grounds to prevent one murder even at the cost of forty-nine accidental deaths that we could otherwise have prevented. These are not in fact consequences of a deontological prohibition against murder with a threshold, because it does not say that the occurrence of a certain kind of act is a bad thing, and therefore to be prevented, but rather tells everyone to *refrain* from such acts, except under certain conditions. In fact, it is perfectly compatible with a deontological prohibition against murder to hold that, considered as an outcome, a murder has *no* more disvalue than an accidental death. While the admission of thresholds would reduce the starkness of the conflicts discussed here, I do not think it would make them disappear, or change their basic character. They would persist in the clash between any deontological requirement and utilitarian values somewhat lower than its threshold.

Finally, let me remark on a frequent criticism of absolutism that depends on a misunderstanding. It is sometimes suggested that such prohibitions depend on a kind of moral self-interest, a primary obligation to preserve one's own moral purity, to keep one's hands clean no matter what happens to the rest of the world. If this were the position, it might be exposed to the charge of self-indulgence. After all, what gives one man a right to put the purity of his soul or the cleanness of his hands above the lives or welfare of large numbers of other people? It might be argued that a public servant like Truman has no right to put himself first in that way; therefore if he is convinced that the alternatives would be worse, he must give the order to drop the bombs, and take the burden of those deaths on himself, as he must do other distasteful things for the general good.

But there are two confusions behind the view that moral self-interest underlies moral absolutism. First, it is a confusion to suggest that the need to preserve one's moral purity might be the *source* of an obligation. For if by committing murder one sacrifices one's moral purity or integrity, that can only be because there is *already* something wrong with murder. The general reason against committing murder cannot therefore be merely that it makes one an immoral person. Secondly, the notion that one might sacrifice one's moral integrity justifiably, in the service of a sufficiently worthy end, is an incoherent notion. For if one were justified in making such a sacrifice (or even morally required to make it), then one would not be sacrificing one's moral integrity by adopting that course: one would be preserving it.

Moral absolutism is not unique among moral theories in requiring each person to do what will preserve his own moral purity in all circumstances. This is equally true of utilitarianism, or of any other theory which distinguishes between right and wrong. Any theory which defines the right course of action in various circumstances and asserts that one should adopt that course, *ipso facto* asserts that one should do what will preserve one's moral purity, simply because the right course of action *is* what will preserve one's moral purity in those circumstances. Of course utilitarianism does not assert that this is *why* one should adopt that course, but we have seen that the same is true of absolutism.

V

It is easier to dispose of false explanations of absolutism than to produce a true one. A positive account of the matter must begin with the observation that war, conflict, and aggression are relations between persons. The view that it can be wrong to consider merely the overall effect of one's action on the general welfare comes into prominence when those actions involve relations with others. A man's acts usually affect more people than he deals with directly, and those effects must naturally be considered in his decisions. But if there are special principles governing the manner in which he should *treat* people, that will require special attention to the particular persons toward whom the act is directed, rather than just to its total effect.

Absolutist restrictions in warfare appear to be of two types: restrictions on the class of persons at whom aggression or violence may be directed and restrictions on the manner of attack, given that the object falls within that class. These can be combined, however, under the principle that hostile treatment of any person must be justified in terms of something *about that person* which makes the treatment appropriate. Hostility is a personal relation, and it must be suited to its target. One consequence of this condition will be that certain persons may not be subjected to hostile treatment in war at all, since nothing about them justifies such treatment. Others will be proper objects of hostility only in certain circumstances, or when they are engaged in certain pursuits. And the appropriate manner and extent of hostile treatment will depend on what is justified by the particular case.

A coherent view of this type will hold that extremely hostile behaviour toward another is compatible with treating him as a person—even perhaps as an end in himself. This is possible only if one has not automatically stopped treating him as a person as soon as one starts to fight with him. If hostile, aggressive, or combative treatment of others always violated the condition that they be treated as human beings, it would be difficult to make further distinctions on that score *within* the class of hostile actions. That point of view, on the level of international relations, leads to the position that if complete pacifism is not accepted, no holds need be barred at all, and we may slaughter and massacre to our hearts' content, if it seems advisable. Such a position is often expressed in discussions of war crimes.

But the fact is that ordinary people do not believe this about conflicts, physical or otherwise, between individuals, and there is no more reason why it should be true of conflicts between nations. There seems to be a perfectly natural conception of the distinction between fighting clean and fighting dirty. To fight dirty is to direct one's hostility or aggression not at its proper object, but at a peripheral target which may be more vulnerable, and through which the proper object can be attacked indirectly. This applies in a fist fight, an election campaign, a duel, or a philosophical argument. If the concept is general enough to apply to all these matters, it should apply to war—both to the conduct of individual soldiers and to the conduct of nations.

Suppose that you are a candidate for public office, convinced that the election of your opponent would be a disaster, that he is an unscrupulous demagogue who will serve a narrow range of interests and seriously infringe the rights of those who disagree with him; and suppose you are convinced that you cannot defeat him by conventional means. Now imagine that various unconventional means present themselves as possibilities: you possess information about his sex life which would scandalize the electorate if made public; or you learn that his wife is an alcoholic or that in his youth he was associated for a brief period with a proscribed political party, and you believe that this information could be used to blackmail him into withdrawing his candidacy; or you can have a team of your supporters flatten the tyres of a crucial subset of his supporters on election day; or you are in a position to stuff the ballot boxes; or, more simply, you can have him assassinated. What is wrong with these methods, given that they will achieve an overwhelmingly desirable result?

There are, of course, many things wrong with them: some are against the law; some infringe the procedures of an electoral process to which you are presumably committed by taking part in it; very importantly, some may backfire, and it is in the interest of all political candidates to adhere to an unspoken agreement not to allow certain personal matters to intrude into a campaign. But that is not all. We have in addition the feeling that these measures, these methods of attack, are *irrelevant* to the issue between you and your opponent, that in taking them up you would not be directing yourself to that which makes him an object of your opposition. You would be directing your attack not at the true target of your hostility, but at peripheral targets that happen to be vulnerable.

The same is true of a fight or argument outside the framework of any system of regulations or law. In an altercation with a taxi driver over an excessive fare, it is inappropriate to taunt him about his accent, flatten one of his tyres, or smear chewing-gum on his windshield; and it remains inappropriate even if he casts aspersions on your race, politics, or religion, or dumps the contents of your suitcase into the street.[6]

[6] Why, on the other hand, does it seem appropriate, rather than irrelevant, to punch someone in the mouth if he insults you? The answer is that in our culture it is an insult to punch someone in the mouth, and not just an injury. This reveals, by the way, a perfectly unobjectionable sense in which convention may play a part in determining exactly what falls under an absolutist restriction and what does not. I am indebted to Robert Fogelin for this point.

The importance of such restrictions may vary with the seriousness of the case; and what is unjustifiable in one case may be justified in a more extreme one. But they all derive from a single principle: that hostility or aggression should be directed at its true object. This means both that it should be directed at the person or persons who provoke it and that it should aim more specifically at what is provocative about them. The second condition will determine what form the hostility may appropriately take.

It is evident that some idea of the relation in which one should stand to other people underlies this principle, but the idea is difficult to state. I believe it is roughly this: whatever one does to another person intentionally must be aimed at him as a subject, with the intention that he receive it as a subject. It should manifest an attitude to *him* rather than just to the situation, and he should be able to recognize it and identify himself as its object. The procedures by which such an attitude is manifested need not be addressed to the person directly. Surgery, for example, is not a form of personal confrontation but part of a medical treatment that can be offered to a patient face to face and received by him as a response to his needs and the natural outcome of an attitude toward *him*.

Hostile treatment, unlike surgery, is already addressed *to* a person, and does not take its interpersonal meaning from a wider context. But hostile acts can serve as the expression or implementation of only a limited range of attitudes to the person who is attacked. Those attitudes in turn have as objects certain real or presumed characteristics or activities of the person which are thought to justify them. When this background is absent, hostile or aggressive behaviour can no longer be intended for the reception of the victim as a subject. Instead it takes on the character of a purely bureaucratic operation. This occurs when one attacks someone who is not the true object of one's hostility—the true object may be someone else, who can be attacked through the victim; or one may not be manifesting a hostile attitude toward anyone, but merely using the easiest available path to some desired goal. One finds oneself not facing or addressing the victim at all, but operating on him—without the larger context of personal interaction that surrounds a surgical operation.

If absolutism is to defend its claim to priority over considerations of utility, it must hold that the maintenance of a direct inter-personal response to the people one deals with is a requirement which no advantages can justify one in abandoning. The require-ment is absolute only if it rules out any calculation of what would justify its violation. I have said earlier that there may be circumstances so extreme that they render an absolutist position untenable. One may find then that one has no choice but to do something terrible. Nevertheless, even in such cases absolutism retains its force in that one cannot claim *justification* for the violation. It does not become *all right*.

As a tentative effort to explain this, let me try to connect absolutist limitations with the possibility of justifying *to the victim* what is being done to him. If one abandons a person in the course of rescuing several others from a fire or a sinking ship, one *could* say to him, 'You understand, I have to leave you to save the others.' Similarly, if one subjects an unwilling child to a painful surgical procedure, one can say to him, 'If you could understand, you would realize that I am doing this to help you.' One could *even* say, as one bayonets an enemy soldier, 'It's either you or me.' But one cannot really say while torturing a prisoner, 'You understand, I have to pull out your finger-nails because it is absolutely essential that we have the names of your confederates'; nor can one say to the victims of Hiroshima, 'You understand, we have to incinerate you to provide the Japanese government with an incentive to surrender.'

This does not take us very far, of course, since a utilitarian would presumably be willing to offer justifications of the latter sort to his victims, in cases where he thought they were sufficient. They are really justifications to the world at large, which the victim, as a reasonable man, would be expected to appreciate. However, there seems to me something wrong with this view, for it ignores the possibility that to treat someone else horribly puts you in a special relation to him, which may have to be defended in terms of other features of your relation to him. The suggestion needs much more development; but it may help us to understand how there may be requirements which are absolute in the sense that there can be no justification for violating them. If the justification for what one did to another person had to be such that it could be offered to him specifically, rather than just to the world at large, that would be a significant source of restraint.

If the account is to be deepened, I would hope for some results along the following lines. Absolutism is associated with a view of oneself as a small being interacting with others in a large world. The justifications it requires are primarily interpersonal. Utilitarianism is associated with a view of oneself as a benevolent bureaucrat distributing such benefits as one can control to countless other beings, with whom one may have various relations or none. The justifications it requires are primarily administrative. The argument between the two moral attitudes may depend on the relative priority of these two conceptions.[7]

VI

Some of the restrictions on methods of warfare which have been adhered to from time to time are to be explained by the mutual interests of the involved parties: restrictions on weaponry, treatment of prisoners, etc. But that is not all there is to it. The conditions of directness and relevance which I have argued apply to relations of conflict and aggression apply to war as well. I have said that there are two types of absolutist restrictions on the conduct of war: those that limit the legitimate targets of hostility and those that limit its character, even when the target is acceptable. I shall say something about each of these. As will become clear, the principle I have sketched does not yield an unambiguous answer in every case.

First let us see how it implies that attacks on some people are allowed, but not attacks on others. It may seem paradoxical to assert that to fire a machine-gun at someone who is throwing hand-grenades at your emplacement is to treat him as a human being. Yet the relation with him is direct and straightforward.[8]

---

[7] Finally, I should mention a different possibility, suggested by Robert Nozick: that there is a strong general presumption against benefiting from the calamity of another, whether or not it has been deliberately inflicted for that or any other reason. This broader principle may well lend its force to the absolutist position.

[8] Marshall Cohen once remarked that, according to my view, shooting at someone establishes an I-thou relationship.

The attack is aimed specifically against the threat presented by a dangerous adversary, and not against a peripheral target through which he happens to be vulnerable but which has nothing to do with that threat. For example, you might stop him by machine-gunning his wife and children, who are standing nearby, thus distracting him from his aim of blowing you up and enabling you to capture him. But if his wife and children are not threatening your life, that would be to treat them as means with a vengeance.

This, however, is just Hiroshima on a smaller scale. One objection to weapons of mass annihilation—nuclear, thermo-nuclear, biological, or chemical—is that their indiscriminateness disqualifies them as direct instruments for the expression of hostile relations. In attacking the civilian population, one treats neither the military enemy nor the civilians with that minimal respect which is owed to them as human beings. This is clearly true of the direct attack on people who present no threat at all. But it is also true of the character of the attack on those who *are* threatening you, i.e., the government and military forces of the enemy. Your aggression is directed against an area of vulnerability quite distinct from any threat presented by them which you may be justified in meeting. You are taking aim at them through the mundane life and survival of their countrymen, instead of aiming at the destruction of their military capacity. And of course it does not require hydrogen bombs to commit such crimes.

This way of looking at the matter also helps us to understand the importance of the distinction between combatants and non-combatants, and the irrelevance of much of the criticism offered against its intelligibility and moral significance. According to an absolutist position, deliberate killing of the innocent is murder, and in warfare the role of the innocent is filled by non-combatants. This has been thought to raise two sorts of problems: first, the widely imagined difficulty of making a division, in modern warfare, between combatants and non-combatants; second, problems deriving from the connotation of the word 'innocence'.

Let me take up the latter question first.[9] In the absolutist position, the operative notion of innocence is not moral innocence,

---

[9] What I say on this subject derives from Anscombe.

and it is not opposed to moral guilt. If it were, then we would be justified in killing a wicked but non-combatant hairdresser in an enemy city who supported the evil policies of his government, and unjustified in killing a morally pure conscript who was driving a tank toward us with the profoundest regrets and nothing but love in his heart. But moral innocence has very little to do with it, for in the definition of murder 'innocent' means 'currently harmless', and it is opposed not to 'guilty' but to 'doing harm'. It should be noted that such an analysis has the consequence that in war we may often be justified in killing people who do not deserve to die, and unjustified in killing people who do deserve to die, if anyone does.

So we must distinguish combatants from non-combatants on the basis of their immediate threat or harmfulness. I do not claim that the line is a sharp one, but it is not so difficult as is often supposed to place individuals on one side of it or the other. Children are not combatants even though they may join the armed forces if they are allowed to grow up. Women are not combatants just because they bear children or offer comfort to the soldiers. More problematic are the supporting personnel, whether in or out of uniform, from drivers of munitions trucks and army cooks to civilian munitions workers and farmers. I believe they can be plausibly classified by applying the condition that the prosecution of conflict must direct itself to the cause of danger, and not to what is peripheral. (The threat presented by an army and its members does not consist merely in the fact that they are men, but in the fact that they are armed and are using their arms in the pursuit of certain objectives. Contributions to their arms and logistics are contributions to this threat; contributions to their mere existence as men are not.) It is therefore wrong to direct an attack against those who merely serve the combatants' needs as human beings, such as farmers and food suppliers, even though survival as a human being is a necessary condition of efficient functioning as a soldier.

This brings us to the second group of restrictions: those that limit what may be done even to combatants. These limits are harder to explain clearly. Some of them may be arbitrary or conventional, and some may have to be derived from other sources; but I believe that the condition of directness and relevance in hostile relations accounts for them to a considerable extent.

Consider first a case which involves both a protected class of non-combatants and a restriction on the measures that may be used against combatants. One provision of the rules of war which is universally recognized, though it seems to be turning into a dead letter in Vietnam, is the special status of medical personnel and the wounded in warfare. It might be more efficient to shoot medical officers on sight and to let the enemy wounded die rather than be patched up to fight another day. But someone with medical insignia is supposed to be left alone and permitted to tend and retrieve the wounded. I believe this is because medical attention is a species of attention to completely general human needs, not specifically the needs of a combat soldier, and our conflict with the soldier is not with his existence as a human being.

By extending the application of this idea, one can justify prohibitions against certain particularly cruel weapons: starvation, poisoning, infectious diseases (supposing they could be inflicted on combatants only), weapons designed to maim or disfigure or torture the opponent rather than merely to stop him. It is not, I think, mere casuistry to claim that such weapons attack the men, not the soldiers. The effect of dum-dum bullets, for example, is much more extended than necessary to cope with the combat situation in which they are used. They abandon any attempt to discriminate in their effects between the combatant and the human being. For this reason the use of flame-throwers and napalm is an atrocity in all circumstances that I can imagine, whoever the target may be. Burns are both extremely painful and extremely disfiguring—far more than any other category of wound. That this well-known fact plays no (inhibiting) part in the determination of US weapons policy suggests that moral sensitivity among public officials has not increased markedly since the Spanish Inquisition.[10]

---

[10] Beyond this I feel uncertain. Ordinary bullets, after all, can cause death, and nothing is more permanent than that. I am not at all sure why we are justified in trying to kill those who are trying to kill us (rather than merely in trying to stop them with force which may also result in their deaths). It is often argued that incapacitating gases are a relatively humane weapon (when not used, as in Vietnam, merely to make people easier to shoot). Perhaps the legitimacy of restrictions against them must depend on the dangers of escalation, and the great

Finally, the same condition of appropriateness to the true object of hostility should limit the scope of attacks on an enemy country: its economy, agriculture, transportation system, and so forth. Even if the parties to a military conflict are considered to be not armies or governments but entire nations (which is usually a grave error), that does not justify one nation in warring against every aspect or element of another nation. That is not justified in a conflict between individuals, and nations are even more complex than individuals, so the same reasons apply. Like a human being, a nation is engaged in countless other pursuits while waging war, and it is not in those respects that it is an enemy.

The burden of the argument has been that absolutism about murder has a foundation in principles governing all one's relations to other persons, whether aggressive or amiable, and that these principles and that absolutism apply to warfare as well, with the result that certain measures are impermissible no matter what the consequences.[11] I do not mean to romanticize war. It is sufficiently Utopian to suggest that when nations conflict they might rise to the level of limited barbarity that typically characterizes violent conflict between individuals, rather than wallowing in the moral pit where they appear to have settled, surrounded by enormous arsenals.

VII

Having described the elements of the absolutist position, we now must return to the conflict between it and utilitarianism. Even if certain types of dirty tactics become acceptable when the stakes

utility of maintaining *any* conventional category of restriction so long as nations are willing to adhere to it. Let me make clear that I do not regard my argument as a defence of the moral immutability of the Hague and Geneva Conventions. Rather, I believe that they rest partly on a moral foundation, and that modifications of them should also be assessed on moral grounds.

[11] It is possible to draw a more radical conclusion, which I shall not pursue here. Perhaps the technology and organization of modern war are such as to make it impossible to wage as an acceptable form of interpersonal or even international hostility. Perhaps it is too impersonal and large-scale for that. If so, then absolutism would in practice imply pacifism, given the present state of things. On the other hand, I am sceptical about the unstated assumption that a technology dictates its own use.

are high enough, the most serious of the prohibited acts, like murder and torture, are not just supposed to require unusually strong justification. They are supposed *never* to be done, because no quantity of resulting benefit is thought capable of *justifying* such treatment of a person.

The fact remains that when an absolutist knows or believes that the utilitarian cost of refusing to adopt a prohibited course will be very high, he may hold to his refusal to adopt it, but he will find it difficult to feel that a moral dilemma has been satisfactorily resolved. The same may be true of someone who rejects an absolutist requirement and adopts instead the course yielding the most acceptable consequences. In either case, it is possible to feel that one has acted for reasons insufficient to justify violation of the opposing principle. In situations of deadly conflict, particularly where a weaker party is threatened with annihilation or enslavement by a stronger one, the argument for resorting to atrocities can be powerful, and the dilemma acute.

There may exist principles, not yet codified, which would enable us to resolve such dilemmas. But then again there may not. We must face the pessimistic alternative that these two forms of moral intuition are not capable of being brought together into a single, coherent moral system, and that the world can present us with situations in which there is no honourable or moral course for a man to take, no course free of guilt and responsibility for evil.[12]

The idea of a moral blind alley is a perfectly intelligible one. It is possible to get into such a situation by one's own fault, and people do it all the time. If, for example, one makes two incompatible promises or commitments—becomes engaged to two people, for example—then there is no course one can take which is not wrong, for one must break one's promise to at least one of them. Making a clean breast of the whole thing will not be enough to remove one's

---

[12] In his reply to this essay ('Rules of War and Moral Reasoning', *Philosophy and Public Affairs* 1, no. 2 (Winter 1972), 167). R. M. Hare pointed out the apparent discrepancy between my acceptance of such a possibility here and my earlier claim in Section IV that absolutism must be formulated so as to avoid the consequence that in certain cases nothing one could do would be morally permissible. The difference is that in those cases the moral incoherence would result from the application of a single principle, whereas the dilemmas described here result from a conflict between two fundamentally different types of principle.

reprehensibility. The existence of such cases is not morally disturbing, however, because we feel that the situation was not unavoidable: one had to do something wrong in the first place to get into it. But what if the world itself, or someone else's actions, could face a previously innocent person with a choice between morally abominable courses of action, and leave him no way to escape with his honour? Our intuitions rebel at the ideal, for we feel that the constructibility of such a case must show a contradiction in our moral views. But it is not in itself a contradiction to say that someone can do X or not do X, and that for him to take either course would be wrong. It merely contradicts the supposition that *ought* implies *can*—since presumably one ought to refrain from what is wrong, and in such a case it is impossible to do so.[13] Given the limitations on human action, it is naïve to suppose that there is a solution to every moral problem with which the world can face us. We have always known that the world is a bad place. It appears that it may be an evil place as well.

[13] This was first pointed out to me by Christopher Boorse. The point is also made in E. J. Lemmon's 'Moral Dilemmas', *Philosophical Review* 71 (Apr. 1962), 150.

4

RIGHTS, GOALS, AND FAIRNESS

T. M. SCANLON

CRITICS of utilitarianism frequently call attention to the abhorrent policies that unrestricted aggregative reasoning might justify under certain possible, or even actual, circumstances. They invite the conclusion that to do justice to the firm intuition that such horrors are clearly unjustifiable one must adopt a deontological moral framework that places limits on what appeals to maximum aggregate well-being can justify. As one who has often argued in this way, however, I am compelled to recognize that this position has its own weakness. In attacking utilitarianism one is inclined to appeal to individual rights, which mere considerations of social utility cannot justify us in overriding. But rights themselves need to be justified somehow, and how other than by appeal to the human interests their recognition promotes and protects? This seems to be the uncontrovertible insight of the classical utilitarians. Further, unless rights are to be taken as defined by rather implausible rigid formulae, it seems that we must invoke what looks very much like the consideration of consequences in order to determine what they rule out and what they allow. Thus, for example, in order to determine whether a given policy violates the right of freedom of expression it is not enough to know merely that it restricts speech. We may need to consider also its effects: how it would affect access to the means of expression and what the

T. M. Scanlon, 'Rights, Goals, and Fairness', from *Public and Private Morality*, ed. Stuart Hampshire (Cambridge University Press, 1978), pp. 93–111. An earlier version appeared in *Erkenntnis*, Vol. II, No. 1, 1977, pp. 81–95. Reprinted by permission of D. Reidel Publishing Company, Dordrecht-Holland.

consequences would be of granting to government the kind of regulatory powers it confers.

I am thus drawn toward a two-tier view: one that gives an important role to consequences in the justification and interpretation of rights but which takes rights seriously as placing limits on consequentialist reasoning at the level of casuistry. Such a view looks like what has been called rule utilitarianism, a theory subject to a number of very serious objections. First, rule utilitarians are hard pressed to explain why, if at base they are convinced utilitarians, they are not thoroughgoing ones. How can they square their utilitarianism with the acceptance of individual actions that are not in accord with the utilitarian formula? Second, rule utilitarianism seems to be open to some of the same objections levelled against utilitarianism in its pure form; in particular it seems no more able than act utilitarianism is to give a satisfactory place to considerations of distributive justice. Third, in attempting to specify which rules it is that are to be applied in the appraisal of acts and policies rule utilitarians of the usual sort are faced with an acute dilemma. If it is some set of ideal rules that are to be applied—those rules general conformity to which would have the best consequences—then the utilitarian case for a concern with rules, rather than merely with the consequences of isolated acts, appears lost. For this case must rest on benefits that flow from the general observance of rules but not from each individual act, and such benefits can be gained only if the rules are in fact generally observed. But if, on the other hand, the rules that are to be applied must be ones that are generally observed, the critical force of the theory seems to be greatly weakened.

The problem, then, is to explain how a theory can have, at least in part, a two-tier structure; how it can retain the basic appeal of utilitarianism, at least as it applies to the foundation of rights, and yet avoid the problems that have plagued traditional rule utilitarianism. As a start towards describing such a theory I will consider three questions. (1) What consequences are to be considered, and how is their value to be determined? (2) How do considerations of distributive justice enter the theory? (3) How does one justify taking rights (or various moral rules) as constraints on the production of valued consequences?

76   T. M. SCANLON

1. CONSEQUENCES AND THEIR VALUES

Here I have two remarks, one of foundation, the other of content. First, as I have argued elsewhere[1] but can here only assert, I depart from the classical utilitarians and many of their modern followers in rejecting subjective preferences as the basis for the valuation of outcomes. This role is to be played instead by an ethically significant, objective notion of the relative importance of various benefits and burdens.

Second, as to content, the benefits and burdens with which the theory is concerned must include not only the things that may happen to people but also factors affecting the ability of individuals to determine what will happen. Some of these factors are the concern of what are generally called rights, commonly[2] distinguished into (claim-) rights to command particular things, where others have a correlative duty to comply; liberties to do or refrain from certain things, where others have no such correlative duties; powers to change people's rights or status; and immunities from powers exercised by others. I take it to be the case that the familiar civil rights, as well as such things as rights of privacy and 'the right to life', are complexes of such elements. The *de facto* ability effectively to choose among certain options and the *de facto* absence of interference by others with one's choices are not the same thing as rights, although if it is generally believed that a person has a particular right, say a claim-right, this may contribute to his having such *de facto* ability or lack of interference. But, however they are created, such abilities and protections are important goods with which any moral theory must be concerned, and the allocation of rights is one way in which this importance receives theoretical recognition.

[1] In 'Preference and Urgency'.
[2] Following Hohfeld and others. See W. N. Hohfeld, *Fundamental Legal Conceptions* (New Haven, 1923), and also S. Kanger, 'New Foundations for Ethical Theory' in R. Hilpinen, ed., *Deontic Logic: Introductory and Systematic Readings* (Dordrecht, 1971), pp. 36–58. On the distinction between concern with outcomes and concern with the allocation of competences to determine outcomes see C. Fried, 'Two Concepts of Interests: Some Reflections of the Supreme Court's Balancing Test', *The Harvard Law Review* 76 (1963), 755–78.

Any theory of right, since it deals with what agents should and may do, is in a broad sense concerned with the assignment of rights and liberties. It is relevant to ask, concerning such a theory, how much latitude it gives a person in satisfying moral requirements and how much protection it gives a person through the constraints it places on the actions of others. Traditional utilitarianism has been seen as extreme on both these counts. It is maximally specific in the requirements it imposes on an agent, and, since there are no limits to what it may require to be done, it provides a minimum of reliable protection from interference by others. Objections to utilitarianism have often focused on its demanding and intrusive character,[3] and other theories of right may grant individuals both greater discretion and better protection. But these are goods with costs. When one individual is given a claim-right or liberty with respect to a certain option, the control that others are able to exercise over their own options is to some degree diminished. Further, if we take the assignment of rights to various individuals as, in at least some cases, an end-point of justification, then we must be prepared to accept the situation resulting from their exercise of these rights even if, considered in itself, it may be unattractive or at least not optimal. Both these points have been urged by Robert Nozick,[4] the latter especially in his attack on 'end-state' and 'patterned' theories. What follows from these observations, however, is not Nozick's particular theory of entitlements but rather a general moral about the kind of comparison and balancing that a justification of rights requires: the abilities and protections that rights confer must be assigned values that are comparable not only with competing values of the same kind but also with the values attached to the production of particular end-results.

The same moral is to be drawn from some of Bernard Williams's objections to utilitarianism.[5] Williams objects that utilitarianism, in demanding total devotion to the inclusive goal of maximum

---

[3] See B. Williams, 'A Critique of Utilitarianism', in J. J. C. Smart and B. Williams, *Utilitarianism: For and Against.* [Reprinted in part as Chapter 2 in this volume—Ed.]

[4] In *Anarchy, State, and Utopia,* esp. pp. 32–5 and Chapter 7.

[5] In sec. 5 of 'A Critique of Utilitarianism'. [Section 4 of Chapter 2 in this volume—Ed.]

happiness, fails to give adequate recognition to the importance, for each individual, of the particular projects which give his life content. The problem with such an objection is that taken alone it may be made to sound like pure self-indulgence. Simply to demand freedom from moral requirements in the name of freedom to pursue one's individual projects is unconvincing. It neglects the fact that these requirements may protect interests of others that are at least as important as one's own. To rise clearly above the level of special pleading these objections must be made general. They must base themselves on a general claim about how important the interests they seek to protect are for any person as compared with the interests served by conflicting claims.

The two preceding remarks—of foundation and of content—are related in the following way. Since the ability to influence outcomes and protection from interference or control by others are things people care about, they will be taken into account in any subjective utilitarian theory. I will later raise doubts as to whether such a theory can take account of them in the right way, but my present concern is with the question what value is to be assigned to these concerns. On a subjective theory these values will be determined by the existing individual preferences in the society in question. I would maintain, however, that prevailing preferences are not an adequate basis for the justification of rights. It is not relevant, for example, to the determination of rights of religious freedom that the majority group in a society is feverishly committed to the goal of making its practices universal while the minority is quite tepid about all matters of religion. This is of course just an instance of the general objection to subjective theories stated above. The equally general response is that one has no basis on which to 'impose' values that run contrary to individual preferences. This objection draws its force from the idea that individual autonomy ought to be respected and that it is offensive to frustrate an individual's considered preferences in the name of serving his 'true interests'. This idea does not itself rest on preferences. Rather, it functions as the objective moral basis for giving preferences a fundamental role as the ground of ethically relevant valuations. But one may question whether this theoretical move is an adequate response to the intuitive idea from which it springs. To be concerned with individual autonomy is to be concerned with the rights, liberties, and other conditions necessary for individuals to develop their own aims and interests and to make their preferences effective in shaping their own lives and contributing to the formation of social policy. Among these will be rights protecting people against various forms of paternalistic intervention. A theory that respects autonomy will be one that assigns all of these factors their proper weight. There is no reason to think that this will be accomplished merely by allowing these weights, and all others, to be determined by the existing configuration of preferences.

2. FAIRNESS AND EQUALITY

Rather than speaking generally of 'distributive justice', which can encompass a great variety of considerations, I will speak instead of fairness, as a property of processes (e.g. of competitions), and equality, as a property of resultant distributions. The question is how these considerations enter a theory of the kind I am describing. One way in which a notion of equality can be built into a consequentialist theory is through the requirement that, in evaluating states of affairs to be promoted, we give equal consideration to the interests of every person. This principle of equal consideration of interests has minimal egalitarian content. As stated, it is compatible with classical utilitarianism which, after all, 'counts each for one and none for more than one'. Yet many have felt, with justification, that utilitarianism gives insufficient weight to distributive considerations. How might this weight be increased? Let me distinguish two ways. The first would be to strengthen the principle of equal consideration of interests in such a way as to make it incompatible with pure utilitarianism. 'Equal consideration' could, for example, be held to mean that in any justification by appeal to consequences we must give priority to those individual interests that are 'most urgent'. To neglect such interests in order to serve instead less urgent interests even of a great number of people would, on this interpretation, violate 'equality of consideration'. Adoption of this interpretation would ward off some objections to utilitarianism based on its insensitivity to distributive considerations but would at the same time preserve other characteristic features of the doctrine, e.g. some of its radically redistributive implications. Such a 'lexical interpretation' has, of course, its own problems. Its strength (and plausibility) is obviously dependent on the ranking we choose for determining the urgency of various interests.

The nature of such a ranking is an important problem, but one I cannot pursue here. Whatever the degree of distributive content that is built into the way individual interests are reckoned in moral argument, however, there is a second way in which distributive considerations enter a theory of the kind I wish to propose: equality of distributions and fairness of processes are among the properties that make states of affairs worth promoting. Equality in the distribution of particular classes of goods is at least sometimes of value as a means to the attainment of other valued ends, and in other cases fairness and equality are valuable in their own right.

Classical utilitarianism, of course, already counts equality as a means, namely as a means to maximum aggregate utility. Taken alone, this seems inadequate—too instrumental to account for the moral importance equality has for us. Yet I do think that in many of the cases in which we are most concerned with the promotion of equality we desire greater equality as a means to the attainment of some further end. In many cases, for example, the desire to eliminate great inequalities is motivated primarily by humanitarian concern for the plight of those who have least. Redistribution is desirable in large part because it is a means of alleviating their suffering (without giving rise to comparable suffering elsewhere). A second source of moral concern with redistribution in the contemporary world lies in the fact that great inequalities in wealth give to those who have more an unacceptable degree of control over the lives of others. Here again the case for greater equality is instrumental. Were these two grounds for redistribution to be eliminated (by, say, greatly increasing the standard of living of all concerned and preventing the gap between rich and poor, which remains unchanged, from allowing the rich to dominate) the moral case for inequality would not be eliminated, but I believe that it would seem less pressing.

Beyond these and other instrumental arguments, fairness and

equality often figure in moral argument as independently valuable states of affairs. So considered, they differ from the ends promoted in standard utilitarian theories in that their value does not rest on their being good things *for* particular individuals: fairness and equality do not represent ways in which individuals may be *better off*.[6] They are, rather, special morally desirable features of states of affairs or of social institutions. In admitting such moral features into the evaluation of consequences, the theory I am describing departs from standard consequentialist theories, which generally resist the introduction of explicitly moral considerations into the maximand. It diverges also from recent deontological theories, which bring in fairness and equality as specific moral requirements rather than as moral goals. I am inclined to pursue this 'third way' for several reasons.

First, it is not easy to come up with a moral argument for substantive equality (as distinct from mere formal equality or equal consideration of interests) which makes it look like an absolute moral requirement. Second, considerations of fairness and equality are multiple. There are many different processes that may be more or less fair, and we are concerned with equality in the distribution of many different and separable benefits and burdens. These are not all of equal importance; the strength of claims of equality and fairness depends on the goods whose distribution is at issue. Third, these claims do not seem to be absolute. Attempts to achieve equality or fairness in one area may conflict with the pursuit of these goals in other areas. In order to achieve greater equality we may, for example, change our processes in ways that involve unfairness in the handling of some individual cases. Perhaps the various forms of fairness and equality can be brought together under one all-encompassing notion of distributive justice which is always to be increased, but it is not obvious that this is so. In any event, it would remain the case that attempts to increase fairness and equality can have costs in other terms; they may interfere with processes whose efficiency is important to us, or

[6] Here I am indebted to Kurt Baier. Defending the claim that fairness and equality are intrinsically valuable is of course a further difficult task. Perhaps all convincing appeals to these notions can be reduced to instrumental arguments, but I do not at present see how. Such a reduction would move my theory even closer to traditional utilitarianism.

involve unwelcome intrusions into individuals' lives. In such cases of conflict it does not seem that considerations of fairness and equality, as such, are always dominant. An increase in equality may in some cases not be worth its cost; whether it is will depend in part on what it is equality *of*.

Economists often speak of 'trade-offs' between equality and other concerns (usually efficiency). I have in the past been inclined, perhaps intolerantly, to regard this as crassness, but I am no longer certain that it is in principle mistaken. The suggestion that equality can be 'traded-off' against other goods arouses suspicion because it seems to pave the way for defences of the status quo. Measures designed to decrease inequality in present societies are often opposed on the ground that they involve too great a sacrifice in efficiency or in individual liberty, and one way to head off such objections is to hold that equality is to be pursued whatever the cost. But one can hold that appeals to liberty and efficiency do not justify maintaining the status quo—and in fact that considerations of individual liberty provide some of the strongest arguments in favour of increased equality of income and wealth—without holding that considerations of equality are, as such, absolute and take priority over all other values.

3. RIGHTS

Why give rights a special place in a basically consequentialist theory? How can a two-tier theory be justified? One common view of the place of rights, and moral rules generally, within utilitarianism holds that they are useful as means to the co-ordination of action. The need for such aids does not depend on imperfect motivation; it might exist even in a society of perfect altruists. A standard example is a rule regulating water consumption during a drought. A restriction to one bucket a day per household might be a useful norm for a society of utilitarians even though their reasons for taking more water than this would be entirely altruistic. Its usefulness does not depend on self-interest. But the value of such a rule does depend on the fact that the agents are assumed to act independently of one another in partial ignorance of what the others have done or will do. If Dudley knows what others will do, and knows that this will leave some water in the well, then there is no utilitarian reason why he should not violate the rule and take more than his share for some suitable purpose—as the story goes, to water the flowers in the public garden.

I am of two minds about such examples. On the one hand, I can feel the force of the utilitarian's insistence that if the water is not going to be used how can we object to Dudley's taking it? On the other hand, I do not find this line of reply wholly satisfying. Why should *he* be entitled to do what others were not? Well, because he knows and they didn't; he alone has the opportunity. But just because he has it does that mean he can exercise it unilaterally? Perhaps, to be unbearably priggish, he should call the surplus to the attention of the others so that they can all decide how to use it. If this alternative is available is it all right for him to pass it up and act on his own? A utilitarian might respond here that he is not saying that Dudley is entitled to do whatever he wishes with the surplus water; he is entitled to do with it what the principle of utility requires and nothing else.

Here a difference of view is shown. Permission to act outside the rule is seen by the non-utilitarian as a kind of freedom for the agent, an exemption, but it is seen by a utilitarian as a specific moral requirement. Dudley is required to do something that is different from what the others do because his situation is different, but he has no greater latitude for the exercise of discretion or personal preference than anyone else does. This suggests that one can look at an assignment of rights in either of two ways: as a way of constraining individual decisions in order to promote some desired further effect (as in the case of a system of rules defining a division of labour between co-workers) or as a way of parceling out valued forms of discretion over which individuals are in conflict. To be avoided, I think, is a narrow utilitarianism that construes all rights on the first model, e.g. as mechanisms of co-ordination or as hedges against individual errors in judgement. So construed, rights have no weight against deviant actions that can be shown to be the most effective way of advancing the shared goal.

If, however, the possibility of construing some rights on the second model is kept open, then rights can be given a more substantial role within a theory that is still broadly utilitarian. When, as seems plausible on one view of the water-shortage example, the purpose of an assignment of rights is to ensure an equitable distribution of a form of control over outcomes, then these rights are supported by considerations which persist even when contrary actions would promote optimum results. This could remain true for a society of conscientious (though perhaps not single-minded) consequentialists, provided that they are concerned with 'consequences' of the sort I have described above. But to say that a rule or a right is not in general subject to exceptions justified on act-utilitarian grounds is not to say that it is absolute. One can ask how important it is to preserve an equitable distribution of control of the kind in question, and there will undoubtedly be some things that outweigh this value. There is no point in observing the one-bucket restriction when the pump-house is on fire. Further, the intent of an assignment of rights on the second model is apt to be to forestall certain particularly tempting or likely patterns of behaviour. If this is so, there may be some acts which are literally contrary to the formula in which the right is usually stated but which do not strike us as actual violations of the right. We are inclined to allow them even though the purposes they serve may be less important than the values the right is intended to secure. Restrictions on speech which none the less are not violations of freedom of expression are a good example of such 'apparent exceptions'.

Reflections of this kind suggest to me that the view that there is a moral right of a certain sort is generally backed by something like the following:

(i) An empirical claim about how individuals would behave or how institutions would work in the absence of this particular assignment of rights (claim-rights, liberties, etc.).

(ii) A claim that this result would be unacceptable. This claim will be based on valuation of consequences of the sort described in Section I above, taking into account also considerations of fairness and equality.

(iii) A further empirical claim about how the envisaged assignment of rights will produce a different outcome.

The empirical parts of this schema play a larger or at least more conspicuous role in some rights than in others. In the case of the right to freedom of expression this role is a large one and fairly well recognized. Neglecting this empirical element leads rights to degenerate into implausible rigid formulae. The impossibility of taking such a formula literally, as defining an absolute moral bar, lends plausibility to a 'balancing' view, according to which such a right merely represents one important value among others, and decisions must be reached by striking the proper balance between them. Keeping in mind the empirical basis of a right counters this tendency and provides a ground (1) for seeing that 'apparent exceptions' of the kind mentioned above are not justified simply by balancing one right against another; (2) for seeing where genuine balancing of interests is called for and what its proper terms are; and (3) for seeing how the content of a right must change as conditions change. These remarks hold, I think, not only for freedom of expression but also for other rights, for example, rights of due process and rights of privacy. In each of these cases a fairly complex set of institutional arrangements and assumptions about how these arrangements operate stands, so to speak, between the formula through which the right is identified and the goals to which it is addressed. This dependence on empirical considerations is less evident in the case of rights, like the right to life, that lie more in the domain of individual morality. I will argue below, however, that this right too can profitably be seen as a system of authorizations and limitations of discretion justified on the basis of an argument of the form just described.

This view of rights is in a broad sense consequentialist in that it holds rights to be justified by appeal to the states of affairs they promote. It seems to differ from the usual forms of rule utilitarianism, however, in that it does not appear to be a maximizing doctrine. The case for most familiar rights—freedom of expression, due process, religious toleration—seems to be more concerned with the avoidance of particular bad consequences than with promoting maximum benefit. But this difference is in part only apparent. The dangers that these rights are supposed to ward off are major ones, not likely to be overshadowed by everyday considerations. Where they are overshadowed, the theory I have described allows for the rights in question to be set aside. Further, the justification for the particular form that such a right takes allows for the consideration of costs. If a revised form of some right would do the intended job as well as the standard form at clearly reduced costs to peripheral interests, then this form would obviously be preferred. It should be noted, however, that if something is being maximized here it can not, in view of the role that the goals of fairness and equality play in the theory, be simply the sum of individual benefits. Moreover, this recognition of an element of maximization does not mean that just any possible improvement in the way people generally behave will become the subject of a right. Rights concern the alleviation of certain major problems, and incremental gains in other goods become relevant to rights in the way just mentioned only when they flow from improvements in our ways of dealing with such problems.

I have suggested that the case for rights derives in large part from the goal of promoting an acceptable distribution of control over important factors in our lives. This general goal is one that would be of importance to people in a wide range of societies. But the particular rights it calls for may vary from society to society. Thus, in particular, the rights we have on the view I have proposed are probably not identical with the rights that would be recognized under the system of rules, general conformity to which in our society would have the best consequences. The problems to which our rights are addressed are ones that arise given the distribution of power and the prevailing patterns of motivation in the societies in which we live. These problems may not be ones that would arise were an ideal code of behaviour to prevail.[7] (And they might not

---

[7] How much this separates my view of rights from an ideal rule utilitarian theory will depend on how that theory construes the notion of an ideal system of rules being 'in force' in a society. In Brandt's sophisticated version, for example, what is required is that it be true, and known in the society, that a high proportion of adults subscribe to these rules, that is, chiefly, that they are to some extent motivated to avoid violating the rules and feel guilty when they believe they have done so. ('Some Merits of One Form of Rule Utilitarianism' in Gorovitz, ed., *Mill: Utilitarianism, with Critical Essays* (Indianapolis, Ind., 1971).) This may not insure that the level of conformity with these rules is much greater than the level of moral behaviour in societies we are familiar with. If it does not, then Brandt's theory may not be much more 'ideal' than the theory of rights offered here. The two theories appear to

be the same either as those we would face in a 'state of nature'.) Concern with rights does not involve accepting these background conditions as desirable or as morally unimpeachable; it only involves seeing them as relatively fixed features of the environment with which we must deal.

Which features of one's society are to be held fixed in this way for purposes of moral argument about rights? This can be a controversial moral question and presents a difficult theoretical issue for anyone holding a view like rule utilitarianism. As more and more is held fixed, including more about what other agents are in fact doing, the view converges toward act utilitarianism. If, on the other hand, very little is held fixed then the problems of ideal forms of rule utilitarianism seem to loom larger: we seem to risk demanding individual observance of rights when this is pointless given the lack of general conformity.

This dilemma is most acute to the degree that the case for rights (or moral rules) is seen to rest on their role in promoting maximum utility through the co-ordination of individual action. Where this is actually the case—as it is with many rules and perhaps some rights—it is of undoubted importance what others are in fact doing—to what degree these rights and rules are generally observed and how individual action will affect general observance. I suggest, however, that this is not the case with most rights. On the view I propose, a central concern of most rights is the promotion and maintenance of an acceptable distribution of control over important factors in our lives. Where a certain curtailment of individual discretion or official authority is clearly required for this purpose, the fact that this right is not generally observed does not undermine the case for its observance in a given instance. The case against allowing some to dictate the private religious observances of others, for example, does not depend on the existence of a general practice of religious toleration. Some of

differ, however, on the issues discussed in Sections 1 and 2 above. These issues also divide my view from R. M. Hare's version of rule utilitarianism, with which I am otherwise in much agreement. See his 'Ethical Theory and Utilitarianism', in H. D. Lewis, ed., *Contemporary British Philosophy, Fourth Series* (London, 1976). Like these more general theories, the account of rights offered here has a great deal in common with the view put forward by Mill in the final chapter of *Utilitarianism* (particularly if Mill's remarks about 'justice' are set aside).

the benefits at which rights of religious freedom are aimed—the benefits of a general climate of religious toleration—are secured only when there is general compliance with these rights. But the case for enforcing these rights does not depend in every instance on these benefits.

For these reasons, the view of rights I have proposed is not prey to objections often raised against ideal rule utilitarian theories. A further question is whether it is genuinely distinct from an act-consequentialist doctrine. It may seem that, for reasons given above, it cannot be: if an act in violation of a given right yields some consequence that is of greater value than those with which the right is concerned, then on my view the right is to be set aside. If the act does not have such consequences then, in virtue of its conflicts with the right and the values that right protects, it seems that the act would not be justifiable on act-consequentialist grounds anyway. But this rests on a mistake. The values supporting a particular right need not all stand to be lost in every case in which the right is violated. In defending the claim that there is a right of a certain sort, e.g., a particular right of privacy, we must be prepared to compare the advantages of having this right—the advantages, e.g., of being free to decline to be searched—against competing considerations—e.g., the security benefits derived from a more lenient policy of search and seizure. But what stands to be gained or lost in any given instance in which a policeman would like to search me need not coincide with either of these values. It may be that in that particular case I don't care.[8]

There is, then, no incoherence in distinguishing between the value of having a right and the cost of having it violated on a particular occasion. And it is just the values of the former sort that we must appeal to in justifying a two-tier view. What more can be said about these values? From an act-consequentialist point of view the value attached to the kind of control and protection that rights confer seems to rest on mistrust of others. If everyone could be relied upon to do the correct thing from an act-consequentialist standpoint would we still be so concerned with rights? This way of

---

[8] On the importance of establishing the proper terms of balancing see Fried. 'Two Concepts of Interests', p. 758.

putting the matter obscures several important elements. First, it supposes that we can all agree on the best thing to be done in each case. But concern with rights is based largely on the warranted supposition that we have significantly differing ideas of the good and that we are interested in the freedom to put our own conceptions into practice. Second, the objection assumes that we are concerned only with the correct choice being made and have no independent concern with who makes it. This also seems clearly false. The independent value we attach to being able to make our own choices should, however, be distinguished from the further value we may attach to having it recognized that we are *entitled* to make them. This we may also value in itself as a sign of respect and personhood, but there is a question to what degree this value is an artefact of our moral beliefs and customs rather than a basis for them. Where a moral framework of rights is established and recognized, it will be important for a person to have his status as a right holder generally acknowledged. But is there something analogous to this importance that is lost for everyone in a society of conscientious act consequentialists where no one holds rights? It is not clear to me that there is, but, however this may be, my account emphasizes the value attached to rights for the sake of what they may bring rather than their value as signs of respect.

If the factors just enumerated were the whole basis for concern with rights then one would expect the case for them to weaken and the force of act-consequentialist considerations to grow relatively stronger as (1) the importance attached to outcomes becomes absolutely greater and hence, presumably, also relatively greater as compared with the independent value of making choices one's self, and as (2) the assignment of values to the relevant outcomes becomes less controversial. To some extent both these things happen in cases where life and death are at stake, and here mistrust emerges as the more plausible basis for concern with rights.

4. CASES OF LIFE AND DEATH

From the point of view suggested in this paper, the right to life is to be seen as a complex of elements including particular liberties to

act in one's own defence and to preserve one's life, claim-rights to
aid and perhaps to the necessities of life, and restrictions on the
liberty of others to kill or endanger. Let me focus here on elements
in these last two categories, namely limits on the liberty to act in
ways that lead to a person's death. An act-consequentialist
standard could allow a person to take action leading to the death
of another whenever this is necessary to avoid greater loss of life
elsewhere. Many find this policy too permissive, and one
explanation of this reaction is that it represents a kind of blind
conservatism. We know that our lives are always in jeopardy in
many ways. Tomorrow I may die of a heart attack or a blood clot. I
may be hit by a falling tree or discover that I have a failing liver or
find myself stood up against a wall by a group of terrorists. But we
are reluctant to open the door to a further form of deadly risk by
licensing others to take our life should this be necessary to
minimize loss of life overall. We are reluctant to do this even when
the effect would be to increase our net chances of living a long life
by decreasing the likelihood that we will actually die when one of
the natural hazards of life befalls us. We adopt, as it were, the
attitude of hoping against hope not to run afoul of any of these
hazards, and we place less stock on the prospect of escaping alive
should we be so unlucky. It would not be irrational for a person to
decide to increase his chances of survival by joining a transplant-
insurance scheme, i.e. an arrangement guaranteeing one a heart or
kidney should he need one provided he agrees to sacrifice himself
to become a donor if he is chosen to do so. But such a decision is
sufficiently controversial and the stakes so high that it is not a
decision that can be taken to have been made for us as part of a
unanimously acceptable basis for the assignment of rights. What I
have here called conservatism is, however, uncomfortably close to
a bias of the lucky against the unlucky in so far as it rests on a
conscious turning of attention away from the prospect of our being
one of the unlucky ones.

A substitute for conservatism is mistrust. We are reluctant to
place our life in *anyone's* hands. We are even more reluctant to
place our lives in *everyone's* hands as the act-consequentialist
standard would have us do. Such mistrust is the main factor
supporting the observed difference between the rationality of

joining a voluntary transplant-insurance scheme and the permissibility of having a compulsory one (let alone the universally administered one that unrestricted act consequentialism could amount to). A person who joins a voluntary scheme has the chance to see who will be making the decisions and to examine the safeguards on the process. In assessing the force of these considerations one should also bear in mind that what they are to be weighed against is not 'the value of life itself' but only a small increase in the probability of living a somewhat longer life.

These appeals to 'conservatism' and mistrust, if accepted, would support something like the distinction between killing and letting die: we are willing to grant to others the liberty not to save us from threat of death when this is necessary to save others, but we are unwilling to license them to put us under threat of death when we have otherwise escaped it. As is well known, however, the killing/ letting die distinction appears to permit some actions leading to a person's death that are not intuitively permissible. These are actions in which an agent refrains from aiding someone already under threat of death and does so because that person's death has results he considers advantageous. (I will assume that they are thought advantageous to someone other than the person who is about to die.) The intuition that such actions are not permitted would be served by a restriction on the liberty to fail to save, specifying that this course of action cannot be undertaken on the basis of conceived advantages of having the person out of the way. Opponents of the law of double effect have sometimes objected that it is strange to make the permissibility of an action depend on quite subtle features of its rationale. In the context of the present theory, however, the distinction just proposed is not formally anomalous. Conferrals of authority and limitations on it often take the form not simply of licensing certain actions or barring them but rather of restricting the grounds on which actions can be undertaken. Freedom of expression embodies restrictions of this kind, for example, and this is one factor responsible for the distinction between real and apparent violations mentioned above.[9]

[9] For a view of freedom of expression embodying this feature, see Scanlon, 'A Theory of Freedom of Expression', *Philosophy and Public Affairs* (1972), 204–26.

Reasons for such a restriction in the present case are easy to come by. People have such powerful and tempting reasons for wanting others removed from the scene that it is obviously a serious step to open the door to calculations taking these reasons into account. Obviously, what would be proposed would be a qualified restriction, allowing consideration of the utilitarian, but not the purely self-interested, advantages to be gained from a person's death. But a potential agent's perception of this distinction does not seem to be a factor worth depending on.

The restriction proposed here may appear odd when compared to our apparent policy regarding mutual aid. If, as seems to be the case, we are prepared to allow a person to fail to save another when doing so would involve a moderately heavy sacrifice, why not allow him to do the same for the sake of a much greater benefit, to be gained from that person's death? The answer seems to be that, while a principle of mutual aid giving less consideration to the donor's sacrifice strikes us as too demanding, it is not nearly as threatening as a policy allowing one to consider the benefits to be gained from a person's death.

These appeals to 'conservatism' and mistrust do not seem to me to provide adequate justification for the distinctions in question. They may explain, however, why these distinctions have some appeal for us and yet remain matters of considerable controversy.

5

ALIENATION, CONSEQUENTIALISM, AND THE DEMANDS OF MORALITY

PETER RAILTON

INTRODUCTION

Living up to the demands of morality may bring with it alienation—from one's personal commitments, from one's feelings or sentiments, from other people, or even from morality itself. In this article I will discuss several apparent instances of such alienation, and attempt a preliminary assessment of their bearing on questions about the acceptability of certain moral theories. Of special concern will be the question whether problems about alienation show consequentialist moral theories to be self-defeating.

I will not attempt a full or general characterization of alienation. Indeed, at a perfectly general level alienation can be characterized only very roughly as a kind of estrangement, distancing, or separateness (not necessarily consciously attended to) resulting in some sort of loss (not necessarily consciously noticed).[1] Rather

Peter Railton, 'Alienation, Consequentialism, and the Demands of Morality', *Philosophy and Public Affairs* Vol. 13, No. 2 (Spring 1984). Copyright © 1984 by Princeton University Press. Reprinted by permission.

[1] The loss in question need not be a loss of something of value, and *a fortiori* need not be a bad thing overall: there are some people, institutions, or cultures alienation from which would be a boon. Alienation is a more or less troubling phenomenon depending upon what is lost; and in the cases to be considered, what is lost is for the most part of substantial value. It does not follow, as we will see in Section 5, that in all such cases alienation is a bad thing on balance. Moreover, I do not assume that the loss in question represents an actual *decline* in some value as the result of a separation coming into being where once there was none. It seems reasonable to say that an individual can experience a loss in being alienated from nature, for example, without assuming that he was ever in communion with it, much as we say it is a loss for someone never to receive an education or never to appreciate music. Regrettably, various relevant kinds and sources of alienation cannot be discussed here. A general, historical discussion of alienation may be found in R. Schacht, *Alienation* (Garden City, NY: Doubleday, 1971).

than seek a general analysis I will rely upon examples to convey a sense of what is involved in the sorts of alienation with which I am concerned. There is nothing in a word, and the phenomena to be discussed below could all be considered while avoiding the controversial term 'alienation'. My sense, however, is that there is some point in using this formidable term, if only to draw attention to commonalities among problems not always noticed. For example, in the final section of this article I will suggest that one important form of alienation in moral practice, the sense that morality confronts us as an alien set of demands, distant and disconnected from our actual concerns, can be mitigated by dealing with other sorts of alienation morality may induce. Finally, there are historical reasons, which will not be entered into here, for bringing these phenomena under a single label; part of the explanation of their existence lies in the conditions of modern 'civil society', and in the philosophical traditions of empiricism and rationalism—which include a certain picture of the self's relation to the world—that have flourished in it.

Let us begin with two examples.

1. JOHN AND ANNE AND LISA AND HELEN

To many, John has always seemed a model husband. He almost invariably shows great sensitivity to his wife's needs, and he willingly goes out of his way to meet them. He plainly feels great affection for her. When a friend remarks upon the extraordinary quality of John's concern for his wife, John responds without any self-indulgence or self-congratulation. 'I've always thought that people should help each other when they're in a specially good position to do so. I know Anne better than anyone else does, so I know better what she wants and needs. Besides, I have such affection for her that it's no great burden—instead, I get a lot of satisfaction out of it. Just think how awful marriage would be, or life itself, if people didn't take special care of the ones they love.' His friend accuses John of being unduly modest, but John's manner convinces him that he is telling the truth: this is really how he feels.

Lisa has gone through a series of disappointments over a short period, and has been profoundly depressed. In the end, however, with the help of others she has emerged from the long night of anxiety and melancholy. Only now is she able to talk openly with friends about her state of mind, and she turns to her oldest friend, Helen, who was a mainstay throughout. She'd like to find a way to thank Helen, since she's only too aware of how much of a burden she's been over these months, how much of a drag and a bore, as she puts it. 'You don't have to thank me, Lisa,' Helen replies, 'you deserved it. It was the least I could do after all you've done for me. We're friends, remember? And we said a long time ago that we'd stick together no matter what. Some day I'll probably ask the same thing of you, and I know you'll come through. What else are friends for?' Lisa wonders whether Helen is saying this simply to avoid creating feelings of guilt, but Helen replies that she means every word—she couldn't bring herself to lie to Lisa if she tried.

2. WHAT'S MISSING?

What is troubling about the words of John and Helen? Both show stout character and moral awareness. John's remarks have a benevolent, consequentialist cast, while Helen reasons in a deontological language of duties, reciprocity, and respect. They are not self-centred or without feeling. Yet something seems wrong.

The place to look is not so much at what they say as what they don't say. Think, for example, of how John's remarks might sound to his wife. Anne might have hoped that it was, in some ultimate sense, in part for *her* sake and the sake of their love as such that John pays such special attention to her. That he devotes himself to her because of the characteristically good consequences of doing so seems to leave her, and their relationship as such, too far out of the picture—this despite the fact that these characteristically good consequences depend in important ways on his special relation to her. She is being taken into account by John, but it might seem she is justified in being hurt by the way she is being taken into account. It is as if John viewed her, their relationship, and even his own affection for her from a distant, objective point of view—a moral point of view where reasons must be reasons for any rational agent and so must have an impersonal character even when they deal with personal matters. His wife might think a more personal point of view would also be appropriate, a point of view from which 'It's my wife' or 'It's Anne' would have direct and special relevance, and play an unmediated role in his answer to the question '*Why* do you attend to her so?'

Something similar is missing from Helen's account of why she stood by Lisa. While we understood that the specific duties she feels toward Lisa depend upon particular features of their relationship, still we would not be surprised if Lisa finds Helen's response to her expression of gratitude quite distant, even chilling. We need not question whether she has strong feeling for Lisa, but we may wonder at how that feeling finds expression in Helen's thinking.[2]

John and Helen both show alienation: there would seem to be an estrangement between their affections and their rational, deliberative selves; an abstract and universalizing point of view mediates their responses to others and to their own sentiments. We should not assume that they have been caught in an uncharacteristic moment of moral reflection or after-the-fact rationalization; it is a settled part of their characters to think and act from a moral point of view. It is as if the world were for them a fabric of obligations and permissions in which personal considerations deserve recognition only to the extent that, and in the way that, such considerations find a place in this fabric.

To call John and Helen alienated from their affections or their intimates is not of itself to condemn them, nor is it to say that they are experiencing any sort of distress. One may be alienated from something without recognizing this as such or suffering in any conscious way from it, much as one may simply be uninterested in something without awareness or conscious suffering. But alienation is not mere lack of interest: John and Helen are not *uninterested* in their affections or in their intimates; rather, their interest takes a certain alienated form. While this alienation may not itself be a psychological affliction, it may be the basis of such afflictions—

[2] This is not to say that no questions arise about whether Helen's (or John's) feelings and attitudes constitute the fullest sort of affection, as will be seen shortly.

such as a sense of loneliness or emptiness—or of the loss of certain things of value—such as a sense of belonging or the pleasures of spontaneity. Moreover, their alienation may cause psychological distress in others, and make certain valuable sorts of relationships impossible.

However, we must be on guard lest oversimple categories distort our diagnosis. It seems to me wrong to picture the self as ordinarily divided into cognitive and affective halves, with deliberation and rationality belonging to the first, and sentiments belonging to the second. John's alienation is not a problem on the boundary of naturally given cognitive and affective selves, but a problem partially constituted by the bifurcation of his psyche into these separate spheres. *John*'s deliberate self seems remarkably divorced from his affections, but not all psyches need be so divided. That there is a cognitive element in affection—that affection is not a mere 'feeling' that is a given for the deliberative self but rather involves as well certain characteristic modes of thought and perception—is suggested by the difficulty some may have in believing that John really does love Anne if he persistently thinks about her in the way suggested by his remarks. Indeed, his affection for Anne does seem to have been demoted to a mere 'feeling'. For this reason among others, we should not think of John's alienation from his affections and his alienation from Anne as wholly independent phenomena, the one the cause of the other.[3] Of course, similar remarks apply to Helen.

3. THE MORAL POINT OF VIEW

Perhaps the lives of John and Anne or Helen and Lisa would be happier or fuller if none of the alienation mentioned were present. But is this a problem for *morality*? If, as some have contended, to have a morality is to make normative judgements from a moral point of view and be guided by them, and if by its nature a moral point of view must exclude considerations that lack universality,

---

[3] Moreover, there is a sense in which someone whose responses to his affections or feelings are characteristically mediated by a calculating point of view may fail to know himself fully, or may seem in a way unknowable to others, and this 'cognitive distance' may itself be part of his alienation. I am indebted here to Allan Gibbard.

then any genuinely moral way of going about life would seem
liable to produce the sorts of alienation mentioned above.[4] Thus it
would be a conceptual confusion to ask that we never be required
by morality to go beyond a personal point of view, since to fail
ever to look at things from an impersonal (or non-personal) point
of view would be to fail ever to *be* distinctively moral—not
immoralism, perhaps, but ammoralism. This would not be to say
that there are not other points of view on life worthy of our
attention,[5] or that taking a moral point of view is always
appropriate—one could say that John and Helen show no moral
defect in thinking so impersonally, although they do moralize to
excess. But the fact that a particular morality requires us to take an
impersonal point of view could not sensibly be held against it, for
that would be what makes it a morality at all.

This sort of position strikes me as entirely too complacent. First,
we must somehow give an account of practical reasoning that does
not merely multiply points of view and divide the self—a more
unified account is needed. Second, we must recognize that loving
relationships, friendships, group loyalties, and spontaneous actions
are among the most important contributors to whatever it is that
makes life worthwhile; any moral theory deserving serious
consideration must itself give them serious consideration. As
William K. Frankena has written, 'Morality is made for man, not

---

[4] There is a wide range of views about the nature of the moral point of view and
its proper role in moral life. Is it necessary that one actually act on universal
principles, or merely that one be willing to universalize the principles upon which
one acts? Does the moral point of view by its nature require us to consider
everyone alike? Here I am using a rather strong reading of the moral point of view,
according to which taking the moral point of view involves universalization and the
equal consideration of all.

[5] A moral point of view theorist might make use of the three points of view
distinguished by Mill: the moral, the aesthetic, and the sympathetic. 'The first
addresses itself to our reason and conscience; the second to our imagination; the
third to our human fellow-feeling,' from 'Bentham', reprinted in *John Stuart Mill:
Utilitarianism and Other Writings*, ed. M. Warnock (New York: New American
Library, 1962), p. 121. What is morally right, in his view, may fail to be 'loveable'
(e.g., a parent strictly disciplining a child) or 'beautiful' (e.g., an inauthentic
gesture). Thus, the three points of view need not concur in their positive or
negative assessments. Notice, however, that Mill has divided the self into three
realms, of 'reason and conscience', of 'imagination', and of 'human fellow-feeling';
notice, too, that he has chosen the word 'feeling' to characterize human affections.

man for morality.'[6] Moral considerations are often supposed to be overriding in practical reasoning. If we were to find that adopting a particular morality led to irreconcilable conflict with central types of human well being—as cases akin to John's and Helen's have led some to suspect—then this surely would give us good reason to doubt its claims.[7]

For example, in the closing sentences of *A Theory of Justice* John Rawls considers the 'perspective of eternity', which is impartial across all individuals and times, and writes that this is a 'form of *thought and feeling* that rational persons can adopt in the world'. 'Purity of heart', he concludes, 'would be to see clearly and act with grace and self-command from this point of view.'[8] This may or may not be purity of heart, but it could not be the standpoint of actual life without radically detaching the individual from a range of personal concerns and commitments. Presumably we should not read Rawls as recommending that we adopt this point of view in the bulk of our actions in daily life, but the fact that so purely abstracted a perspective is portrayed as a kind of moral ideal should at least start us wondering.[9] If to be more perfectly moral is to ascend even higher toward *sub specie aeternitatis* abstraction, perhaps we made a mistake in boarding the moral escalator in the first place. Some of the very 'weaknesses' that prevent us from achieving this moral ideal—strong attach-

[6] W. K. Frankena, *Ethics*, 2nd edn. (Englewood Cliffs, NJ: Prentice-Hall, 1973), p. 116. Moralities that do not accord with this dictum—or a modified version of it that includes all sentient beings—might be deemed alienated in a Feuerbachian sense.

[7] Mill, for instance, calls the moral point of view 'unquestionably the first and most important', and while he thinks it the error of the moralizer (such as Bentham) to elevate the moral point of view and 'sink the [aesthetic and sympathetic] entirely', he does not explain how to avoid such a result if the moral point of view is to be, as he says it ought, 'paramount'. See his 'Bentham', pp. 121 f.

Philosophers who have recently raised doubts about moralities for such reasons include B. Williams, in 'A Critique of Utilitarianism', in J. J. C. Smart and B. Williams, *Utilitarianism: For and Against*, and Michael Stocker, in 'The Schizophrenia of Modern Ethical Theories', *Journal of Philosophy* 73 (1976), 453–66. [Williams's essay is reprinted in part as chapter 2 in this collection—Ed.]

[8] J. Rawls, *A Theory of Justice*, p. 587, emphasis added.

[9] I am not claiming that we should interpret all of Rawls's intricate moral theory in light of these few remarks. They are cited here merely to illustrate a certain tendency in moral thought, especially that of a Kantian inspiration.

ments to persons or projects—seem to be part of a considerably more compelling human ideal.

Should we say at this point that the lesson is that we should give a more prominent role to the value of non-alienation in our moral reasoning? That would be too little too late: the problem seems to be the way in which morality asks us to look at things, not just the things it asks us to look at.

4. THE 'PARADOX OF HEDONISM'

Rather than enter directly into the question whether being moral is a matter of taking a moral point of view and whether there is thus some sort of necessary connection between being moral and being alienated in a way detrimental to human flourishing, I will consider a related problem, the solution to which may suggest a way of steering around obstacles to a more direct approach.

One version of the so-called 'paradox of hedonism' is that adopting as one's exclusive ultimate end in life the pursuit of maximum happiness may well prevent one from having certain experiences or engaging in certain sorts of relationships or commitments that are among the greatest sources of happiness.[10] The hedonist, looking around him, may discover that some of those who are less concerned with their own happiness than he is, and who view people and projects less instrumentally than he does, actually manage to live happier lives than he despite his dogged pursuit of happiness. The 'paradox' is pragmatic, not logical, but it looks deep none the less: the hedonist, it would appear, ought not to be a hedonist. It seems, then, as if we have come across a second case in which mediating one's relations to people or projects by a particular point of view—in this case, a hedonistic point of view—may prevent one from attaining the fullest possible realization of sought-after values.

However, it is important to notice that, even though adopting a hedonistic life project may tend to interfere with realizing that

---

[10] This is a 'paradox' for individual, egoistic hedonists. Other forms the 'paradox of hedonism' may take are social in character: a society of egoistic hedonists might arguably achieve less total happiness than a society of more benevolent beings; or, taking happiness as the sole social goal might lead to a less happy society overall than could exist if a wider range of goals were pursued.

very project, there is no such natural exclusion between acting for the sake of another or a cause as such and recognizing how important this is to one's happiness. A spouse who acts for the sake of his mate may know full well that this is a source of deep satisfaction for him—in addition to providing him with reasons for acting internal to it, the relationship may also promote the external goal of achieving happiness. Moreover, while the pursuit of happiness may not be the reason he entered or sustains the relationship, he may also recognize that if it had not seemed likely to make him happy he would not have entered it, and that if it proved over time to be inconsistent with his happiness he would consider ending it.

It might be objected that one cannot really regard a person or a project as an end as such if one's commitment is in this way contingent or overridable. But were this so, we would be able to have very few commitments to ends as such. For example, one could not be committed to both one's spouse and one's child as ends as such, since at most one of these commitments could be overriding in cases of conflict. It is easy to confuse the notion of a commitment to an end *as such* (or *for its own sake*) with that of an *overriding* commitment, but strength is not the same as structure. To be committed to an end as such is a matter of (among other things) whether it furnishes one with reasons for acting that are not mediated by other concerns. It does not follow that these reasons must always outweigh whatever opposing reasons one may have, or that one may not at the same time have other, mediating reasons that also incline one to act on behalf of that end.

Actual commitments to ends as such, even when very strong, are subject to various qualifications and contingencies.[11] If a friend grows too predictable or moves off to a different part of the world, or if a planned life project proves less engaging or practical than one had imagined, commitments and affections naturally change. If a relationship were highly vulnerable to the least change, it would be strained to speak of genuine affection rather than, say, infatuation. But if members of a relationship came to believe that they would be better off without it, this ordinarily would be a non-trivial change, and it is not difficult to imagine that their

---

[11] This is not to deny that there are indexical components to commitments.

commitment to the relationship might be contingent in this way but none the less real. Of course, a relationship involves a shared history and shared expectations as well as momentary experiences, and it is unusual that affection or concern can be changed overnight, or relationships begun or ended at will. Moreover, the sorts of affections and commitments that can play a decisive role in shaping one's life and in making possible the deeper sorts of satisfactions are not those that are easily overridden or subject to constant reassessment or second-guessing. Thus a sensible hedonist would not forever be subjecting his affections or commitments to egoistic calculation, nor would he attempt to break off a relationship or commitment merely because it might seem to him at a given moment that some other arrangement would make him happier. Commitments to others or to causes as such may be very closely linked to the self, and a hedonist who knows what he's about will not be one who turns on his self at the slightest provocation. Contingency is not expendability, and while some commitments are remarkably non-contingent—such as those of parent to child or patriot to country—it cannot be said that commitments of a more contingent sort are never genuine, or never conduce to the profounder sorts of happiness.[12]

Following these observations, we may reduce the force of the 'paradox of hedonism' if we distinguish two forms of hedonism. *Subjective hedonism* is the view that one should adopt the hedonistic point of view in action, that is, that one should whenever possible attempt to determine which act seems most likely to contribute optimally to one's happiness, and behave accordingly. *Objective hedonism* is the view that one should follow

[12] It does seem likely to matter just what the commitment is contingent upon as well as just how contingent it is. I think it is an open question whether commitments contingent upon the satisfaction of egoistic hedonist criteria are of the sort that might figure in the happiest sorts of lives ordinarily available. We will return to this problem presently.

Those who have had close relationships often develop a sense of *duty* to one another that may outlast affection or emotional commitment, that is, they may have a sense of obligation to one another that is less contingent than affection or emotional commitment, and that should not simply be confused with them. If such a sense of obligation is in conflict with self-interest, and if it is a normal part of the most satisfying sorts of close relationships, then this may pose a problem for the egoistic hedonist.

that course of action which would in fact most contribute to one's happiness, even when this would involve *not* adopting the hedonistic point of view in action. An act will be called *subjectively hedonistic* if it is done from a hedonistic point of view; an act is *objectively hedonistic* if it is that act, of those available to the agent, which would most contribute to his happiness.[13] Let us call someone a *sophisticated hedonist* if he aims to lead an objectively hedonistic life (that is, the happiest life available to him in the circumstances) and yet is not committed to subjective hedonism. Thus, within the limits of what is psychologically possible, a sophisticated hedonist is prepared to eschew the hedonistic point of view whenever taking this point of view conflicts with following an objectively hedonistic course of action. The so-called paradox of hedonism shows that there will be such conflicts: certain acts or courses of action may be objectively hedonistic only if not' subjectively hedonistic. When things are put this way, it seems that the sophisticated hedonist faces a problem rather than a paradox: how to act in order to achieve maximum possible happiness if this is at times—or even often—*not* a matter of carrying out hedonistic deliberations.

The answer in any particular case will be complex and contextual—it seems unlikely that any one method of decision making would always promote thought and action most conducive to one's happiness. A sophisticated hedonist might proceed precisely by looking at at the complex and contextual: observing the actual modes of thought and action of those people who are in some ways like himself and who seem most happy. If our

[13] A few remarks are needed. First. I will say that an act is available to an agent if he would succeed in performing it if he tried. Second, here and elsewhere in this article I mean to include quite 'thick' descriptions of actions, so that it may be part of an action that one perform it with a certain intention or goal. In the short run (but not so much the long run) intentions, goals, motives, and the like are usually less subject to our deliberate control than overt behaviour—it is easier to say 'I'm sorry' than to say it and mean it. This, however, is a fact about the relative availability of acts to the agent at a given time, and should not dictate what is to count as an act. Third, here and elsewhere I ignore for simplicity's sake the possibility that more than one course of action may be maximally valuable. And fourth, for reasons I will not enter into here, I have formulated objective hedonism in terms of actual outcomes rather than expected values (relative to the information available to the agent). One could make virtually the same argument using an expected value formulation.

assumptions are right, he will find that few such individuals are subjective hedonists; instead, they act for the sake of a variety of ends as such. He may then set out to develop in himself the traits of character, ways of thought, types of commitment, and so on, that seem common in happy lives. For example, if he notes that the happiest people often have strong loyalties to friends, he must ask how he can become a more loyal friend—not merely how he can seem to be a loyal friend (since those he has observed are not happy because they merely seem loyal), but how he can in fact be one.

Could one really make such changes if one had as a goal leading an optimally happy life? The answer seems to me a qualified *yes*, but let us first look at a simpler case. A highly competitive tennis player comes to realize that his obsession with winning is keeping him from playing his best. A pro tells him that if he wants to win he must devote himself more to the game and its play as such and think less about his performance. In the commitment and concentration made possible by this devotion, he is told, lies the secret of successful tennis. So he spends a good deal of time developing an enduring devotion to many aspects of the activity, and finds it peculiarly satisfying to become so absorbed in it. He plays better, and would have given up the programme of change if he did not, but he now finds that he plays tennis more for its own sake, enjoying greater internal as well as external rewards from the sport. Such a person would not keeping thinking—on or off the court—'No matter how I play, the only thing I really care about is whether I win!' He would recognize such thoughts as self-defeating, as evidence that his old, unhelpful way of looking at things was returning. Nor would such a person be self-deceiving. He need not hide from himself his goal of winning, for this goal is consistent with his increased devotion to the game. His commitment to the activity is not eclipsed by, but made more vivid by, his desire to succeed at it.

The same sort of story might be told about a sophisticated hedonist and friendship. An individual could realize that his instrumental attitude toward his friends prevents him from achieving the fullest happiness friendship affords. He could then attempt to focus more on his friends as such, doing this somewhat deliberately, perhaps, until it comes more naturally. He might then find his friendships improved and himself happier. If he found instead that his relationships were deteriorating or his happiness declining, he would reconsider the idea. None of this need be hidden from himself: the external goal of happiness reinforces the internal goals of his relationships. The sophisticated hedonist's motivational structure should therefore meet a *counterfactual condition*: he need not always act for the sake of happiness, since he may do various things for their own sake or for the sake of others, but he would not act as he does if it were not compatible with his leading an objectively hedonistic life. Of course, a sophisticated hedonist cannot guarantee that he will meet this counterfactual condition, but only attempt to meet it as fully as possible.

Success at tennis is a relatively circumscribed goal, leaving much else about one's life undefined. Maximizing one's happiness, by contrast, seems all-consuming. Could commitments to other ends survive alongside it? Consider an analogy. Ned needs to make a living. More than that, he needs to make as much money as he can—he has expensive tastes, a second marriage, and children reaching college age, and he does not have extensive means. He sets out to invest his money and his labour in ways he thinks will maximize return. Yet it does not follow that he acts as he does solely for the sake of earning as much as possible.[14] Although it is obviously true that he does what he does because he believes that it will maximize return, this does not preclude his doing it for other reasons as well, for example, for the sake of living well or taking care of his children. This may continue to be the case even if Ned comes to want money for its own sake, that is, if he comes to see the accumulation of wealth as intrinsically as well as extrinsically attractive.[15] Similarly, the stricture that one seek the objectively

[14] M. Stocker considers related cases in 'Morally Good Intentions', *The Monist* 54 (1970), 124–41. I am much indebted to his discussion.

[15] There may be a parallelism of sorts between Ned's coming to seek money for its own sake and a certain pattern of moral development: what is originally sought in order to live up to familial or social expectations may come to be an end in itself.

It might be objected that the goal of earning as much money as possible is quite unlike the goal of being as happy as possible, since money is plainly instrumentally valuable even when it is sought for its own sake. But happiness, too, is instrumentally valuable, for it may contribute to realizing such goals as being a likeable or successful person.

hedonistic life certainly provides one with considerable guidance, but it does not supply the whole of one's motives and goals in action.

My claim that the sophisticated hedonist can escape the paradox of hedonism was, however, qualified. It still seems possible that the happiest sorts of lives ordinarily attainable are those led by people who would reject even sophisticated hedonism, people whose character is such that if they were presented with a choice between two entire lives, one of which contains less total happiness but none the less realizes some other values more fully, they might well knowingly choose against maximal happiness. If this were so, it would show that a sophisticated hedonist might have reason for changing his beliefs so that he no longer accepts hedonism in any form. This still would not refute objective hedonism as an account of the (rational, prudential, or moral) *criterion* one's acts should meet, for it would be precisely in order to meet this criterion that the sophisticated hedonist would change his beliefs.[16]

5. THE PLACE OF NON-ALIENATION AMONG HUMAN VALUES

Before discussing the applicability of what has been said about hedonism to morality, we should notice that alienation is not always a bad thing, that we may not want to overcome all forms of alienation, and that other values, which may conflict with non-alienation in particular cases, may at times have a greater claim on us. Let us look at a few such cases.

It has often been argued that a morality of duties and obligations may appropriately come into play in familial or friendly relationships when the relevant sentiments have given out, for instance, when one is exasperated with a friend, when love is tried, and so on.[17] 'Ought' implies 'can' (or, at least, 'could'), and while it may be better in human terms when we do what we ought to do at least in part out of feelings of love, friendship, or sympathy, there are

---

[16] An important objection to the claim that objective hedonism may serve as the *moral* criterion one's acts should meet, even if this means not believing in hedonism, is that moral principles must meet a *publicity* condition. I will discuss this objection in Section 6.

[17] See, for example, Stocker, 'The Schizophrenia of Modern Ethical Theories'.

times when we simply cannot muster these sentiments, and the right thing to do is to act as love or friendship or sympathy would have directed rather than refuse to perform any act done merely from a sense of duty.

But we should add a further role for unspontaneous, morally motivated action: even when love or concern is strong, it is often desirable that people achieve some distance from their sentiments or one another. A spouse may act toward his mate in a grossly overprotective way: a friend may indulge another's ultimately destructive tendencies; a parent may favour one child inordinately. Strong and immediate affection may overwhelm one's ability to see what another person actually needs or deserves. In such cases a certain distance between people or between an individual and his sentiments, and an intrusion of moral considerations into the gap thus created, may be a good thing, and part of genuine affection or commitment. The opposite view, that no such mediation is desirable as long as affection is strong, seems to me a piece of romanticism. Concern over alienation therefore ought not to take the form of a cult of 'authenticity at any price'.

Moreover, there will occur regular conflicts between avoiding alienation and achieving other important individual goals. One such goal is autonomy. Bernard Williams has emphasized that many of us have developed certain 'ground projects' that give shape and meaning to our lives, and has drawn attention to the damage an individual may suffer if he is alienated from his ground projects by being forced to look at them as potentially overridable by moral considerations.[18] But against this it may be urged that it is crucial for autonomy that one hold one's commitments up for inspection—even one's ground projects. Our ground projects are often formed in our youth, in a particular family, class, or cultural background. It may be alienating and even disorienting to call these into question, but to fail to do so is to lose autonomy. Of course, autonomy could not sensibly require that we question all of our values and commitments at once, nor need it require us to be forever detached from what we are doing. It is quite possible to submit basic aspects of one's life to scrutiny and arrive at a set of autonomously chosen commitments that form the basis of an

[18] Williams, 'A Critique of Utilitarianism'.

integrated life. Indeed, psychological conflicts and practical obstacles give us occasion for re-examining our basic commitments rather more often than we'd like.

At the same time, the tension between autonomy and non-alienation should not be exaggerated. Part of avoiding exaggeration is giving up the Kantian notion that autonomy is a matter of escaping determination by any contingency whatsoever. Part, too, is refusing to conflate autonomy with sheer independence from others. Both Rousseau and Marx emphasized that achieving control over one's own life requires participation in certain sorts of social relations—in fact, relations in which various kinds of alienation have been minimized.

Autonomy is but one value that may enter into complex trade-offs with non-alienation. Alienation and inauthenticity do have their uses. The alienation of some individuals or groups from their milieu may at times be necessary for fundamental social criticism or cultural innovation. And without some degree of inauthenticity, it is doubtful whether civil relations among people could long be maintained. It would take little ingenuity, but too much of the reader's patience, to construct here examples involving troubling conflicts between non-alienation and virtually any other worthy goal.

6. REDUCING ALIENATION IN MORALITY

Let us now move to morality proper. To do this with any definiteness, we must have a particular morality in mind. For various reasons, I think that the most plausible sort of morality is consequentialist in form, assessing rightness in terms of contribution to the good. In attempting to sketch how we might reduce alienation in moral theory and practice, therefore, I will work within a consequentialist framework (although a number of the arguments I will make could be made, *mutatis mutandis*, by a deontologist).

Of course, one has adopted no morality in particular even in adopting consequentialism unless one says what the good is. Let us, then, dwell briefly on axiology. One mistake of dominant consequentialist theories, I believe, is their failure to see that things other than subjective states can have intrinsic value. Allied to this is a tendency to reduce all intrinsic values to one—happiness. Both of these features of classical utilitarianism reflect forms of alienation. First, in divorcing subjective states from their objective counterparts, and claiming that we seek the latter exclusively for the sake of the former, utilitarianism cuts us off from the world in a way made graphic by examples such as that of the experience machine, a hypothetical device that can be programmed to provide one with whatever subjective states he may desire. The experience machine affords us decisive subjective advantages over actual life: few, if any, in actual life think they have achieved all that they could want, but the machine makes possible for each an existence that he cannot distinguish from such a happy state of affairs.[19] Despite this striking advantage, most rebel at the notion of the experience machine. As Robert Nozick and others have pointed out, it seems to matter to us what we actually *do* and *are* as well as how life *appears* to us.[20] We see the point of our lives as bound up with the world and other people in ways not captured by subjectivism, and our sense of loss in contemplating a life tied to an experience machine, quite literally alienated from the surrounding world, suggests where subjectivism has gone astray. Second, the reduction of all goals to the purely abstract goal of happiness or pleasure, as in hedonistic utilitarianism, treats all other goals instrumentally. Knowledge or friendship may promote happiness, but is it a fair characterization of our commitment to these goals to say that this is the only sense in which they are ultimately valuable? Doesn't the insistence that there is an abstract and uniform goal lying behind all of our ends bespeak an alienation from these particular ends?

Rather than pursue these questions further here, let me suggest an approach to the good that seems to me less hopeless as a way of capturing human value: a pluralistic approach in which several goods are viewed as intrinsically, non-morally valuable—such as happiness, knowledge, purposeful activity, autonomy, solidarity,

---

[19] At least one qualification is needed: the subjective states must be psychologically possible. Perhaps some of us desire what are, in effect, psychologically impossible states.

[20] R. Nozick, *Anarchy, State, and Utopia*, pp. 42 ff.

respect, and beauty.[21] These goods need not be ranked lexically, but may be attributed weights, and the criterion of rightness for an act would be that it most contribute to the weighted sum of these values in the long run. This creates the possibility of trade-offs among values of the kinds discussed in the previous section. However, I will not stop here to develop or defend such an account of the good and the right, since our task is to show how certain problems of alienation that arise in moral contexts might be dealt with if morality is assumed to have such a basis.

Consider, then, Juan, who, like John, has always seemed a model husband. When a friend remarks on the extraordinary concern he

---

[21] To my knowledge, the best-developed method for justifying claims about intrinsic value involves thought-experiments of a familiar sort, in which, for example, we imagine two lives, or two worlds, alike in all but one respect, and then attempt to determine whether rational, well-informed, widely experienced individuals would (when vividly aware of both alternatives) be indifferent between the two or have a settled preference for one over the other. Since no one is ideally rational, fully informed, or infinitely experienced, the best we can do is to take more seriously the judgements of those who come nearer to approximating these conditions. Worse yet: the best we can do is to take more seriously the judgements of those we *think* better approximate these conditions. (I am not supposing that facts or experience somehow entail values, but that, in rational agents, beliefs and values show a marked mutual influence and coherence.) We may overcome some narrowness if we look at behaviour and preferences in other societies and other epochs, but even here we must rely upon interpretations coloured by our own beliefs and values. Within the confines of this article I must leave unanswered a host of deep and troubling questions about the nature of values and value judgements. Suffice it to say that there is no reason to think that we are in a position to give anything but a tentative list of intrinsic goods.

It becomes a complex matter to describe the psychology of intrinsic value. For example, should we say that one values a relationship of solidarity, say, a friendship, *because it is* a friendship? That makes it sound as if it were somehow instrumental to the realization of some abstract value, friendship. Surely this is a misdescription. We may be able to get a clearer idea of what is involved by considering the case of happiness. We certainly do not value a particular bit of experienced happiness because it is instrumental in the realization of the abstract goal, happiness—we value the experience for its own sake because it is a happy experience. Similarly, a friendship is itself the valued thing, the thing of a valued kind. Of course, one can say that one values friendship and therefore seeks friends, just as one can say one values happiness and therefore seeks happy experiences. But this locution must be contrasted with what is being said when, for example, one talks of seeking *things that make one happy*. Friends are not 'things that make one achieve friendship'—they partially constitute friendships, just as particular happy experiences partially constitute happiness for an individual. Thus taking friendship as an intrinsic value does not entail viewing particular friendships instrumentally.

shows for his wife, Juan characteristically responds: 'I love Linda. I even *like* her. So it means a lot to me to do things for her. After all we've been through, it's almost a part of me to do it.' But his friend knows that Juan is a principled individual, and asks Juan how his marriage fits into that larger scheme. After all, he asks, it's fine for Juan and his wife to have such a close relationship, but what about all the other, needier people Juan could help if he broadened his horizon still further? Juan replies, 'Look, it's a better world when people can have a relationship like ours—and nobody could if everyone were always asking themselves who's got the most need. It's not easy to make things work in this world, and one of the best things that happens to people is to have a close relationship like ours. You'd make things worse in a hurry if you broke up those close relationships for the sake of some higher goal. Anyhow, I know that you can't always put family first. The world isn't such a wonderful place that it's OK just to retreat into your own little circle. But still, you need that little circle. People get burned out, or lose touch, if they try to save the world by themselves. The ones who can stick with it and do a good job of making things better are usually the ones who can make that fit into a life that does not make them miserable. I haven't met any real saints lately, and I don't trust people who think they *are* saints.'

If we contrast Juan with John, we do not find that the one allows moral considerations to enter his personal life while the other does not. Nor do we find that one is less serious in his moral concern. Rather, what Juan recognizes to be morally required is not by its nature incompatible with acting directly for the sake of another. It is important to Juan to subject his life to moral scrutiny—he is not merely stumped when asked for a defence of his acts above a personal level, he does not *just* say 'Of course I take care of her, she's my wife!' or 'It's Linda' and refuse to listen to the more impersonal considerations raised by his friend. It is consistent with what he says to imagine that his motivational structure has a form akin to that of the sophisticated hedonist, that is, his motivational structure meets a counterfactual condition: while he ordinarily does not do what he does simply for the sake of doing what's right, he would seek to lead a different sort of life if he did not think his were morally defensible. His love is not a romantic submersion in the other to the exclusion of worldly responsibilities, and to that extent it may be said to involve a degree of alienation from Linda. But this does not seem to drain human value from their relationship. Nor need one imagine that Linda would be saddened to hear Juan's words the way Anne might have been saddened to overhear the remarks of John.[22]

Moreover, because of his very willingness to question his life morally, Juan avoids a sort of alienation not sufficiently discussed—alienation from others, beyond one's intimate ties. Individuals who will not or cannot allow questions to arise about what they are doing from a broader perspective are in an important way cut off from their society and the larger world. They may not be troubled by this in any very direct way, but even so they may fail to experience that powerful sense of purpose and meaning that comes from seeing oneself as part of something larger and more enduring than oneself or one's intimate circle. The search for such a sense of purpose and meaning seems to me ubiquitous—surely much of the impulse to religion, to ethnic or regional identification (most strikingly, in the 'rediscovery' of such identities), or to institutional loyalty stems from this desire to see ourselves as part of a more general, lasting, and worthwhile scheme of things.[23] This presumably is part of what is meant by saying that secularization

---

[22] If one objects that Juan's commitment to Linda is lacking because it is contingent in some ways, the objector must show that the *kinds* of contingencies involved would destroy his relationship with Linda, especially since moral character often figures in commitments—the character of the other, or the compatibility of a commitment with one's having the sort of character one values—and the contingencies in Juan's case are due to his moral character.

[23] I do not mean to suggest that such identities are always matters of choice for individuals. Quite the reverse, identities often arise through socialization, prejudice, and similar influences. The point rather is that there is a very general phenomenon of identification, badly in need of explanation, that to an important extent underlies such phenomena as socialization and prejudice, and that suggests the existence of certain needs in virtually all members of society—needs to which identification with entities beyond the self answers.

Many of us who resist raising questions about our lives from broader perspectives do so, I fear, not out of a sense that it would be difficult or impossible to lead a meaningful life if one entertained such perspectives, but rather out of a sense that our lives would not stand up to much scrutiny therefrom, so that leading a life that *would* seem meaningful from such perspectives would require us to change in some significant way.

has led to a sense of meaninglessness, or that the decline of traditional communities and societies has meant an increase in anomie. (The sophisticated hedonist, too, should take note: one way to gain a firmer sense that one's life is worth while, a sense that may be important to realizing various values in one's own life, is to overcome alienation from others.)

Drawing upon our earlier discussion of two kinds of hedonism, let us now distinguish two kinds of consequentialism. *Subjective consequentialism* is the view that whenever one faces a choice of actions, one should attempt to determine which act of those available would most promote the good, and should then try to act accordingly. One is behaving as subjective consequentialism requires—that is, leading a *subjectively consequentialist life*—to the extent that one uses and follows a distinctively consequentialist mode of decision making, consciously aiming at the overall good and conscientiously using the best available information with the greatest possible rigour. *Objective consequentialism* is the view that the criterion of the rightness of an act or course of action is whether it in fact would most promote the good of those acts available to the agent. Subjective consequentialism, like subjective hedonism, is a view that prescribes following a particular mode of deliberation in action; objective consequentialism, like objective hedonism, concerns the outcomes actually brought about, and thus deals with the question of deliberation only in terms of the tendencies of certain forms of decision making to promote appropriate outcomes. Let us reserve the expression *objectively consequentialist act (or life)* for those acts (or that life) of those available to the agent that would bring about the best outcomes.[24]

[24] Although the language here is causal—'promoting' and 'bring about'—it should be said that the relation of an act to the good need not always be causal. An act of learning may non-causally involve coming to have knowledge (an intrinsic good by my reckoning) as well as contributing causally to later realizations of intrinsic value. Causal consequences as such do not have a privileged status. As in the case of objective hedonism, I have formulated objective consequentialism in terms of actual outcomes (so-called 'objective duty') rather than expected values relative to what is rational for the agent to believe ('subjective duty'). The main arguments of this article could be made using expected value, since the course of action with highest expected value need not in general be the subjectively consequentialist one. See also notes 13 and 21.

Are there any subjective consequentialists? Well, various theorists have claimed

To complete the parallel, let us say that a *sophisticated consequentialist* is someone who has a standing commitment to leading an objectively consequentialist life, but who need not set special stock in any particular form of decision making and therefore does not necessarily seek to lead a subjectively consequentialist life. Juan, it might be argued (if the details were filled in), is a sophisticated consequentialist, since he seems to believe he should act for the best but does not seem to feel it appropriate to bring a consequentialist calculus to bear on his every act.

Is it bizarre, or contradictory, that being a sophisticated consequentialist may involve rejecting subjective consequentialism? After all, doesn't an adherent of subjective consequentialism also seek to lead an objectively consequentialist life? He may, but then he is mistaken in thinking that this means he should always undertake a distinctively consequentialist deliberation when faced with a choice. To see his mistake, we need only consider some examples.

It is well known that in certain emergencies, the best outcome requires action so swift as to preclude consequentialist deliberation. Thus a sophisticated consequentialist has reason to inculcate in himself certain dispositions to act rapidly in obvious emergencies. The disposition is not a mere reflex, but a developed pattern of action deliberately acquired. A simple example, but it should dispel the air of paradox.

Many decisions are too insignificant to warrant consequentialist deliberation ('Which shoelace should I do up first?') or too predictable in outcome ('Should I meet my morning class today as scheduled or should I linger over the newspaper?'). A famous old conundrum for consequentialism falls into a smaller category: before I deliberate about an act, it seems I must decide how much time would be optimal to allocate for this deliberation; but then I must first decide how much time would be optimal to allocate for this time-allocation decision; but before that I must decide how much time would be optimal to allocate for *that* decision; and so on. The sophisticated consequentialist can block this paralysing

that a consequentialist must be a subjective consequentialist in order to be genuine—see Williams, 'A Critique of Utilitarianism', p. 135, and Rawls, *A Theory of Justice*, p. 182.

regress by noting that often the best thing to do is not to ask questions about time allocation at all; instead, he may develop standing dispositions to give more or less time to decisions depending upon their perceived importance, the amount of information available, the predictability of his choice, and so on. I think we all have dispositions of this sort, which account for our patience with some prolonged deliberations but not others.

There are somewhat more intriguing examples that have more to do with psychological interference than mere time efficiency: the timid, put-upon employee who knows that if he deliberates about whether to ask for a raise he will succumb to his timidity and fail to demand what he actually deserves; the self-conscious man who knows that if, at social gatherings, he is forever wondering how he should act, his behaviour will be awkward and unnatural, contrary to his goal of acting naturally and appropriately; the tightrope walker who knows he must not reflect on the value of keeping his concentration; and so on. People can learn to avoid certain characteristically self-defeating lines of thought—just as the tennis player in an earlier example learned to avoid thinking constantly about winning—and the sophisticated consequentialist may learn that consequentialist deliberation is in a variety of cases self-defeating, so that other habits of thought should be cultivated.

The sophisticated consequentialist need not be deceiving himself or acting in bad faith when he avoids consequentialist reasoning. He can fully recognize that he is developing the dispositions he does because they are necessary for promoting the good. Of course, he cannot be preoccupied with this fact all the while, but then one cannot be *preoccupied* with anything without this interfering with normal or appropriate patterns of thought and action.

To the list of cases of interference we may add John, whose all-purpose willingness to look at things by subjective consequentialist lights prevents the realization in him and in his relationships with others of values that he would recognize to be crucially important.

Bernard Williams has said that it shows consequentialism to be in grave trouble that it may have to usher itself from the scene as a mode of decision making in a number of important areas of life.[25]

[25] Williams, 'A Critique of Utilitarianism', p. 135.

Though I think he has exaggerated the extent to which we would have to exclude consequentialist considerations from our lives in order to avoid disastrous results, it is fair to ask: if maximizing the good were in fact to require that consequentialist reasoning be *wholly* excluded, would this refute consequentialism? Imagine an all-knowing demon who controls the fate of the world and who visits unspeakable punishment upon man to the extent that he does not employ a Kantian morality. (Obviously, the demon is not himself a Kantian.) If such a demon existed, sophisticated consequentialists would have reason to convert to Kantianism, perhaps even to make whatever provisions could be made to erase consequentialism from the human memory and prevent any resurgence of it.

Does this possibility show that objective consequentialism is self-defeating? On the contrary, it shows that objective consequentialism has the virtue of not blurring the distinction between the *truth-conditions* of an ethical theory and its *acceptance-conditions* in particular contexts, a distinction philosophers have generally recognized for theories concerning other subject matters. It might be objected that, unlike other theories, ethical theories must meet a condition of publicity, roughly to the effect that it must be possible under all circumstances for us to recognize a true ethical theory as such and to promulgate it publicly without thereby violating that theory itself.[26] Such a condition might be thought to follow from the social nature of morality. But any such condition would be question-begging against consequentialist theories, since it would require that one class of actions—acts of adopting or promulgating an ethical theory—*not* be assessed in terms of their consequences. Moreover, I fail to see how such a condition could emanate from the social character of morality. To prescribe the adoption and promulgation of a mode of decision making regardless of its consequences seems to me radically detached from human concerns, social or otherwise. If it is argued that an ethical theory that fails to meet the publicity requirement could under certain conditions endorse a course of action leading

---

[26] For discussion of a publicity condition, see Rawls, *A Theory of Justice*, pp. 133, 177–82, 582. The question whether a publicity condition can be justified is a difficult one, deserving fuller discussion than I am able to give it here.

to the abuse and manipulation of man by man, we need only reflect that no psychologically possible decision procedure can guarantee that its widespread adoption could never have such a result. A 'consequentialist demon' might increase the amount of abuse and manipulation in the world in direct proportion to the extent that people act according to the categorical imperative. Objective consequentialism (unlike certain deontological theories) has valuable flexibility in permitting us to take consequences into account in assessing the appropriateness of certain modes of decision making, thereby avoiding any sort of self-defeating decision procedure worship.

A further objection is that the lack of any direct link between objective consequentialism and a particular mode of decision making leaves the view too vague to provide adequate guidance in practice. On the contrary, objective consequentialism sets a definite and distinctive criterion of right action, and it becomes an empirical question (though not an easy one) which modes of decision making should be employed and when. It would be a mistake for an objective consequentialist to attempt to tighten the connection between his criterion of rightness and any particular mode of decision making: someone who recommended a particular mode of decision making regardless of consequences would not be a hard-nosed, non-evasive objective consequentialist, but a self-contradicting one.

7. CONTRASTING APPROACHES

The seeming 'indirectness' of objective consequentialism may invite its confusion with familiar indirect consequentialist theories, such as rule-consequentialism. In fact, the subjective/objective distinction cuts across the rule/act distinction, and there are subjective and objective forms of both rule- and act-based theories. Thus far, we have dealt only with subjective and objective forms of act-consequentialism. By contrast, a *subjective rule*-consequentialist holds (roughly) that in deliberation we should always attempt to determine which act, of those available, conforms to that set of rules general acceptance of which would most promote the good; we then should attempt to perform this act. An *objective rule*-consequentialist sets actual conformity to the rules with the highest acceptance value as his criterion of right action, recognizing the possibility that the best set of rules might in some cases—or even always—recommend that one not perform rule-consequentialist deliberation.

Because I believe this last possibility must be taken seriously, I find the objective form of rule-consequentialism more plausible. Ultimately, however, I suspect that rule-consequentialism is untenable in either form, for it could recommend acts that (subjectively or objectively) accord with the best set of rules even when these rules are *not* in fact generally accepted, and when as a result these acts would have devastatingly bad consequences. 'Let the rules with greatest acceptance utility be followed, though the heavens fall!' is no more plausible than '*Fiat justitia, ruat coelum!*'—and a good bit less ringing. Hence, the arguments in this article are based entirely upon act-consequentialism.

Indeed, once the subjective/objective distinction has been drawn, an act-consequentialist can capture some of the intuitions that have made rule- or trait-consequentialism appealing.[27] Surely part of the attraction of these indirect consequentialisms is the idea that one should have certain traits of character, or commitments to persons or principles, that are sturdy enough that one would at least sometimes refuse to forsake them even when this refusal is known to conflict with making some gain—perhaps small—in total utility. Unlike his subjective counterpart, the objective act-consequentialist is able to endorse characters and commitments that are sturdy in just this sense.

To see why, let us first return briefly to one of the simple examples of Section 6. A sophisticated act-consequentialist may recognize that if he were to develop a standing disposition to render prompt assistance in emergencies without going through elaborate act-consequentialist deliberation, there would almost certainly be cases in which he would perform acts worse than those he would have performed had he stopped to deliberate, for example, when his prompt action is misguided in a way he would have noticed had he thought the matter through. It may still be

[27] For an example of trait-consequentialism, see R. M. Adams, 'Motive Utilitarianism'.

right for him to develop this disposition, for without it he would act rightly in emergencies still less often—a quick response is appropriate much more often than not, and it is not practically possible to develop a disposition that would lead one to respond promptly in exactly those cases where this would have the best results. While one can attempt to cultivate dispositions that are responsive to various factors which might indicate whether promptness is of greater importance than further thought, such refinements have their own costs and, given the limits of human resources, even the best cultivated dispositions will sometimes lead one astray. The objective act-consequentialist would thus recommend cultivating dispositions that will sometimes lead him to violate his own criterion of right action. Still, he will not, as a trait-consequentialist would, shift his criterion and say that an act is right if it stems from the traits it would be best overall to have (given the limits of what is humanly achievable, the balance of costs and benefits, and so on). Instead, he continues to believe that an act may stem from the disposition it would be best to have, and yet be wrong (because it would produce worse consequences than other acts available to the agent in the circumstances).[28]

This line of argument can be extended to patterns of motivation, traits of character, and rules. A sophistiated act-consequentialist should realize that certain goods are reliably attainable—or attainable at all—only if people have well-developed characters;

---

[28] By way of contrast, when Robert Adams considers application of a motive-utilitarian view to the ethics of actions, he suggests 'conscience utilitarianism', the view that 'we have a *moral duty* to do an act, if and only if it would be demanded of us by the most useful kind of conscience we could have', 'Motive Utilitarianism', p. 479. Presumably, this means that it would be morally wrong to perform an act contrary to the demands of the most useful sort of conscience. I have resisted this sort of redefinition of rightness for actions, since I believe that the most useful sort of conscience may on occasion demand of us an act that does not have the best overall consequences of those available, and that performing this act would be wrong.

Of course, some difficulties attend the interpretation of this last sentence. I have assumed throughout that an act is available to an agent if he would succeed in performing it if he tried. I have also taken a rather simple view of the complex matter of attaching outcomes to specific acts. In those rare cases in which the performance of even one exceptional (purportedly optimizing) act would completely undermine the agent's standing (optimal) disposition, it might not be possible after all to say that the exceptional act would be the right one to perform in the circumstances. (This question will arise again shortly.)

that the human psyche is capable of only so much self-regulation and refinement; and that human perception and reasoning are liable to a host of biases and errors. Therefore, individuals may be more likely to act rightly if they possess certain enduring motivational patterns, character traits, or prima-facie commitments to rules in addition to whatever commitment they have to act for the best. Because such individuals would not consider consequences in all cases, they would miss a number of opportunities to maximize the good; but if they were instead always to attempt to assess outcomes, the overall result would be worse, for they would act correctly less often.[29]

We may now strengthen the argument to show that the objective act-consequentialist can approve of dispositions, characters, or commitments to rules that are sturdy in the sense mentioned above, that is, that do not merely supplement a commitment to act for the best, but sometimes override it, so that one knowingly does what is contrary to maximizing the good. Consider again Juan and Linda, whom we imagine to have a commuting marriage. They normally get together only every other week, but one week she seems a bit depressed and harried, and so he decides to take an extra trip in order to be with her. If he did not travel, he would save a fairly large sum that he could send Oxfam to dig a well in a drought-stricken village. Even reckoning in Linda's uninterrupted malaise, Juan's guilt, and any ill effects on their relationship, it may be that for Juan to contribute the fare to Oxfam would produce better consequences overall than the unscheduled trip. Let us suppose that Juan knows this, and that he could stay home and write the cheque if he tried. Still, given Juan's character, he in

---

[29] One conclusion of this discussion is that we cannot realistically expect people's behaviour to be in strict compliance with the counterfactual condition even if they are committed sophisticated consequentialists. At best, a sophisticated consequentialist tries to meet this condition. But it should be no surprise that in practice we are unlikely to be morally ideal. Imperfections in information alone are enough to make it very improbable that individuals will lead objectively consequentialist lives. Whether or when to *blame* people for real or apparent failures to behave ideally is, of course, another matter.

Note that we must take into account not just the frequency with which right acts are performed, but the actual balance of gains and losses to overall well-being that results. Relative frequency of right action will settle the matter only in the (unusual) case where the amount of good at stake in each act of a given kind—for example, each emergency one comes across—is the same.

fact will not try to perform this more beneficial act but will travel to see Linda instead. The objective act-consequentialist will say that Juan performed the wrong act on this occasion. Yet he may also say that if Juan had had a character that would have led him to perform the better act (or made him more inclined to do so), he would have had to have been less devoted to Linda. Given the ways Juan can affect the world, it may be that if he were less devoted to Linda his overall contribution to human well-being would be less in the end, perhaps because he would become more cynical and self-centred. Thus it may be that Juan should have (should develop, encourage, and so on) a character such that he sometimes knowingly and deliberately acts contrary to his objective consequentialist duty. Any other character, of those actually available to him, would lead him to depart still further from an objectively consequentialist life. The issue is not whether staying home would *change* Juan's character—for we may suppose that it would not—but whether he would in fact decide to stay home if he had that character, of those available, that would lead him to perform the most beneficial overall sequence of acts. In some cases, then, there will exist an objective act-consequentialist argument for developing and sustaining characters of a kind Sidgwick and others have thought an act-consequentialist must condemn.[30]

[30] In *The Methods of Ethics*, Bk. IV, ch. 5, sec. 4, Sidgwick discusses 'the Ideal of character and conduct' that a utilitarian should recognize as 'the sum of excellences or Perfections', and writes that 'a Utilitarian must hold that it is always wrong for a man knowingly to do anything other than what he believes to be most conducive to Universal Happiness' (p. 492). Here Sidgwick is uncharacteristically confused—and in two ways. First, considering act-by-act evaluation, an objective utilitarian can hold that an agent may simply be wrong in believing that a given course of action is most conducive to universal happiness, and therefore it may be right for him knowingly to do something other than this. Second, following Sidgwick's concern in this passage and looking at enduring traits of character rather than isolated acts, and even assuming the agent's belief to be correct, an objective utilitarian can hold that the ideal character for an individual, or for people in general, may involve a willingness knowingly to act contrary to maximal happiness when this is done for the sake of certain deep personal commitments. See H. Sidgwick, *The Methods of Ethics*, p. 492.

It might be thought counterintuitive to say, in the example given, that it is not right for Juan to travel to see Linda. But it must be kept in mind that for an act-consequentialist to say that an action is not right is not to say that it is without merit, only that it is not the very best act available to the agent. And an intuitive

8. DEMANDS AND DISRUPTIONS

Before ending this discussion of consequentialism, let me mention one other large problem involving alienation that has seemed uniquely troubling for consequentialist theories and that shows how coming to terms with problems of alienation may be a social matter as well as a matter of individual psychology. Because consequentialist criteria of rightness are linked to maximal contribution to the good, whenever one does not perform the very best act one can, one is 'negatively responsible' for any shortfall in total well-being that results. Bernard Williams has argued that to accept such a burden of responsibility would force most of us to abandon or be prepared to abandon many of our most basic individual commitments, alienating ourselves from the very things that mean the most to us.[31]

To be sure, objective act-consequentialism of the sort considered here is a demanding and potentially disruptive morality, even after allowances have been made for the psychological phenomena thus far discussed and for the difference between saying an act is wrong and saying that the agent ought to be blamed for it. But just *how* demanding or disruptive it would be for an individual is a function—as it arguably should be—of how bad the state of the world is, how others typically act, what institutions exist, and how much that individual is capable of doing. If wealth were more equitably distributed, if political systems were less repressive and more responsive to the needs of their citizens, and if people were more generally prepared to accept certain responsibilities, then individuals' everyday lives would not have to be constantly disrupted for the sake of the good.

For example, in a society where there are no organized forms of disaster relief, it may be the case that, if disaster were to strike a

sense of the rightness of visiting Linda may be due less to an evaluation of the act itself than to a reaction to the sort of character a person would have to have in order to stay home and write a cheque to Oxfam under the circumstances. Perhaps he would have to be too distant or righteous to have much appeal to us—especially in view of the fact that it is his spouse's anguish that is at stake. We have already seen how an act-consequentialist may share this sort of character assessment.

[31] Williams, 'A Critique of Utilitarianism', sec. 3. [Section 2 of Chapter 2 in this volume—Ed.]

particular region, people all over the country would be obliged to make a special effort to provide aid. If, on the other hand, an adequate system of publicly financed disaster relief existed, then it probably would be a very poor idea for people to interrupt their normal lives and attempt to help—their efforts would probably be uncoordinated, ill-informed, an interference with skilled relief work, and economically disruptive (perhaps even damaging to the society's ability to pay for the relief effort).

By altering social and political arrangements we can lessen the disruptiveness of moral demands on our lives, and in the long run achieve better results than free-lance good-doing. A consequentialist theory is therefore likely to recommend that accepting negative responsibility is more a matter of supporting certain social and political arrangements (or rearrangements) than of setting out individually to save the world. Moreover, it is clear that such social and political changes cannot be made unless the lives of individuals are psychologically supportable in the meanwhile, and this provides substantial reason for rejecting the notion that we should abandon all that matters to us as individuals and devote ourselves solely to net social welfare. Finally, in many cases what matters most is *perceived* rather than actual demandingness or disruptiveness, and this will be a relative matter, depending upon normal expectations. If certain social or political arrangements encourage higher contribution as a matter of course, individuals may not sense these moral demands as excessively intrusive.

To speak of social and political changes is, of course, to suggest eliminating the social and political preconditions for a number of existing projects and relationships, and such changes are likely to produce some degree of alienation in those whose lives have been disrupted. To an extent such people may be able to find new projects and relationships as well as maintain a number of old projects and relationships, and thereby avoid intolerable alienation. But not all will escape serious alienation. We thus have a case in which alienation will exist whichever course of action we follow— either the alienation of those who find the loss of the old order disorienting, or the continuing alienation of those who under the present order cannot lead lives expressive of their individuality or goals. It would seem that to follow the logic of Williams's position would have the unduly conservative result of favouring those less alienated in the present state of affairs over those who might lead more satisfactory lives if certain changes were to occur. Such conservativism could hardly be warranted by a concern about alienation if the changes in question would bring about social and political preconditions for a more widespread enjoyment of meaningful lives. For example, it is disruptive of the ground projects of many men that women have begun to demand and receive greater equality in social and personal spheres, but such disruption may be offset by the opening of more avenues of self-development to a greater number of people.

In responding to Williams's objection regarding negative responsibility, I have focused more on the problem of disruptiveness than on the problem of demandingness, and more on the social than on the personal level. More would need to be said than I am able to say here to come fully to terms with his objection, although some very general remarks may be in order. The consequentialist starts out from the relatively simple idea that certain things seem to matter to people above all else. His root conception of moral rightness is therefore that it should matter above all else whether people, in so far as possible, actually realize these ends.[32] Consequentialist moralities of the sort considered here undeniably set a demanding standard, calling upon us to do more for one another than is now the practice. But this standard plainly does not require that most people lead intolerable lives for the sake of some

---

[32] I appealed to this 'root conception' in rejecting rule-consequentialism in Section 7. Although consequentialism is often condemned for failing to provide an account of morality consistent with respect for persons, this root conception provides the basis for a highly plausible notion of such respect. I doubt, however, that any fundamental ethical dispute between consequentialists and deontologists can be resolved by appeal to the idea of respect for persons. The deontologist has his notion of respect—e.g., that we not use people in certain ways—and the consequentialist has *his*—e.g., that the good of every person has an equal claim upon us, a claim unmediated by any notion of right or contract, so that we should do the most possible to bring about outcomes that actually advance the good of persons. For every consequentially justified act of manipulation to which the deontologist can point with alarm there is a deontologically justified act that fails to promote the well-being of some person(s) as fully as possible to which the consequentialist can point, appalled. Which notion takes 'respect for persons' more seriously? There may be no non-question-begging answer, especially once the consequentialist has recognized such things as autonomy or respect as intrinsically valuable.

greater good: the greater good is empirically equivalent to the best possible lives for the largest possible number of people.[33] Objective consequentialism gives full expression to this root intuition by setting as the criterion of rightness actual contribution to the realization of human value, allowing practices and forms of reasoning to take whatever shape this requires. It is thus not equivalent to requiring a certain, alienated way of thinking about ourselves, our commitments, or how to act.

Samuel Scheffler has recently suggested that one response to the problems Williams raises about the impersonality and demandingness of consequentialism could be to depart from consequentialism at least far enough to recognize as a fundamental moral principle an agent-centred prerogative, roughly to the effect that one is not always obliged to maximize the good, although one is always permitted to do so if one wishes. This prerogative would make room for agents to give special attention to personal projects and commitments. However, the argument of this article, if successful, shows there to be a firm place in moral practice for prerogatives that afford such room even if one accepts a fully consequentialist fundamental moral theory.[34]

9. ALIENATION FROM MORALITY

By way of conclusion, I would like to turn to alienation from morality itself, the experience (conscious or unconscious) of morality as an external set of demands not rooted in our lives or accommodating to our perspectives. Giving a convincing answer to the question 'Why should I be moral?' must involve diminishing the extent that morality appears alien.

[33] The qualification 'empirically equivalent to' is needed because in certain empirically unrealistic cases, such as utility monsters, the injunction 'Maximize overall realization of human value' cannot be met by improving the lives of as large a proportion of the population as possible. However, under plausible assumptions about this world (including diminishing marginal value) the equivalence holds.

[34] For Scheffler's view, see *The Rejection of Consequentialism: A Philosophical Investigation of the Considerations Underlying Rival Moral Conceptions*. The consequentialist may also argue that at least some of the debate set in motion by Williams is more properly concerned with the question of the relation between moral imperatives and imperatives of rationality than with the content of moral imperatives as such. (See note 42.)

Part of constructing such an answer is a matter of showing that abiding by morality need not alienate us from the particular commitments that make life worthwhile, and in the previous sections we have begun to see how this might be possible within an objective act-consequentialist account of what morality requires. We saw how in general various sorts of projects or relationships can continue to be a source of intrinsic value even though one recognizes that they might have to undergo changes if they could not be defended in their present form on moral grounds. And again, knowing that a commitment is morally defensible may well deepen its value for us, and may also make it possible for us to feel part of a larger world in a way that is itself of great value. If our commitments are regarded by others as responsible and valuable (or if we have reason to think that others should so regard them), this may enhance the meaning or value they have for ourselves, while if they are regarded by others as irresponsible or worthless (especially, if we suspect that others regard them so justly), this may make it more difficult for us to identify with them or find purpose or value in them. Our almost universal urge to rationalize our acts and lives attests our wish to see what we do as defensible from a more general point of view. I do not deny that bringing a more general perspective to bear on one's life may be costly to the self—it may cause re-evaluations that lower self-esteem, produce guilt, alienation, and even problems of identity. But I do want to challenge the simple story often told in which there is a personal point of view from which we glimpse meanings which then vanish into insignificance when we adopt a more general perspective. In thought and action we shuttle back and forth from more personal to less personal standpoints, and both play an important role in the process whereby purpose, meaning, and identity are generated and sustained.[35] Moreover, it may be part of mature commitments, even of the most intimate sort, that a measure of perspective beyond the personal be maintained.

These remarks about the role of general perspectives in

[35] For example, posterity may figure in our thinking in ways we seldom articulate. Thus, nihilism has seemed to some an appropriate response to the idea that mankind will soon destroy itself. 'Everything would lose its point' is a reaction quite distinct from 'Then we should enjoy ourselves as much as possible in the meantime', and perhaps equally comprehensible.

individual lives lead us to what I think is an equally important part of answering the question 'Why should I be moral?': reconceptualization of the terms of the discussion to avoid starting off in an alienated fashion and ending up with the result that morality still seems alien. Before pursuing the idea, let us quickly glance at two existing approaches to the question.

Morality may be conceived of as in essence selfless, impartial, impersonal. To act morally is to subordinate the self and all contingencies concerning the self's relations with others or the world to a set of imperatives binding on us solely as rational beings. We should be moral, in this view, because it is ideally rational. However, morality thus conceived seems bound to appear as alien in daily life. 'Purity of heart' in Rawls's sense would be essential to acting morally, and the moral way of life would appear well removed from our actual existence, enmeshed as we are in a web of 'particularistic' commitments—which happen to supply our *raisons d'être*.

A common alternative conception of morality is not as an elevated purity of heart but as a good strategy for the self. Hobbesian atomic individuals are posited and appeal is made to game theory to show that pay-offs to such individuals may be greater in certain conflict situations—such as reiterated prisoners' dilemmas—if they abide by certain constraints of a moral kind (at least, with regard to those who may reciprocate) rather than act merely prudentially. Behaving morally, then, may be an advantageous policy in certain social settings. However, it is not likely to be the *most* advantageous policy in general, when compared to a strategy that cunningly mixes some compliance with norms and some non-compliance; and presumably the Hobbesian individual is interested only in maximal self-advantage. Yet even if we leave aside worries about how far such arguments might be pushed, it needs to be said that morality as such would confront such an entrepreneurial self as an alien set of demands, for central to morality is the idea that others' interests must sometimes be given weight for reasons unrelated to one's own advantage.

Whatever their differences, these two apparently antithetical approaches to the question 'why should I be moral?' have remarkably similar underlying pictures of the problem. In these pictures, a presocial, rational, abstract individual is the starting-point, and the task is to construct proper interpersonal relations out of such individuals. Of course, this conceit inverts reality: the rational individual of these approaches is a social and historical *product*. But that is old hat. We are not supposed to see this as any sort of history, we are told, but rather as a way of conceptualizing the questions of morality. Yet why when conceptualizing are we drawn to such asocial and ahistorical images? My modest proposal is that we should keep our attention fixed on society and history at least long enough to try recasting the problem in more naturalistic terms.[36]

As a start, let us begin with individuals situated in society, complete with identities, commitments, and social relations. What are the ingedients of such identities, commitments, and relations? When one studies relationships of deep commitment—of parent to child, or wife to husband—at close range, it becomes artificial to impose a dichotomy between what is done for the self and what is done for the other. We cannot decompose such relationships into a vector of self-concern and a vector of other-concern, even though concern for the self and the other are both present. The other has come to figure in the self in a fundamental way—or, perhaps a better way of putting it, the other has become a reference point of the self. If it is part of one's identity to be the parent of Jill or the husband of Linda, then the self has reference points beyond the ego, and that which affects these reference points may affect the self in an unmediated way.[37] These reference points do not all fall within the circle of intimate relationships, either. Among the most important constituents of

---

[36] I 'do not deny that considerations about pay-offs of strategies in conflict situations may play a role in cultural or biological evolutionary explanations of certain moral sentiments or norms. Rather, I mean to suggest that there are characteristic sorts of abstractions and simplifications involved in game-theoretic analysis that may render it blind to certain phenomena crucial for understanding morality and its history, and for answering the question 'Why should I be moral?' when posed by actual individuals.

[37] Again we see the inadequacy of subjectivism about values. If, for example, part of one's identity is to be Jill's parent, then should Jill cease to exist, one's life could be said to have lost some of its purpose even if one were not aware of her death. As the example of the experience machine suggested earlier, there is an objective side to talk about purpose.

identities are social, cultural, or religious ties—one is a Jew, a Southerner, a farmer, or an alumnus of Old Ivy. Our identities exist in relational, not absolute, space, and except as they are fixed by reference points in others, in society, in culture, or in some larger constellation still, they are not fixed at all.[38]

There is a worthwhile analogy between meaning in lives and meaning in language. It has been a while since philosophers have thought it helpful to imagine that language is the arrangement resulting when we hook our private meanings up to a system of shared symbols. Meaning, we are told, resides to a crucial degree in use, in public contexts, in referential systems—it is possible for the self to use a language with meanings because the self is embedded in a set of social and historical practices. But ethical philosophers have continued to speak of the meaning of life in surprisingly private terms. Among recent attempts to give a foundation for morality, Nozick's perhaps places greatest weight on the idea of the meaning of life, which he sees as a matter of an individual's 'ability to regulate and guide [his] life in accordance with some overall conception [he] chooses to accept', emphasizing the idea that an individual creates meaning through choice of a life plan; clearly, however, in order for choice to play a self-defining role, the options among which one chooses must already have some meaning independent of one's decisions.[39]

---

[38] Here I do not have in mind identity in the sense usually at stake in discussions of personal identity. The issue is not identity as principle of individuation, but as *experienced*, as a sense of self—the stuff actual identity crises are made of.

[39] Nozick, *Anarchy, State, and Utopia*, p. 49. (I ignore here Nozick's more recent remarks about the meaning of life in his *Philosophical Explanations* (Cambridge, Mass.: Harvard University Press, 1981). The notion of a 'rationally chosen life plan' has figured prominently in the literature recently, in part due to Rawls's use of it in characterizing the good (see Rawls, *A Theory of Justice*, ch. 7, 'Goodness as Rationality'). Rawls's theory of the good is a complex matter, and it is difficult to connect his claims in any direct way to a view about the meaning of life. However, see T. M. Scanlon, 'Rawls' Theory of Justice', *University of Pennsylvania Law Review* 121 (1973), 1020–69, for an interpretation of Rawls in which the notion of an individual as above all a rational chooser—more committed to maintaining his status as a rational agent able to adopt and modify his goals than to any particular set of goals—functions as the ideal of a person implicit in Rawls's theory. On such a reading, we might interpolate into the original text the idea that meaning derives from autonomous individual choice, but this is highly speculative. In any event, recent discussions of rationally chosen life plans as the bearers of

It is not only 'the meaning of life' that carries such pre-suppositions. Consider, for example, another notion that has played a central role in moral discourse: respect. If the esteem of others is to matter to an individual those others must themselves have some significance to the individual; in order for their esteem to constitute the sought-after respect, the individual must himself have some degree of respect for them and their judgement.[40] If the self loses significance for others, this threatens its significance even for itself; if others lose significance for the self, this threatens to remove the basis for self-significance. It is a commonplace of psychology and sociology that bereaved or deracinated individuals suffer not only a sense of loss owing to broken connections with others, but also a loss in the solidity of the self, and may therefore come to lose interest in the self or even a clear sense of identity. Reconstructing the self and self-interest in such cases is as much a matter of constructing new relations to others and the world as it is a feat of self-supporting self-reconstruction. Distracted by the picture of a hypothetical, presocial individual, philosophers have found it very easy to assume, wrongly, that in the actual world concern for oneself and one's goals is quite automatic, needing no outside support, while a direct concern for others is inevitably problematic, needing some further rationale.

It does not follow that there is any sort of categorical imperative to care about others or the world beyond the self as such. It is quite possible to have few external reference points and go through life in an alienated way. Life need not have much meaning in order to go on, and one does not even have to care whether life goes on. We cannot show that moral scepticism is necessarily irrational by pointing to facts about meaning, but a naturalistic approach to morality need no more refute radical scepticism than does a naturalistic approach to epistemology. For actual people, there may be surprisingly little distance between asking in earnest 'Why

ultimate significance or value do not appear to me to do full justice to the ways in which lives actually come to be invested with meaning, especially since some meanings would have to be presupposed by any rational choice of a plan of life.

[40] To be sure, this is but one of the forms of respect that are of importance to moral psychology. But as we see, self-respect has a number of interesting connections with respect for, and from, others.

should I take any interest in anyone else?' and asking 'Why should I take any interest in myself?'[41] The proper response to the former is not merely to point out the indirect benefits of caring about things beyond the self, although this surely should be done, but to show how denying the significance of anything beyond the self may undercut the basis of significance for the self. There is again a close, but not exact parallel in language: people can get along without a language, although certainly not as well as they can with it; if someone were to ask 'Why should I use my words the same way as others?' the proper response would not only be to point out the obvious benefits of using his words in this way, but also to point out that by refusing to use words the way others do he is undermining the basis of meaning in his own use of language.

These remarks need not lead us to a conservative traditionalism. We must share and preserve meanings in order to have a language at all, but we may use a common language to disagree and innovate. Contemporary philosophy of language makes us distrust any strict dichotomy between meaning, on the one hand, and belief and value, on the other; but there is obviously room within a system of meanings for divergence and change on empirical and normative matters. Language itself has undergone considerable change over the course of history, coevolving with beliefs and norms without in general violating the essential conditions of meaningfulness. Similarly, moral values and social practices may undergo change without obliterating the basis of meaningful lives, so long as certain essential conditions are fulfilled. (History does record some changes, such as the uprooting of tribal peoples, where these conditions were not met, with devastating results.)

A system of available, shared meanings would seem to be a

---

[41] This may be most evident in extreme cases. Survivors of Nazi death camps speak of the effort it sometimes took to sustain a will to survive, and of the importance of others, and of the sense of others, to this. A survivor of Treblinka recalls, 'In our group we shared everything; and at the moment one of the group ate something without sharing it, we knew it was the beginning of the end for him.' (Quoted in T. Des Pres, *The Survivor: An Anatomy of Life in the Death Camps* (New York: Oxford University Press, 1976), p. 96.) Many survivors say that the idea of staying alive to 'bear witness', in order that the deaths of so many would not escape the world's notice, was decisive in sustaining their own commitment to survival.

precondition for sustaining the meaningfulness of individual lives in familiar sorts of social arrangements. Moreover, in such arrangements identity and self-significance seem to depend in part upon the significance of others to the self. If we are prepared to say that a sense of meaningfulness is a precondition for much else in life, then we may be on the way to answering the question 'Why should I be moral?' for we have gone beyond pure egocentrism precisely by appealing to facts about the self.[42] Our earlier discussions have yielded two considerations that make the rest of the task of answering this question more tractable. First, we noted in discussing hedonism that individual lives seem most enjoyable when they involve commitments to causes beyond the self or to others as such. Further, we remarked that it is plausible that the happiest sorts of lives do not involve a commitment to hedonism even of a sophisticated sort. If a firm sense of meaningfulness is a precondition of the fullest happiness, this speculation becomes still

---

[42] One need not be a sceptic about morality or alienated from it in any general sense in order for the question 'Why should I be moral?' to arise with great urgency. If in a given instance doing what is right or having the best sort of character were to conflict head-on with acting on behalf of a person or a project that one simply could not go against without devastating the self, then it may fail to be reasonable from the agent's standpoint to do what is right. It is always *morally* wrong (though not always morally blameworthy) to fail to perform morally required acts, but in certain circumstances that may be the most reasonable thing to do—not because of some larger moral scheme, but because of what matters to particular individuals. Therefore, in seeking an answer to 'Why should I be moral?' I do not assume that it must always be possible to show that the moral course of action is ideally rational or otherwise optimal from the standpoint of the agent. (I could be more specific here if I had a clearer idea of what rationality is.) It would seem ambitious enough to attempt to show that, in general, there are highly desirable lives available to individuals consistent with their being moral. While we might hope for something stronger, this could be enough—given what can also be said on behalf of morality from more general viewpoints—to make morality a worthy candidate for our allegiance as individuals.

It should perhaps be said that on an objective consequentialist account, being moral need not be a matter of consciously following distinctively moral imperatives, so that what is at stake in asking 'Why should I be moral?' in connection with such a theory is whether one has good reason to lead one's life in such a way that an objective consequentialist criterion of rightness is met as nearly as possible. In a given instance, this criterion might be met by acting out of a deeply felt emotion or an entrenched trait of character, without consulting morality or even directly in the face of it. This, once more, is an indication of objective consequentialism's flexibility: the idea is to *be* and *do* good, not necessarily to *pursue* goodness.

more plausible. Second, we sketched a morality that began by taking seriously the various forms of human non-moral value, and then made room for morality in our lives by showing that we can raise moral questions without thereby destroying the possibility of realizing various intrinsic values from particular relationships and activities. That is, we saw how being moral might be compatible (at least in these respects) with living a desirable life. It would take another article, and a long one, to show how these various pieces of the answer to 'why should I be moral?' might be made less rough and fitted together into a more solid structure. But by adopting a non-alienated starting-point—that of situated rather than presocial individuals—and by showing how some of the alienation associated with bringing morality to bear on our lives might be avoided, perhaps we have reduced the extent to which morality seems alien to us by its nature.

6

SIDE CONSTRAINTS*

ROBERT NOZICK

1. THE MINIMAL STATE AND THE ULTRAMINIMAL STATE

The night-watchman state of classical liberal theory, limited to the functions of protecting all its citizens against violence, theft, and fraud, and to the enforcement of contracts, and so on, appears to be redistributive.[1] We can imagine at least one social arrangement intermediate between the scheme of private protective associations and the night-watchman state. Since the night-watchman state is often called a minimal state, we shall call this other arrangement the *ultraminimal state*. An ultraminimal state maintains a monopoly over all use of force except that necessary in immediate self-defence, and so excludes private (or agency) retaliation for wrong and exaction of compensation; but it provides protection and enforcement services *only* to those who purchase its protection and enforcement policies. People who don't buy a protection contract from the monopoly don't get protected. The minimal (night-watchman) state is equivalent to the ultraminimal state conjoined with a (clearly redistributive) Friedmanesque voucher plan, financed from tax revenues.[2] Under this plan all people, or some (for example, those in need), are given tax-funded vouchers

*This is not the title of the original printing.

[1] Here and in the next section I draw upon and amplify my discussion of these issues in footnote 4 of 'On the Randian Argument', *The Personalist* (Spring 1971).

[2] M. Friedman, *Capitalism and Freedom* (Chicago: University of Chicago Press, 1962), ch. 6. Friedman's school vouchers, of course, allow a choice about who is to supply the product, and so differ from the protection vouchers imagined here.

that can be used only for their purchase of a protection policy from the ultraminimal state.

Since the night-watchman state appears redistributive to the extent that it compels some people to pay for the protection of others, its proponents must explain why this redistributive function of the state is unique. If some redistribution is legitimate in order to protect everyone, why is redistribution not legitimate for other attractive and desirable purposes as well? What rationale specifically selects protective services as the sole subject of legitimate redistributive activities? A rationale, once found, may show that this provision of protective services is *not* redistributive. More precisely, the term 'redistributive' applies to types of *reasons* for an arrangement, rather than to an arrangement itself. We might elliptically call an arrangement 'redistributive' if its major (only possible) supporting reasons are themselves redistributive. ('Paternalistic' functions similarly.) Finding compelling non-redistributive reasons would cause us to drop this label. Whether we say an institution that takes money from some and gives it to others is redistributive will depend upon *why* we think it does so. Returning stolen money or compensating for violations of rights are *not* redistributive reasons. I have spoken until now of the night-watchman state's *appearing* to be redistributive, to leave open the possibility that non-redistributive types of reasons might be found to justify the provision of protective services for some by others (I explore some such reasons in Chapters 4 and 5 of Part I.)[3]

A proponent of the ultraminimal state may seem to occupy an inconsistent position, even though he avoids the question of what makes protection uniquely suitable for redistributive provision. Greatly concerned to protect rights against violation, he makes this the sole legitimate function of the state; and he protests that all other functions are illegitimate because they themselves involve the violation of rights. Since he accords paramount place to the protection and non-violation of rights, how can he support the ultraminimal state, which would seem to leave some persons' rights unprotected or ill protected? How can he support this *in the name of* the non-violation of rights?

---

[3] [Not reprinted in this collection—Ed.]

2. MORAL CONSTRAINTS AND MORAL GOALS

This question assumes that a moral concern can function only as a moral *goal*, as an end state for some activities to achieve as their result. It may, indeed, seem to be a necessary truth that 'right', 'ought', 'should', and so on, are to be explained in terms of what is, or is intended to be, productive of the greatest good, with all goals built into the good.[4] Thus it is often thought that what is wrong with utilitarianism (which *is* of this form) is its too narrow conception of good. Utilitarianism doesn't, it is said, properly take rights and their non-violation into account; it instead leaves them a derivative status. Many of the counter-example cases to utilitarianism fit under this objection, for example, punishing an innocent man to save a neighbourhood from a vengeful rampage. But a theory may include in a primary way the non-violation of rights, yet include it in the wrong place and the wrong manner. For suppose some condition about minimizing the total (weighted) amount of violations of rights is built into the desirable end state to be achieved. We then would have something like a 'utilitarianism of rights'; violations of rights (to be *minimized*) merely would replace the total happiness as the relevant end state in the utilitarian structure. (Note that we do not hold the non-violation of our rights as our sole greatest good or even rank it first lexicographically to exclude trade-offs, if there is some desirable society we would choose to inhabit even though in it some rights of ours sometimes are violated, rather than move to a desert island where we could survive alone.) This still would require us to violate someone's rights when doing so minimizes the total (weighted) amount of the violation of rights in the society. For example, violating someone's rights might deflect others from *their* intended action of gravely violating rights, or might remove their motive for doing so, or might divert their attention, and so on. A mob rampaging through a part of town killing and burning *will* violate the rights of those living there. Therefore, someone might try to justify his punishing another *he* knows to be innocent of a crime that enraged a mob, on the grounds that punishing this

[4] For a clear statement that this view is mistaken, see J. Rawls, *A Theory of Justice*, pp. 30, 565–6.

innocent person would help to avoid even greater violations of rights by others, and so would lead to a minimum weighted score for rights violations in the society.

In contrast to incorporating rights into the end state to be achieved, one might place them as side constraints upon the actions to be done: don't violate constraints C. The rights of others determine the constraints upon your actions. (A *goal-directed* view with constraints added would be: among those acts available to you that don't violate contraints C, act so as to maximize goal G. Here, the rights of others would contrain your goal-directed behaviour. I do not mean to imply that the correct moral view includes mandatory goals that must be pursued, even within the constraints.) This view differs from one that tries to build the side constraints C *into* the goal G. The side-constraint view forbids you to violate these moral constraints in the pursuit of your goals: whereas the view whose objective is to minimize the violation of these rights allows you to violate the rights (the constraints) in order to lessen their total violation in the society.[5]

[5] Unfortunately, too few models of the structure of moral views have been specified heretofore, though there are surely other interesting structures. Hence an argument for a side-constraint structure that consists largely in arguing against an end-state maximization structure is inconclusive, for these alternatives are not exhaustive. An array of structures must be precisely formulated and investigated; perhaps some novel structure then will seem most appropriate.

The issue of whether a side-constraint view can be put in the form of the goal-without-side-constraint view is a tricky one. One might think, for example, that each person could distinguish in his goal between *his* violating rights and someone else's doing it. Give the former infinite (negative) weight in his goal, and no amount of stopping others from violating rights can outweigh his violating someone's rights. In addition to a component of a goal receiving infinite weight, indexical expressions also appear, for example, '*my* doing something'. A careful statement delimiting 'constraint views' would exclude these gimmicky ways of transforming side contraints into the form of an end-state view as sufficient to constitute a view as end state. Mathematical methods of transforming a constrained minimization problem into a sequence of unconstrained minimizations of an auxiliary function are presented in A. Fiacco and G. McCormick, *Nonlinear Programming: Sequential Unconstrained Minimization Techniques* (New York: Wiley, 1968). The book is interesting both for its methods and for their limitations in illuminating our area of concern; note the way in which the penalty functions include the constraints, the variation in weights of penalty functions (sec. 7.1), and so on.

The question of whether these side constraints are absolute, or whether they may be violated in order to avoid catastrophic moral horror, and, if the latter, what the resulting structure might look like, is one I hope largely to avoid.

The claim that the proponent of the ultraminimal state is inconsistent, we now can see, assumes that he is a 'utilitarian of rights'. It assumes that his goal is, for example, to minimize the weighted amount of the violation of rights in the society, and that he should pursue this goal even through means that themselves violate people's rights. Instead, he may place the non-violation of rights as a constraint upon action, rather than (or in addition to) building it into the end state to be realized. The position held by this proponent of the ultraminimal state will be a consistent one if his conception of rights holds that your being *forced* to contribute to another's welfare violates your rights, whereas someone else's not providing you with things you need greatly, including things essential to the protection of your rights, does not *itself* violate your rights, even though it avoids making it more difficult for someone else to violate them. (That conception will be consistent provided it does not construe the monopoly element of the ultraminimal state as itself a violation of rights.) That it is a consistent position does not, of course, show that it is an acceptable one.

3. WHY SIDE CONSTRAINTS?

Isn't it *irrational* to accept a side constraint C, rather than a view that directs minimizing the violations of C? (The latter view treats C as a condition rather than a constraint.) If non-violation of C is so important, shouldn't that be the goal? How can a concern for the non-violation of C lead to the refusal to violate C even when this would prevent other more extensive violations of C? What is the rationale for placing the non-violation of rights as a side constraint upon action instead of including it solely as a goal of one's actions?

Side constraints upon action reflect the underlying Kantian principle that individuals are ends and not merely means; they may not be sacrificed or used for the achieving of other ends without their consent. Individuals are inviolable. More should be said to illuminate this talk of ends and means. Consider a prime example of a means, a tool. There is no side constraint on how we may use a tool, other than the moral constraints on how we may use it upon others. There are procedures to be followed to preserve it for future use ('don't leave it out in the rain'), and there are more and less efficient ways of using it. But there is no limit on what we may do to it to best achieve our goals. Now imagine that there was an overridable constraint *C* on some tool's use. For example, the tool might have been lent to you only on the condition that *C* not be violated unless the gain from doing so was above a certain specified amount, or unless it was necessary to achieve a certain specified goal. Here the object is not *completely* your tool, for use according to your wish or whim. But it is a tool nevertheless, even with regard to the overridable constraint. If we add constraints on its use that may not be overridden, then the object may not be used as a tool *in those ways. In those respects*, it is not a tool at all. Can one add enough constraints so that an object cannot be used as a tool at all, in *any* respect?

Can behaviour toward a person be constrained so that he is not to be used for any end except as he chooses? This is an impossibly stringent condition if it requires everyone who provides us with a good to approve positively of every use to which we wish to put it. Even the requirement that he merely should not object to any use we plan would seriously curtail bilateral exchange, not to mention sequences of such exchanges. It is sufficient that the other party stands to gain enough from the exchange so that he is willing to go through with it, even though he objects to one or more of the uses to which you shall put the good. Under such conditions, the other party is not being used solely as a means, in that respect. Another party, however, who would not choose to interact with you if he knew of the uses to which you *intend* to put his actions or good, *is* being used as a means, even if he receives enough to choose (in his ignorance) to interact with you. ('All along, you were just *using* me' can be said by someone who chose to interact only because he was ignorant of another's goals and of the uses to which he himself would be put.) Is it morally incumbent upon someone to reveal his intended uses of an interaction if he has good reason to believe the other would refuse to interact if he knew? Is he *using* the other person, if he does not reveal this? And what of the cases where the other does not choose to be of use at all? In getting pleasure from seeing an attractive person go by, does one use the other solely as a means?[6] Does someone so use an object of sexual fantasies? These and related questions raise very interesting issues for moral philosophy; but not, I think, for political philosophy.

Political philosophy is concerned only with *certain* ways that persons may not use others; primarily, physically aggressing against them. A specific side constraint upon action toward others expresses the fact that others may not be used in the specific ways the side constraint excludes. Side constraints express the inviolability of others, in the ways they specify. These modes of inviolability are expressed by the following injunction: 'Don't use people in specified ways.' An end-state view, on the other hand, would express the view that people are ends and not merely means (if it chooses to express this view at all), by a different injunction: 'Minimize the use in specified ways of persons as means.' Following this precept itself may involve using someone as a means in one of the ways specified. Had Kant held this view, he would have given the second formula of the categorical imperative as, 'So act as to minimize the use of humanity simply as a means ,' rather than the one he actually used: 'Act in such a way that you always treat humanity, whether in your own person or in the person of any other, never simply as a means, but always at the same time as an end.'[7]

Side constraints express the inviolability of other persons. But why may not one violate persons for the greater social good? Individually, we each sometimes choose to undergo some pain or sacrifice for a greater benefit or to avoid a greater harm: we go to the dentist to avoid worse suffering later; we do some unpleasant work for its results; some persons diet to improve their health or looks; some save money to support themselves when they are older. In each case, some cost is borne for the sake of the greater overall good. Why not, *similarly*, hold that some persons have to bear some costs that benefit other persons more, for the sake of the overall social good? But there is no *social entity* with a good

---

[6] Which does which? Often a useful question to ask, as in the following:
—'What is the difference between a Zen master and an analytic philosopher?'
—'One talks riddles and the other riddles talks.'
    [7] *Groundwork of the Metaphysic of Morals.* Translated by H. J. Paton, *The Moral Law* (London: Hutchinson, 1956), p. 96.

that undergoes some sacrifice for its own good. There are only individual people, different individual people, with their own individual lives. Using one of these people for the benefit of others, uses him and benefits the others. Nothing more. What happens is that something is done to him for the sake of others. Talk of an overall social good covers this up. (Intentionally?) To use a person in this way does not sufficiently respect and take account of the fact that he is a separate person,[8] that his is the only life he has. *He* does not get some overbalancing good from his sacrifice, and no one is entitled to force this upon him—least of all a state or government that claims his allegiance (as other individuals do not) and that therefore scrupulously must be *neutral* between its citizens.

[8] See J. Rawls. *A Theory of Justice*, secs. 5, 6, 30. [Section 5 of Rawls's book is reprinted in this collection as Chapter 1—Ed.]

7

AUTONOMY AND DEONTOLOGY*

THOMAS NAGEL

1. THREE KINDS OF AGENT RELATIVITY

In this chapter I want to take up some of the problems that must be faced by any defender of the objectivity of ethics who wishes to make sense of the actual complexity of the subject. The treatment will be general and very incomplete. Essentially I shall discuss some examples in order to suggest that the enterprise is not hopeless.

The discussion will revolve around the distinction between agent-relative and agent-neutral values. I won't try to set forth a full ethical theory, even in outline, but I will try to say something in this chapter and the next[1] about the central problem of ethics: how the lives, interests, and welfare of others make claims on us and how these claims, of various forms, are to be reconciled with the aim of living our own lives. My assumption is that the shape of a moral theory depends on the interplay of forces in the psychic economy of complex rational beings. (I shall not say anything about aesthetic values, whose relation to human interests is obscure, though they are revealed to us by the capacity of certain things outside us to command our interest and respect.)

There is one important component of ethics that is consequen-

Thomas Nagel, 'Autonomy and Deontology', from *The View from Nowhere* (New York: Oxford University Press, 1986), pp. 164–88 (ch. 9). Copyright: Thomas Nagel.

* [This is not the title of the original printing. This selection from *The View from Nowhere* constitutes a revised version of the third of Nagel's Tanner Lectures, to which a number of the contributors to this volume refer. Those lectures were published, with the title 'The Limits of Objectivity', in *The Tanner Lectures on Human Values*, I, ed. S. McMurrin (University of Utah/Cambridge University Press, 1980). Reprinted by permission of the University of Utah Press—Ed.]

[1] [What Nagel refers to as 'the next' chapter is not reprinted in this volume—Ed.]

tialist and impersonal. If what I said in the last chapter is right, some kind of hedonistic, agent-neutral consequentialism describes a significant form of concern that we owe to others. Life is filled with basic pleasures and pains, and they matter. Perhaps other basic human goods, such as health and survival, have the same status, but let me put that aside for the moment. I want now to examine other sorts of objective reasons that complicate the picture. Ethics is concerned not only with what should happen, but also independently with what people should or may *do*. Neutral reasons underlie the former; but relative reasons can affect the latter.[2] In philosophical discussion, the hegemony of neutral reasons and impersonal values is typically challenged by three broad types of reasons that are relative in form, and whose existence seems to be independent of impersonal values.

The first type of reason stems from the desires, projects, commitments, and personal ties of the individual agent, all of which give him reasons to act in the pursuit of ends that are his own. These I shall collect under the general heading of reasons of autonomy (not to be confused with the autonomy of free will).

The second type of reason stems from the claims of other persons not to be maltreated in certain ways. What I have in mind are not neutral reasons for everyone to bring it about that no one is maltreated, but relative reasons for each individual not to maltreat others himself, in his dealings with them (for example by violating their rights, breaking his promises to them, etc.). These I shall collect under the general, ugly, and familiar heading of deontology. Autonomous reasons would limit what we are obliged to do in the service of impersonal values. Deontological reasons would limit what we are *permitted* to do in the service of either impersonal or autonomous ones.

[2] [On pp. 152–3 of *The View from Nowhere*, Nagel explains the distinction between agent-neutral and agent-relative reasons as follows: 'If a reason can be given a general form which does not include an essential reference to the person who has it, it is an *agent-neutral* reason. For example, if it is a reason for anyone to do or want something that it would reduce the amount of wretchedness in the world, then that is a neutral reason. If on the other hand the general form of a reason does include an essential reference to the person who has it, it is an *agent-relative* reason. For example, if it is a reason for anyone to do or want something that it would be in *his* interest, then that is a relative reason.'—Ed.]

The third type of reason stems from the special obligations we have toward those to whom we are closely related: parents, children, spouses, siblings, fellow members of a community or even a nation. Most people would acknowledge a non-contractual obligation to show special concern for some of these others— though there would be disagreement about the strength of the reasons and the width of the net. I'll refer to them as reasons of obligation, even though they don't include a great many obligations that are voluntarily undertaken. I mention them here only for completeness and won't discuss them in detail. I have less confidence here than with regard to the other two categories that in ordinary thought they resist agent-neutral justification.

I am not sure whether all these agent-relative reasons actually exist. The autonomous ones and perhaps the obligatory ones are fairly intelligible; but while the idea behind the deontological ones can I think be explained, it is an explanation which throws some doubt on their validity. The only way to find out what limits there are to what we may or must do in the service of impersonal values is to see what sense can be made of the apparent limits, and to accept or reject them according to whether the maximum sense is good enough.

Taken together, autonomous, obligatory, neutral, and de-ontological reasons cover much of the territory of unreflective bourgeois morality. Common sense suggests that each of us should live his own life (autonomy), give special consideration to certain others (obligation), have some significant concern for the general good (neutral values), and treat the people he deals with decently (deontology). It also suggests that these aims may produce serious inner conflict. Common sense doesn't have the last word in ethics or anywhere else, but it has, as J. L. Austin said about ordinary language, the first word: it should be examined before it is discarded.

Attempts have been made to find room for some version of all three types of apparent exception to impersonal ethics in a more complex impersonal system, using developments of consequentialism like rule-utilitarianism and motive-utilitarianism. A recent example is Hare's two-level version of utilitarianism in *Moral Thinking*. And T. M. Scanlon offers a consequentialist but non-utilitarian justification of deontological rights in 'Rights, Goals, and Fairness'.[3] I shall not try to show that these reductions of the agent-relative to the agent-neutral fail, since I believe they are partly correct. They just aren't the whole truth. I shall try to present an alternative account of how the exceptions might make sense independently. My aim is to explain what it is that eludes justification in neutral terms. Since this is most conspicuous with regard to autonomy and deontology, I shall concentrate on them. The account in both cases depends on certain discrepancies between what can be valued from an objective standpoint and what can be seen from an objective standpoint to have value from a less objective standpoint.

2. REASONS OF AUTONOMY

Not all the sources of subjective reasons are as simple as sensory pleasure and pain. I believe that the most reasonable objectification of the value that we all recognize in our own encounter with these experiences is an impersonal one. Difficult as it may be to carry out, each of us has reason to give significant weight to the simple sensory pleasure or pain of others as well as to his own. When these values occur in isolation, the results can be demanding. If you and a stranger have both been injured, you have one dose of painkiller, and his pain is much more severe than yours, you should give him the painkiller—not for any complicated reasons, but simply because of the relative severity of the two pains, which provides a neutral reason to prefer the relief of the more severe. The same may be said of other basic elements of human good and ill.

But many values are not like this. Though some human interests (and not only pleasure and pain) give rise to impersonal values, I now want to argue that not all of them do. If I have a bad headache, anyone has a reason to want it to stop. But if I badly want to climb to the top of Mount Kilimanjaro, not everyone has a reason to want me to succeed. I have a reason to try to get to the top, and it may be much stronger than my reason for wanting a

---

[3] [Reprinted as chapter 4 in this collection—Ed.]

headache to go away, but other people have very little reason, if any, to care whether I climb the mountain or not. Or suppose I want to become a pianist. Then I have a reason to practise, but other people have little or no reason to care if I practise or not. Why is this?

Why shouldn't the satisfaction of my desire to climb the mountain have impersonal value comparable to the value it has for me—just like the elimination of my headache? As it happens, you may have to put up with severe altitude headaches and nausea to get to the top of a mountain that high: it has to be worth it to you. Why doesn't the objectification of these values preserve the relation among them that exists in the perspective of the climber? This problem was originally formulated by Scanlon. He makes a strong case against the view that the satisfaction of preferences as such provides the raw material for ethics—the basis of our claims to the concern of others. The impersonal value of things that matter to an individual need not correspond to their personal value to him. 'The fact that someone would be willing to forgo a decent diet in order to build a monument to his god does not mean that his claim on others for aid in his project has the same strength as a claim for aid in obtaining enough to eat.'[4]

There are two ways in which a value may be conditional on a desire: the value may lie either outside or inside the conditional, so to speak. In the former case, a person's having X if he desires X has neutral value: satisfaction of the desire has objective utility that everyone has reason to promote. In the latter case, if a person desires X, his having X has relative value for him: susceptibility to the value is conditional on having the desire, and satisfaction of the desire does not have impersonal utility.

It isn't easy to state a general rule for assigning desires to one category or the other. I have claimed that sensory experiences which we strongly like or dislike simply in themselves have agent-neutral value because of those desires. Such immediate likes and dislikes, not resulting from any choice or underlying reason, are very different from the desires that define our broader aims and ambitions. The former result in mental states that are transparently

---

[4] T. M. Scanlon, 'Preference and Urgency', pp. 659–60.

good or bad, because the attitude of the subject is decisive. The latter require more complicated evaluation.

Most of the things we pursue, if not most of the things we avoid, are optional. Their value to us depends on our individual aims, projects, and concerns, including particular concerns for other people that reflect our relations with them; they acquire value only because of the interest we develop in them and the place this gives them in our lives, rather than evoking interest because of their value. When we look at such desires objectively, from outside, we can acknowledge the validity of the reasons they give for action without judging that there is a neutral reason for any of those things to be done. That is because when we move to the objective standpoint, we leave behind the perspective from which the values have to be accepted.

The crucial question is how far the authority of each individual runs in determining the objective value of the satisfaction of his own desires and preferences. From the objective standpoint we see a world which contains multiple individual perspectives. Some of the appearances of value from within those perspectives can just be taken over by the objective self. But I believe that others must remain essentially perspectival—appearances of value only *to the subject*, and valid only from within his life. Their value is not impersonally detachable, because it is too bound up with the idiosyncratic attitudes and aims of the subject, and can't be subsumed under a more universal value of comparable importance, like that of pleasure and pain.

Anyone may of course make the ends of another person his own, but that is a different matter: a matter of personal sympathy rather than of objective acknowledgement. So long as I truly occupy the objective standpoint, I can recognize the value of one of these optional ends only vicariously, through the perspective of the person who has chosen it, and not in its own right.

This is true even if the person is myself. When I regard my life from outside, integration of the two standpoints cannot overcome a certain form of detachment. I can't directly appreciate the value of my climbing Mount Kilimanjaro just because I want to, as I appreciate the value of my being adequately fed and clothed. The *fact* that I want to, viewed from outside, has none of the importance of *wanting to*, experienced from within. I can see a reason here only through the perspective of TN, who has chosen an optional goal which adds to the values operating within his life something beyond the reasons that simply come at him independently of his choices. I cannot see it except as a value for him, and I cannot therefore take it on without qualification as an impersonal value.

While this seems to me true, there is a natural way to dispute it. I have acknowledged that, in the case of sensations, a strong desire or aversion can confer agent-neutral value, and it doesn't require that I have the desire or even fully understand it. Even if, for example, I don't mind the sound of squeaking chalk, I can acknowledge that it is impersonally bad for someone who hates it to be subjected to that sound. The impersonal badness attaches not to the experience conceived merely as a certain sound, but to someone's *having an experience he hates*. The evident awfulness is enough. Now someone might ask, why shouldn't a comparable impersonal value attach to someone's *having (or doing) something he wants*—whatever the desire is? Even if I can't objectively identify with the desire, and therefore can't assign any value to the achievement as such, why can't I judge it to have impersonal value under this more complex description? This would be the universal value under which one could objectively favour all preference-satisfaction.

It isn't easy to make the case convincingly, but I don't believe there is such a universal value. One reason is that the personal projects we are talking about generally involve things happening in the world outside our minds. It seems too much to allow an individual's desires to confer impersonal value on something outside himself, even if he is to some extent involved in it. The impersonal authority of the individual's values diminishes with distance from his inner condition. We can see this clearly, I think, in the limiting case of a personal desire for something which will never impinge on his consciousness: posthumous fame, for example. If someone wants posthumous fame, he may have a reason to do what he thinks will achieve it but one cannot see it as anything but a good *for him*. There is no agent-neutral value whatever in the realization of his hope: the only reason anyone else could have for caring about it would be a specific personal concern for him and his ambitions.

On the other hand, the more a desire has as its object the quality of the subject's experience, and the more immediate and independent of his other values it is, the more it will tend to generate impersonal as well as personal reasons. But to the extent that it transcends his own experience, the achievement of a typical personal project or ambition has no value except from the perspective of its subject—at least none in any way comparable to the value reasonably placed on it by the person whose ambition it is. (I am assuming here that we can abstract from any intrinsic value the achievement may have which does not depend on his interest at all—or else that we are dealing with projects whose actual value, whatever it is, derives entirely from the interest of the subject.) Whereas one clearly can find value in the occurrence/ non-occurrence of a sensory experience that is strongly liked/ disliked for itself, whether or not one has or even empathizes with the reaction. To put it in a way that sounds paradoxical: the more subjective the object of the desire, the more impersonal the value of its satisfaction.

If this is right, then a certain amount of dissociation is inevitable when we bring the two standpoints together. From within I am directly subject to certain agent-relative reasons. From without all I can do is to acknowledge the reasonableness for the person I am of being motivated by those reasons—without being motivated by them myself, *qua* objective self. My objectivity shows up in the acknowledgement that these relative reasons are examples of something general, and could arise for any other agent with optional goals of his own. From a point of view outside the perspective of the ambition to climb Kilimanjaro or become a pianist, it is possible to recognize and understand that perspective and so to acknowledge the reasons that arise inside it; but it is not possible to accept those reasons as one's own, unless one occupies the perspective rather than merely recognizing it.

There is nothing incoherent in wanting to be able to climb Kilimanjaro or play all the Beethoven piano sonatas, while thinking that impersonally it doesn't matter whether one can do this. In fact one would have to be dotty to think it did matter impersonally. It doesn't even matter much impersonally that *if* someone wants to play all the Beethoven sonatas by heart, he should be able to. It matters a little, so that if he is incapable of achieving it, it might be better if he didn't want to—leaving aside whatever value there may be in the ambition itself. The neutral values of pleasure and pain come into effect here. But even that is a rather weak neutral value, since it is not the neutral correlate of the agent-relative reasons deriving directly from the ambition, whose object is not pleasure. If an interest is developed by the agent himself through his choices and actions, then the objective reasons it provides are primarily relative.

Any neutral reasons stemming from it must express values that are independent of the particular perspective and system of preferences of the agent. The general values of pleasure and pain, satisfaction and frustration, fill this role to some extent, as I have said, though only to the extent that they can be detached from the value of the object of desire whose acquisition or loss produces the feeling. (This, incidentally, explains the appeal of hedonism to consequentialists: it reduces all value to the impersonal common denominator of pleasure and pain.) But what there is not, I believe, is a completely general impersonal value of the satisfaction of desires and preferences. The strength of an individual's personal preferences in general determines what they give him reason to do, but it does not determine the impersonal value of his getting what he wants. There is no independent value of preference-satisfaction *per se*, which preserves its force even from an impersonal standpoint.

3. PERSONAL VALUES AND IMPARTIALITY

This may seem harsh, and if we left it at that, it would be. For if agent-neutral reasons derived only from pleasure and pain, we would have no reason to care about many fundamental aspects of other people's welfare which cannot easily be given a hedonistic interpretation—their freedom, their self-respect, their access to opportunities and resources that enable them to live fulfilling lives.

But I believe there is another way in which these things can be seen as having impersonal value—without giving *carte blanche* to individual preferences. These very general human goods share with the much more specific goods of pleasure and freedom from pain a characteristic that generates neutral reasons. Their value does not have to be seen through the particular values of the individual who has or lacks them, or through the particular preferences or projects he has formed.[5] Also, though they do not involve solely the contents of consciousness, such goods are very 'close to home': they determine the character of life from the inside, and this lends authority to the value placed on them by the subject. For both these reasons, when we contemplate our own lives and those of others from outside, the most plausible objectification of these very general goods is not agent-relative.

From the objective standpoint, the fundamental thing leading to the recognition of agent-neutral reasons is a sense that no one is more important than anyone else. The question then is whether we are all equally unimportant or all equally important, and the answer, I think, is somewhere in between. The areas in which we must continue to be concerned about ourselves and others from outside are those whose value comes as close as possible to being universal. If impersonal value is going to be admitted at all, it will naturally attach to liberty, general opportunities, and the basic resources of life, as well as to pleasure and the absence of suffering. This is not equivalent to assigning impersonal value to each person's getting whatever he wants.

The hypothesis of two levels of objectification implies that there is not a significant reason for something to happen corresponding to every reason for someone to do something. Each person has reasons stemming from the perspective of his own life which, though they can be publicly recognized, do not in general provide reasons for others and do not correspond to reasons that

---

[5] This is the rationale behind the choice of primary goods as the common measure of welfare for distributive justice in Rawls, *A Theory of Justice*. See Rawls, 'Social Unity and Primary Goods', for a much fuller treatment. That essay, Scanlon, 'Preference and Urgency', and the present discussion are all treatments of the 'deep problem' described in Rawls, *A Theory of Justice*, pp. 173–5. Dworkin's defence of resources rather than welfare as the correct measure of equality is also in part a response to this problem. ('What is Equality? Part 1: Equality of Welfare' and 'What is Equality? Part 2: Equality of Resources', *Philosophy and Public Affairs* 10 (1981).

the interests of others provide for him. Since the relative reasons are general and not purely subjective, he must acknowledge that the same is true of others with respect to him. A certain objective distance from his own aims is unavoidable; there will be some dissociation of the two standpoints with respect to his individual concerns. The ethical results will depend on the size of the impersonal demands made on him and others by the actual circumstances, and how strongly they weigh against more personal reasons.

One difficult question is whether such a two-tier system implies a significant limit to the degree to which ethics requires us to be impartial between ourselves and others.[6] It would imply this if the agent-relative reasons coming from our personal aims were simply added on to the neutral reasons derived from more universal values. For then I would be permitted to pursue my personal projects in preference to the impersonal good of others just as I can pursue those projects in preference to my own health, comfort, etc.; and I wouldn't have to sacrifice myself in return for the furtherance of *their* personal projects—only for their impersonal good. So it looks as though each person's agent-relative reasons would give him a margin of protection against the claims of others—though of course it could be overridden by sufficiently strong impersonal reasons.

However, there is some reason to doubt that the result will be this straightforward. In weighing our agent-relative reasons against the impersonal claims of others, we may not be able to use the same standards we use within our own lives. To take Scanlon's example again: just as we have more reason to help someone get enough to eat than to help him build a monument to his god—even if he is willing to forgo the food for the monument—so he may have more reason to help feed others than to build the monument, even if he cannot be faulted for starving himself. In other words, we have to give basic impersonal goods more weight when they come from other people's needs than when they compete with personal reasons within our own lives.

---

[6] Impartiality should not be confused with equality. Nothing I say here bears on the question of how much equality is required in the allocation of what has impersonal value. Absolute impartiality is consistent with a denial that equality should be an independent factor at all in settling distributive questions.

I am not sure of the best account of this, or how far it would go toward requiring impartiality. Full impartiality would seem to demand that any tendency toward self-favouritism on the basis of personal reasons be offset by a corresponding decrease in the weight given in one's interpersonal decisions to impersonal reasons deriving from one's own basic needs—so that one's total is not increased, so to speak. All reasons would have to be weighted so that everyone was equally important. But I don't know whether a credible system of this kind could be described, at any rate for the purposes of individual decision making. It seems more likely that interpersonal impartiality, both among others and between oneself and others, would have to be defined in terms of agent-neutral values, and that this would leave room for some partiality toward oneself and one's personal concerns and attachments, the extent of it depending on the comparative importance of relative and neutral reasons in the overall system. A stronger form of impartiality, if one is required, would have to appear at a higher level, in the application of practical reason to the social and political institutions that provide a background to individual choice.

There is one objection to this approach which ought to be mentioned, though probably few people would make it. I have claimed that a neutral objectification of the bulk of individualistic subjective reasons does not make sense. But of course that doesn't entail that a relative objectification is correct instead. There is a radical alternative: it could be that these reasons have no objective validity at all, relative or neutral. That is, it might be said by an uncompromising utilitarian that if there isn't a neutral reason for me to climb Kilimanjaro or learn the Beethoven sonatas—if it wouldn't be a good thing in itself, if the world wouldn't be a better place for my getting to the top of the mountain or being able to play the sonatas—then I have no reason of any kind to do those things, and I had better get rid of my desire to do them as soon as possible. I may not, in other words, accord more personal value to anything in my life than is justified by its impersonal value.

That is a logically possible move, but not a plausible one. It results from the aim of eliminating perspective from the domain of real value to the greatest possible extent, and that aim is not required of us by objectivity, so far as I can see. We should certainly try to harmonize our lives to some extent with how we think the world should be. But there is no necessity, I now believe, to abandon all values that do not correspond to anything desirable from an impersonal standpoint, even though this may be possible as a personal choice—a choice of self-transcendence.

If there are, objectively, both relative and neutral reasons, this raises a problem about how life is to be organized so that both can be given their due. One way of dealing with the problem is to put much of the responsibility for securing impersonal values into the hands of an impersonal institution like the state. A well-designed set of political and social institutions should function as a moral buffer to protect personal life against the ravenous claims of impersonal good, and vice versa. I shall say a bit more about the relation between ethics and political theory later.

Before leaving the subject of autonomy, let me compare what I have said with another recent treatment of the relation between personal and impersonal values in ethical theory: Samuel Scheffler's *The Rejection of Consequentialism*. He proposes an 'agent-centred prerogative', which would permit each individual to accord extra weight to all of his interests in deciding what to do, above that which they contribute to the neutral value of the total outcome of his actions, impersonally viewed.

More specifically, I believe that a plausible agent-centred prerogative would allow each agent to assign a certain proportionately greater weight to his own interests than to the interests of other people. It would then allow the agent to promote the non-optimal outcome of his own choosing, provided only that the degree of its inferiority to each of the superior outcomes he could instead promote in no case exceeded, by more than the specified proportion, the degree of sacrifice necessary for him to promote the superior outcome. (p. 20)

This proposal is different from mine but not strictly incompatible with it. Scheffler does not make the distinction I have made between those interests and desires that do and those that do not generate impersonal values. He is not committed to a particular method of ranking the impersonal value of states of affairs, but his discussion suggests that he believes the satisfaction of most types of human preferences could be counted in determining whether one state of affairs or outcome was impersonally better than another. But whether or not he would accept my distinction, one could accept it and still formulate the proposal of an agent-centred prerogative; for that proposal describes a limit on the requirement always to produce the impersonally best outcome, which is independent of how the comparative impersonal value of outcomes is determined. It might be determined not by all interests but only by some. Then the prerogative would allow an individual to give those interests extra weight if they were his.

The trouble is that on the autonomy view I have put forward, he may already have some unopposed reasons which favour himself, arising from those desires whose satisfaction yields personal but not impersonal value. Perhaps it's going too far in moral indulgence to add to these a further prerogative of favouring himself with respect to the fundamental goods and evils whose impersonal value is clear.

An alternative position, which combines aspects of Scheffler's and mine, might be this. The division between interests that give rise to impersonal values and interests that don't is not sharp; it is a matter of degree. Some interests generate only relative reasons and no neutral ones; some generate neutral reasons that are just as strong as the relative ones; but some generate both relative reasons and somewhat weaker neutral ones. An individual is permitted to favour himself with respect to an interest to the degree to which the agent-relative reason generated by that interest exceeds the corresponding agent-neutral reason. There is no uniform prerogative of assigning a single proportionately greater weight to the cure of one's headaches, the realization of one's musical or athletic ambitions, and the happiness of one's children.

A variable prerogative of this kind would accord better than a uniform prerogative with Scheffler's account of the motivation behind it: the wish to give moral significance to the personal point of view by permitting morality to reflect the way in which concerns and commitments are naturally generated from within a particular point of view. If some interests are more dependent on a particular normative point of view than others, they will more naturally resist assimilation to the unifying claims of impersonal value in the construction of morality. All this emerges from the attempt to combine subjective and objective standpoints toward action and its motives.

On the other hand, even after such adjustments there will still be claims of impersonal morality that seem from an individual point of view excessive, and it may be that the response to this will have to include a more general agent-centred prerogative. I shall take up the problem in the next chapter.

4. DEONTOLOGY

Let me turn now to the obscure topic of deontological constraints. These are agent-relative reasons which depend not on the aims or projects of the agent but on the claims of others. Unlike autonomous reasons, they are not optional. If they exist, they restrict what we may do in the service of either relative or neutral goals.

They complicate an already complicated picture. If there are agent-relative reasons of autonomy that do not give rise to agent-neutral inter-personal claims, then the claims of others must compete with these personal reasons in determining what one should do. Deontological constraints add further agent-relative reasons to the system—reasons not to treat others in certain ways. They are not impersonal claims derived from the interests of others, but personal demands governing one's relations with others.

Whatever their explanation, they are conspicuous among the moral appearances. Here is an example to focus your intuitions.

You have an auto accident one winter night on a lonely road. The other passengers are badly injured, the car is out of commission, and the road is deserted, so you run along it till you find an isolated house. The house turns out to be occupied by an old woman who is looking after her very small grandchild. There is no phone, but there is a car in the garage, and you ask desperately to borrow it, and explain the situation. She doesn't believe you. Terrified by your desperation she runs upstairs and locks herself in the bathroom, leaving you alone with the child. You pound ineffectively on the door and search without success for the car keys. Then it occurs to you that she might be persuaded to tell you where they are if you were to twist the child's arm outside the bathroom door. Should you do it?

It is difficult not to see this is a dilemma, even though the child's getting its armed twisted is a minor evil compared with your friends' not getting to the hospital. The dilemma must be due to a special reason against *doing* such a thing. Otherwise it would be obvious that you should choose the lesser evil and twist the child's arm.

Common moral intuition recognizes several types of deontological reasons—limits on what one may do to people or how one may treat them. There are the special obligations created by promises and agreements; the restrictions against lying and betrayal; the prohibitions against violating various individual rights, rights not to be killed, injured, imprisoned, threatened, tortured, coerced. robbed; the restrictions against imposing certain sacrifices on someone simply as means to an end; and perhaps the special claim of immediacy, which makes distress at a distance so different from distress in the same room. There may also be a deontological requirement of fairness, of evenhandedness or equality in one's treatment of people. (This is to be distinguished from an impersonal value thought to attach to equality in the distribution of benefits, considered as an aspect of the assessment of states of affairs.)

In all these cases it appears that the special reasons, if they exist. cannot be explained simply in terms of neutral values, because the particular relation of the agent to the outcome is essential. Deontological constraints may be overridden by neutral reasons of sufficient strength, but they are not themselves to be understood as the expression of neutral values of any kind. It is clear from the way such reasons work that they cannot be explained by the hypothesis that the violation of a deontological constraint has high negative impersonal value. Deontological reasons have their full force against your doing something—not just against its happening.

For example, if there really are such constraints, the following things seem to be true. It seems that you shouldn't break a promise or tell a lie for the sake of some benefit, even though you would

not be required to forgo a comparable benefit in order to prevent
someone else from breaking a promise or telling a lie. And it
seems that you shouldn't twist the arm of a small child to get its
grandmother to do something, even something important enough
so·that you would not be required to forgo a comparable benefit in
order to prevent someone else from twisting a child's arm. And it
may be that you shouldn't engage in certain kinds of unfair
discriminatory treatment (in an official role, for example) even to
produce a good result which you would not be required to forgo in
order to prevent similar unfairness by others.

Some may simply deny the plausibility of such moral intuitions.
Others may say that their plausibility can be subtly accounted for
in terms of impersonal values, and that they appear to involve a
fundamentally different type of reason for action only if they are
inadequately analysed. As I have said, I don't want to take up
these alternative accounts here. They may provide the best hope
of rationally justifying something that has the rough shape of a set
of deontological restrictions; but offered as complete accounts
they seem to me essentially revisionist. Even if from that point of
view they contain a good deal of truth, they do not shed light on
the independent deontological conceptions they are intended to
replace. Those conceptions still have to be understood, even if
they will eventually be rejected.

Sometimes, particularly when institutions and general practices
are involved in the case, there is a neutral justification for what
looks initially like an agent relative restriction on action. And it is
certainly a help to the acceptance of deontological constraints that
general adherence to them does not produce disastrous results in
the long run. Rules against the direct infliction of harm and against
the violation of widely accepted rights have considerable social
utility, and if it ceased to be so, those rules would lose much of
their moral attractiveness.

But I am convinced that a less indirect, non-statistical form of
evaluation is also at work in support of deontological constraints,
and that it underlies the central, most puzzling intuitions in this
area. This is what would produce a sense of dilemma if it turned
out that general adherence to deontological restrictions worked
consistently contrary to impersonal utility. Right or wrong, it is

this type of view that I want to explore and understand. There is no point in trying to show in advance that such dilemmas cannot arise.

One reason for the resistance to deontological constraints is that they are formally puzzling, in a way that the other reasons we have discussed are not. We can understand how autonomous agent-relative reasons might derive from the specific projects and concerns of the agent, and we can understand how neutral reasons might derive from the interests of others, giving each of us reason to take them into account. But how can there be relative reasons to respect the claims of others? How can there be a reason not to twist someone's arm which is not equally a reason to prevent his arm from being twisted by someone else?

The relative character of the reason cannot come simply from the character of the interest that is being respected, for that alone would justify only a neutral reason to protect the interest. And the relative reason does not come from an aim or project of the individual agent, for it is not conditional on what the agent wants. Deontological restrictions, if they exist, apply to everyone: they are mandatory and may not be given up like personal ambitions or commitments.

It is hard to understand how there could be such a thing. One would expect that reasons stemming from the interests of others would be neutral and not relative. How can a claim based on the interests of others apply to those who may infringe it directly or intentionally in a way that it does not apply to those whose actions may damage that same interest just as much indirectly? After all, it is no worse *for the victim* to be killed or injured deliberately than accidentally, or as an unavoidable side-effect of the dangerous rescue operation. In fact the special features of action that bring these reasons into effect may not add to the impersonal badness of the occurrence at all. To use an example of T. M. Scanlon, if you have to choose between saving someone from being murdered and saving someone else from being killed in a similar manner accidentally, and you have no special relation to either of them, it seems that your choice should depend only on which one you're more likely to succeed in saving. Admittedly the wickedness of a murder is in some sense a bad thing; but when it is a matter of deciding which of them there is more reason to prevent, a murder does not seem to be a significantly worse event, impersonally considered, than an accidental or incidental death. Some entirely different kind of value must be brought in to explain the idea that one should not kill one person even to prevent a number of accidental deaths: murder is not just an evil that everyone has reason to prevent, but an act that everyone has reason to *avoid*.

In any case, even if a murder were a worse event, impersonally considered, than an accidental death, this could not be used to explain the deontological constraint against murder. For that constraint prohibits murder even if it is necessary to prevent other *murders*—not only other deaths.

There is no doubt that ideas of this kind form an important part of common moral phenomenology. Yet their paradoxical flavour tempts one to think that the whole thing is a kind of moral illusion resulting either from innate psychological dispositions or from crude but useful moral indoctrination. Before debunking the intuition, however, we ought to have a better grasp of what it is. No doubt it's a good thing for people to have a deep inhibition against torturing children even for very strong reasons, and the same might be said of other deontological constraints. But that does not explain why we find it almost impossible to regard it as a merely useful inhibition. An illusion involves a judgement or a disposition to judge, and not a mere motivational impulse. The phenomenological fact to be accounted for is that we seem to apprehend in each individual case an extremely powerful agent-relative *reason* not to harm an innocent person. This presents itself as the apprehension of a normative truth, not just as a psychological inhibition. It needs to be analysed and accounted for, and accepted or rejected according to whether the account gives it an adequate justification.

I believe that the traditional principle of double effect, despite problems of application, provides a rough guide to the extension and character of deontological constraints, and that even after the volumes that have been written on the subject in recent years, this remains the right point of convergence for efforts to capture our intuitions.[7] The principle says that to violate deontological

---

[7] A good statement of a view of this type is found in Fried, *Right and Wrong*.

constraints one must maltreat someone else intentionally. The maltreatment must be something that one does or chooses, either as an end or as a means, rather than something one's actions merely cause or fail to prevent but that one doesn't aim at.

It is also possible to foresee that one's actions will cause or fail to prevent a harm that one does not intend to bring about or permit. In that case it does not come under a deontological constraint, though it may still be objectionable for neutral reasons. The precise way to draw this distinction has been the subject of extensive debate, sometimes involving ingenious examples of a runaway trolley which will kill five people unless you . . . , where the dots are filled in by different ways of saving the five, all of which in some way involve one other person's death. I won't try to draw the exact boundaries of the principle. Though I say it with trepidation, I believe that for my purposes they don't matter too much, and I suspect they can't be drawn more than roughly: my deontological intuitions, at least, begin to fail above a certain level of complexity. But one point worth mentioning is that the constraints apply to intentionally permitting as well as to intentionally doing harm. Thus in our example there would be the same kind of objection if with the same end in view you permitted someone else to twist the child's arm. You would have let it happen intentionally, and that would be different from a failure to prevent such an occurrence because you were too engaged in doing something else, which was more important.

5. AGENTS AND VICTIMS

So far this is just moral phenomenology: it does not remove the paradox. Why should we consider ourselves far more responsible for what we do (or permit) intentionally than for consequences of action that we foresee and decide to accept but that do not form part of our aims (intermediate or final)? How can the connection of ends and means conduct responsibility so much more effectively than the connection of foresight and avoidability?

It is as if each action produced a unique normative perspective on the world, determined by intention. When I twist the child's arm intentionally I incorporate that evil into what I do: it is my deliberate creation and the reasons stemming from it are magnified and lit up from my point of view. They overshadow reasons stemming from greater evils that are more 'faint' from this perspective, because they do not fall within the intensifying beam of my intentions even though they are consequences of what I do.

That is the picture, but can it be correct? Isn't it a normatively distorted picture?

This problem is an instance of the collision between subjective and objective points of view. The issue is whether the special, personal perspective of agency has legitimate significance in determining what people have reason to do—whether, because of this perspective, I can have sufficient reason not to do something which, considered from an external standpoint, it would be better if I did. That is, *things* will be better, what *happens* will be better, if I twist the child's arm than if I do not. But I will have done something worse. If considerations of what I may do, and the correlative claims of my victim against me, can outweigh the substantial impersonal value of what will happen, that can only be because the perspective of the agent has an importance in practical reasoning that resists domination by a conception of the world as a place where good and bad things happen whose value is perspective-free.

I have already claimed that the dominance of this neutral conception of value is not complete. It does not swallow up or overwhelm the relative reasons arising from those individual ambitions, commitments, and attachments that are in some sense chosen. But the admission of what I have called autonomous reasons does not imply the possibility of deontological reasons.[8] The two are very different. The peculiarity of deontological reasons is that, although they are agent-relative, they do not express the subjective autonomy of the agent at all. They are demands, not options. The paradox is that this partial, perspectival respect for the interests of others should not give way to an agent-neutral respect free of perspective. The deontological perspective seems primitive, even superstitious, by comparison: merely a stage

---

[8] This is emphasized by Scheffler, who has a cautiously sceptical discussion of deontological constraints under the heading of 'agent-centred restrictions'.

on the way to full objectivity. How can what we *do* in this narrow sense be so important?

Let me try to say where the strength of the deontological view lies. We may begin by considering a curious feature of deontological reasons on which I have not yet remarked. Intention appears to magnify the importance of evil aims by comparison with evil side-effects in a way that it does not magnify the importance of good aims by comparison with good side-effects. We are supposed to avoid using evil means to produce a good end, even though it would be permissible to produce that good end by neutral means with comparably evil side-effects. On the other hand, given two routes to a legitimate end, one of which involves good means and neutral side-effects and the other of which involves neutral means and equally good side-effects, there is no reason to choose the first route. Deontological reasons tell us only not to aim at evil; they don't tell us to aim at good, as a means. Why should this be? What is the relation between evil and intention, or aiming, that makes them clash with such force?

The answer emerges if we ask ourselves what it is to aim at something, what differentiates it from merely producing the result knowingly.

The difference is that action intentionally aimed at a goal is guided by that goal. Whether the goal is an end in itself or only a means, action aimed at it must follow it and be prepared to adjust its pursuit if deflected by altered circumstances—whereas an act that merely produces an effect does not follow it, is not *guided* by it, even if the effect is foreseen.

What does this mean? It means that to aim at evil, even as a means, is to have one's action guided by evil. One must be prepared to adjust it to insure the production of evil: a falling-off in the level of the desired evil becomes a reason for altering what one does so that the evil is restored and maintained. But the essence of evil is that it should *repel* us. If something is evil, our actions should be guided, if they are guided by it at all, toward its elimination rather than toward its maintenance. That is what evil *means*. So when we aim at evil we are swimming head-on against the normative current. Our action is guided by the goal at every point in the direction diametrically opposite to that in which the value of that goal points. To put it another way, if we aim at evil we make what we do in the first instance a positive rather than a negative function of it. At every point, the intentional function is simply the normative function reversed, and from the point of view of the agent, this produces an acute sense of moral dislocation.

If you twist the child's arm, your aim is to produce pain. So when the child cries, 'Stop, it hurts!' his objection corresponds in perfect diametrical opposition to your intention. What he is pleading as your reason to stop is precisely your reason to go on. If it didn't hurt you would twist harder, or try the other arm. There may be cases (e.g. of justified punishment or obloquy) when pain is not intrinsically evil, but this is not one of them: the victim is innocent. You are pushing directly and essentially against the intrinsic normative force of your goal, for it is the production of his pain that guides you. It seems to me that this is the phenomeno-logical nerve of deontological constraints. What feels peculiarly wrong about doing evil intentionally even that good may come of it is the headlong striving against value that is internal to one's aim.

I have discussed a simple case, but naturally there can be complications. One is the possibility of someone volunteering to be subjected to some kind of pain or damage, either for his own good or for some other end which is important to him. In that case the particular evil that you aim at is swallowed up in the larger aim for deontological purposes. So the evil at which we are constrained not to aim is *our victim's* evil, rather than just a particular bad thing, and each individual has considerable authority in defining what will count as harming him for the purpose of this restriction.[9]

All this still leaves unsettled the question of justification. For it will be objected that if one aims at evil as a means only, then even if several people's interests are involved one's action is really being guided not by evil but by overall good, which includes a balance of goods and evils. So when you twist the child's arm, you are guided

[9] The same seems to apply even when informed consent is impossible, as when we cause suffering or damage to a young child for its own greater good—though here there may be a residual inhibition: if we imagine in the case described that the *child's* safety depends on getting the car keys, it doesn't altogether remove the revulsion against twisting his arm to get them.

by the aim of rescuing your injured friends, and the good of that aim dominates the evil of the child's pain. The immediacy of the fact that you must try to produce evil as a subsidiary aim is phenomenologically important, but why should it be morally important? Even though it adds to the personal cost to you, why should it result in a prohibition?

I don't believe there is a decisive answer here. The question is whether to disregard the resistance encountered by my immediate pursuit of what is evil for my victim, in favour of the overall value of the results of what I do. When I view my act from outside and think of it as resulting from a choice of the impersonally considered state of the world in which it occurs, this seems rational. In thinking of the matter this way, I abstract my will and its choices from my person, as it were, and even from my actions, and decide directly among states of the world, as if I were taking a multiple choice test. If the choice is determined by what on balance is impersonally best, then I am guided by good and not by evil.

But the self that is so guided is the objective self, which regards the world impersonally, as a place containing TN and his actions, among other things. It is detached from the perspective of TN, for it views the world from nowhere within it. It chooses, and TN, its instrument, or perhaps one could say its agent, carries out the instructions as best he can. *He* may have to aim at evil, for the impersonally best alternative may involve the production of good ends by evil means. But he is only following orders.

To see the matter in this light is to see both the appeal of agent-neutral, consequentialist ethics and the contrary force of agent-relative, deontological ethics. The detached, objective view takes in everything and provides a standpoint of choice from which all choosers can agree about what should happen. But each of us is not only an objective self but a particular person with a particular perspective; we act in the world from that perspective, and not only from the point of view of a detached will, selecting and rejecting world-states. So our choices are not merely choices of states of the world, but of actions. Every choice is two choices, and from the internal point of view, the pursuit of evil in twisting the child's arm looms large. The production of pain is the immediate aim, and the fact that from an external perspective you are choosing a balance of good over evil does not cover up the fact that this is the intrinsic character of your action.

I have concentrated on the point of view of the agent, as seems suitable in the investigation of an agent-relative constraint. But there is also something to be said about the point of view of the victim. There too we encounter problems having to do with the integration of the two standpoints, and further support for the analysis. Moral principles don't simply tell agents what they may and may not do. They also tell victims what sort of treatment they may and may not object to, resist, or demand.

If I were justified in killing one innocent person to save five others, then he would have no right to object, and on a fully consequentialist view he would have no right to resist. The other five, by contrast, would have the right to object if I *didn't* kill him to save them. A thoroughly impersonal morality would require that victims as well as actors be dominated by impersonal, agent-neutral values in their judgements about how others treat them.

But this seems an excessive demand to make of individuals whose perspective on the world is inherently complex and includes a strong subjective component. Of course none of the six people in this dilemma wants to die, but only one of them is faced with me trying to kill him. This person is not permitted, on a purely agent-neutral consequentialist view, to appeal for his life against my deliberate attempt to take it from him. His special position as my victim doesn't give him any special standing to appeal to me.

Of course the deontological position has a parallel feature. On a deontological view, the five people I could save by killing the one cannot appeal to me for their lives, against my refusal to save them. (They may appeal against *their* killers, if that's the nature of the death threat, but not against me.) But this does not make the two positions symmetrical, for there is a difference. The deontological constraint permits a victim always to object to those who aim at his harm, and this relation has the same special character of normative magnification when seen from the personal perspective of the victim that it has when seen from the personal perspective of the agent. Such a constraint expresses the direct appeal to the point of view of the agent from the point of view of the person on whom he is acting. It operates through that relation. The victim feels outrage when he is deliberately harmed even for the greater good of others, not simply because of the quantity of the harm but because of the assault on his value of having my actions guided by his evil. What I do is immediately directed against his good: it doesn't just in fact harm him.

The five people I could save by killing him can't say the same, if I refrain. They can appeal only to my objective acknowledgement of the impersonal value of their lives. That is not trivial, of course, but it still seems less pressing than the protest available to my victim—a protest he can make not to them but to me, as the possessor of the life I am aiming to destroy.

This merely corroborates the importance of the internal perspective in accounting for the content of deontological intuitions. It does not prove the correctness of those intuitions. But it confirms that a purely impersonal morality requires the general suppression of the personal perspective in moral motivation, not only in its rejection of relative reasons of autonomy but also in its refusal to accept agent-relative deontological restrictions. Such restrictions need not be absolute: they can be thought of as relative reasons with a certain weight, that are among the sources of morality but do not exhaust it. When we regard human relations objectively, it does not seem irrational to admit such reasons at the basic level into the perspective of both agents and victims.

6. MORAL PROGRESS

This account of the force of deontological reasons applies with special clarity to the constraint against doing harm as a means to your ends. A fuller deontological theory would have to explain the different types of normative grain against which one acts in breaking promises, lying, discriminating unfairly, and denying immediate emergency aid. It would also have to deal with problems about what exactly is being aimed at, in cases of action that can be described in several different ways. But I believe that the key to understanding any of these moral intuitions is the distinction between the internal viewpoint of the agent or victim and an external, objective viewpoint which both agent and victim can also adopt. Reasons for action look different from the first two points of view than from the third.

We are faced with a choice. For the purposes of ethics, should we identify with the detached, impersonal will that chooses total outcomes, and act on reasons that are determined accordingly? Or is this a denial of what we are really doing and an avoidance of the full range of reasons that apply to creatures like us? This is a true philosophical dilemma; it arises out of our nature, which includes different points of view on the world. When we ask ourselves how to live, the complexity of what we are makes a unified answer difficult. I believe the human duality of perspectives is too deep for us reasonably to hope to overcome it. A fully agent-neutral morality is not a plausible human goal.

On the other hand, it is conceivable that deontological restrictions now widely accepted may be modified under the pressure of conflict with the impersonal standpoint. Some degree of scepticism about our current moral intuitions is not unreasonable, in light of the importance to moral belief of our starting-points, the social influences pressing on us, and the confusion of our thought. If we aspire to objective truth in this area—that is, truth that is independent of our beliefs—we would be wise to hold many of our views more tentatively than we are naturally inclined to do. In ethics, even without the benefit of many clear examples, we should be open to the possibility of progress as we are in other areas, with a consequent effect of reduced confidence in the finality of our current understanding.[10]

It is evident that we are at a primitive stage of moral development. Even the most civilized human beings have only a haphazard understanding of how to live, how to treat others, how to organize their societies. The idea that the basic principles of morality are *known*, and that the problems all come in their interpretation and application, is one of the most fantastic conceits to which our conceited species has been drawn. (The idea that, if we cannot easily know it, there is no truth here is no less conceited.) Not all of our ignorance in these areas is ethical, but a

---

[10] See Parfit, *Reasons and Persons*, pt. 1, for discussion of some ways common-sense morality might be revised to bring it closer to consequentialism.

lot of it is. And the idea of the possibility of moral progress is an essential condition of moral progress. None of it is inevitable.

The pursuit of objectivity is only a method of getting closer to the truth. It is not guaranteed to succeed, and there is room for scepticism about its specific results in ethics as elsewhere. How far it can take us from the appearances is not clear. The truth here could not be radically inaccessible in the way that the truth about the physical world might be. It is more closely tied to the human perspective and the human motivational capacity because its point is the regulation of human conduct. It has to be suited to govern our lives day by day, in a way in which theoretical understanding of the physical world does not. And to do its work it must be far more widely accepted and internalized than in areas where the public is willing to defer to expert opinion.

There might be forms of morality incommensurable with our own that are appropriate for Martians but to which we do not have access for the same reason that we do not have access to the minds of such creatures. Unless we can understand their lives, experiences, and motives from inside, we will be unable to appreciate the values to which they respond in a way that allows us to objectify them accurately. Objectivity needs subjective material to work on, and for human morality this is found in human life.

How far outside ourselves we can go without losing contact with this essential material—with the forms of life in which values and justifications are rooted—is not certain. But I believe that ethics, unlike aesthetics, requires more than the purification and intensification of internal human perspectives. It requires a detachment from particular perspectives and transcendence of one's time and place. If we did not have this capacity then there would be no alternative to relativism in ethics. But I believe we do have it, and that it is not inevitably a form of false consciousness.

Even the very primitive stage of moral development we have reached was arrived at only by a long and difficult journey. I assume a much longer one lies ahead of us, if we survive. It would be foolish to try to lay down in advance the outlines of a correct method for ethical progress, but it seems reasonable at present to continue the awkward pursuit of objectivity described here. This does not mean that greater detachment always takes us closer to the truth. Sometimes, to be sure, objectivity will lead us to regard our original inclinations as mistaken, and then we will try to replace them or bracket them as ineliminable but illusory. But it would be a mistake to try to eliminate perspective from our conception of ethics entirely—as much of a mistake as it would be to try to eliminate perspective from the universe. This itself must be objectively recognized. Though it may be equally tempting, it would be no more reasonable to eliminate all those reasons for action that cannot be assimilated to the most external, impersonal system of value than it would be to eliminate all facts that cannot be assimilated to physics.

Yet in defending the legitimacy of agent-relative principles, we must guard against self-deception and the escalation of personal claims simply to resist burdensome moral demands. It is not always easy to tell, for example, whether a morality that leaves extensive free space in each individual life for the pursuit of personal interests is not just a disguise for the simplest form of badness: selfishness in the face of the legitimate claims of others. It is hard to be good, as we all know.

I suspect that if we try to develop a system of reasons which harmonizes personal and impersonal claims, then even if it is acknowledged that each of us must live in part from his own point of view, there will be a tendency for the personal components to be altered. As the claims of objectivity are recognized, they may come to form a larger and larger part of each individual's conception of himself, and will influence the range of personal aims and ambitions, and the ideas of his particular relations to others and the claims they justify. I do not think it is Utopian to look forward to the gradual development of a greater universality of moral respect, an internalization of moral objectivity analogous to the gradual internalization of scientific progress that seems to be a feature of modern culture.

On the other hand there is no reason to expect progress to be reductive, though here as elsewhere progress is too easily identified with reduction and simplification. Distinct individuals are still the clients of ethics, and their variety guarantees that pluralism will be an essential aspect of any adequate morality, however advanced.

There have to be principles of practical reason that allow us to take into account values that we do not share but whose force for others we must acknowledge. In general, the problem of how to combine the enormous and disparate wealth of reasons that practical objectivity generates, together with the subjective reasons that remain, by a method that will allow us to act and choose in the world, is dauntingly difficult.

This brings us to a final point. There can be no ethics without politics. A theory of how individuals should act requires a theory—an ethical theory, not just an empirical one—of the institutions under which they should live: institutions which substantially determine their starting-points, the choices they can make, the consequences of what they do, and their relations to one another. Since the standpoint of political theory is necessarily objective and detached, it offers strong temptations to simplify, which it is important to resist. A society must in some sense be organized in accordance with a single set of principles, even though people are very different.

This is inconvenient: it may seem that political theory must be based on a universal human nature, and that if we cannot discover such a thing we have to invent it, for political theory must exist. To avoid such folly, it is necessary to take on the much more difficult task of devising fair uniform social principles for beings whose nature is not uniform and whose values are legitimately diverse. If they were diverse enough, the task might be impossible—there may be no such thing as intergalactic political theory—but within the human species the variation seems to fall within bounds that do not rule out the possibility of at least a partial solution. This would have to be something acceptable from a standpoint external to that of each particular individual, which at the same time acknowledges the plurality of values and reasons arising within all those perspectives. Even though the morality of politics is rightly more impersonal than the morality of private life, the acknowledgement of personal values and autonomy is essential even at the level that requires the greatest impersonality.

There is no telling what kinds of transcendence of individuality will result over the long term from the combined influence of moral and political progress, or decline. A general takeover of

172 THOMAS NAGEL

individual life from the perspective of the universe, or even from the perspective of humanity, seems premature—even if some saints or mystics can manage it. Reasons for action have to be reasons for individuals, and individual perspectives can be expected to retain their moral importance so long as diverse human individuals continue to exist.

8

IS COMMON-SENSE MORALITY
SELF-DEFEATING?[1]

DEREK PARFIT

WHEN is a moral theory self-defeating? I suggest the following.
There are certain things we ought to try to achieve. Call these our
moral aims. Our moral theory would be self-defeating if we
believed we ought to do what will cause our moral aims to be
worse achieved. Is this ever true? If so, what does it show?

I

We ought to try never to act wrongly. Call this our *formal* aim.
Could a moral theory be formally self-defeating? I shall not discuss
this possibilty. By 'aims' I shall mean substantive aims.

There are two ways in which a theory might be substantively
self-defeating. Call this theory *T*, and the aims it gives to each our
T-given aims. Say that we *successfully obey T* when each succeeds
in doing what, of the acts available, best achieves his *T*-given aims.
Call *T*

> *indirectly self-defeating* when it is true that, if we try to achieve
> our *T*-given aims, these aims will be worse achieved.

and

> *directly self-defeating* when it is certain that, if we successfully
> obey *T*, we will thereby cause our *T*-given aims to be worse
> achieved.

Consider first Act Consequentialism, or *AC*. This gives to all

Derek Parfit, 'Is Common-Sense Morality Self-Defeating?', *Journal of Philosophy*
76, No. 10 (October 1979), pp. 533–45. Reprinted by permission of the Editors of
the Journal of Philosophy and the author.

[1] This paper is a shortened version of the last part of my 'Prudence. Morality.
and the Prisoner's Dilemma'.

one common aim: the best possible outcome. If we try to achieve this aim, we may often fail. Even when we succeed, the fact that we are trying might make the outcome worse. AC might thus be indirectly self-defeating. What does this show? A consequentialist might say: 'It shows that AC should be only one part of our moral theory. It should be the part that covers successful acts. When we are certain to succeed, we should aim for the best possible outcome. Our wider theory should be this: we should have the aims and dispositions having which would make the outcome best. This wider theory would not be self-defeating. So the objection has been met.'

Could AC be *directly* self-defeating? Could it be certain that, if we successfully obey AC, we will thereby make the outcome worse? There is one kind of case in which this may seem possible. These are co-ordination problems, where what each ought to do depends upon what others do. In such cases even if we all successfully obey AC this does not ensure that our acts jointly produce the best possible outcome. But it cannot ensure that they do not. If they do, we must be successfully obeying AC. So AC cannot be directly self-defeating. It cannot be *certain* that, if we successfully obey this moral theory, we will thereby cause the aim that it gives us to be worse achieved.[2]

We can widen this conclusion. When any theory T gives us common aims, it cannot be directly self-defeating. If we cause these common aims to be best achieved, we must be successfully obeying T. So it cannot be certain that, if we successfully obey T, we will thereby cause our T-given aims to be worse achieved.

When T gives to different people different aims, this can be certain. But we need a new distinction. Call T

> *directly individually self-defeating* when it is certain that, if someone successfully obeys T, he will thereby cause his T-given aims to be worse achieved,

and

> *directly collectively self-defeating* when it is certain that, if all rather than none successfully obey T, we will thereby cause the T-given aims of each to be worse achieved.

[2] I summarize D. Regan's *Utilitarianism and Co-operation.*

It is the second that is possible. Suppose that T gives to you and me different moral aims. And suppose that each could either (1) promote his own T-given aim or (2) more effectively promote the other's. The outcomes would be these:

	You do (1)	You do (2)
I do (1)	Our T-given aims are third-best achieved	Mine is best achieved, yours worst
I do (2)	Mine is worst achieved, yours best	Our T-given aims are second-best achieved

Suppose finally that neither's choice will affect the other's. It will then be certain that, if I do (1) rather than (2), my T-given aim will be better achieved. This is so whatever you do. And the same holds for you. So we both successfully obey T only if we both do (1) rather than (2). Only then is each doing what, of the acts available, best achieves his T-given aim. But it is certain that if both rather than neither successfully obey T—if both do (1) rather than (2)—we will thereby cause the T-given aims of each to be worse achieved. Theory T is here directly collectively self-defeating.

Such cases can occur whenever

(a) our moral theory gives to each a different aim,
(b) the achievement of each person's aim partly depends on what others do, and
(c) what each does will not affect what these others do.

On the moral theories most of us accept, (a) and (b) often hold. In a case involving only two people, (c) may be unlikely. It may hold only if we cannot communicate. But in cases that involve large numbers of people (c) often holds. What each does would here be unlikely to affect what others do. Partly for this reason, it is the many-person cases which have practical importance. But it will be simpler to discuss two-person versions.

II

Consider first *self-referential altruism*. Most of us believe that there are certain people to whose interests we should give extra weight. Thus each ought to give priority to his children, parents, pupils, patients, members of his own trade union, those whom he represents, or fellow-countrymen. This priority should not be absolute. It would be wrong to save my child's toy rather than a stranger's life. But I ought to save my child from harm rather than save a stranger's child from a somewhat greater harm. I have special duties to my child, which cannot be overridden simply because I could do somewhat greater good elsewhere.

When I try to save my child from harm, what should my aim be? Should it simply be that he is not harmed? Or should it rather be that he is saved from harm by me? If you would have a better chance of saving him from harm, I would be wrong to insist that the attempt be made by me. This suggests that my aim should take the simpler form. Let us assume that this is so.

Consider *Case One*. We cannot communicate. But each could either (1) save his own child from some lesser harm or (2) save the other's child from another somewhat greater harm. The outcomes would be these:

	You do (1)	do (2)
I do (1)	Both our children suffer the greater harm	Mine suffers neither harm, yours both
do (2)	Mine suffers both, yours neither	Both suffer the lesser harm

Since we cannot communicate, neither's choice will affect the other's. If we believe we ought to give priority to our own children, we must believe that each should do (1) rather than (2). Each would thus ensure that, whatever the other does, his own child will be harmed less. But if both do (1) rather than (2) both our children will be harmed more.

Besides trying to protect my child, I should try to give him certain kinds of benefit. What should my aim here be? Should it simply be that he receive these benefits, or should it rather be that he receive these benefits *from me*? Could I be right to insist that it be I who benefits my child, if I knew that this would be worse for him? Some would answer 'No'. But this answer may be too sweeping. It treats parental care as a mere means. We may think it more than that. We may agree that, with some kinds of benefit, my aim should take the simpler form. It should simply be that the outcome be better for my child. But there may be other kinds of benefit which it should be my aim that *I* give my child.

Consider *Case Two*. We cannot communicate. But each could either (1) benefit his own child or (2) benefit the other's child somewhat more. The outcomes would be these:

	You do (1)	do (2)
I do (1)	Third-best for both our children	Best for mine, worst for yours
do (2)	Worst for mine, best for yours	Second-best for both

If my aim should here be that the outcome be better for my child, I should again do (1) rather than (2). That will be better for my child, whatever you do. And the same holds for you. But if both do (1) rather than (2) that will be worse for both our children. Consider next *Case Three*. We cannot communicate. But I could either (1) enable myself to benefit my child or (2) enable you to benefit yours somewhat more. You have the same alternatives with respect to me. The outcomes would be these:

You

	do (1)	do (2)
do (1) **I**	Each can benefit his child	I can benefit mine most, you can benefit yours least
do (2)	I can benefit mine least, you can benefit yours most	Each can benefit his child more

If my aim should here be that I benefit my child, I should again do (1) rather than (2). I can then, whatever you do, benefit my child more. And the same holds for you. But if both do (1) rather than (2) each can benefit his child less. Note the difference between these two examples. In Case Two we are concerned with what happens. The aim of each is that the outcome be better for his child. This is an aim that the other can directly cause to be achieved. In Case Three we are concerned with what we *do*. Since my aim is that *I* benefit my child, you cannot, on my behalf, do so. But you might enable me to do so. You might thus indirectly cause my aim to be achieved.

These two cases are unlikely to occur. But we often face many-person versions. It is often true that, if all rather than none give priority to our own children, that will either be worse for all our children, or will enable each to benefit his children less. One common case involves a *public good*: an outcome that benefits our children whether or not we help to produce it. It can be true of each parent that, if he helps, his contribution adds to the total benefit. But his own children's share of what he himself adds would, in a large community, be small. Nor would his example be widely copied. It may thus be better for his children if he does not contribute. He could spend what he saves—whether in money, time, or energy—directly on them. If we ought to give priority to our own children, it may thus be true of each that he should not contribute. Each would then be doing what is best for his own children, whatever others do. But if none contribute that would be worse for all our children than if all do. Consider next those benefits which it should be the aim of each that *he* give his children. Whether each can do so may in part depend on how much he earns. It is often true that each could either (1) add to his own earnings or (2) add more to the earnings of others. (Choice (2) typically involves some kind of self-restraint.) It will here be true of each that, if he does (1) rather than (2), he can benefit his children more. This is so whatever others do. But if all do (1) rather than (2) each can benefit his children less. These are only two of the ways in which such cases can occur. There are many others. Similar remarks apply to all similar obligations—such as those to parents, pupils, members of our own trade union, or fellow-countrymen. So there are countless many-person cases with the structure of my two examples.

Consider finally those things which we should aim *not* to do— such as infringing people's rights, or harming the innocent. Should we have the common aim that *we* do not do these things, or should each have the aim that they are not done *by him*? We should here distinguish two questions. What should each do when we all do our duty? This assumes what is called *full compliance*. What should each do when there are some others who act wrongly? This assumes *partial compliance*. These two questions may need different answers. Suppose you threaten that, unless I harm one innocent person, you will harm both him and several others. Some claim that, even if I believe your threat, I should here be concerned only with what *I* do. I should refuse to harm the innocent, even if the outcome is that you do so on a larger scale. But this is not the kind of case we are discussing. We are asking what might happen if we all obey our moral theory. So we must change the example. Suppose that, through no fault of yours, it has become true that you must harm certain innocent people. There are two ways in which this might be true. If it would prevent some catastrophe, harming these people might be your duty. Even if we deny this, we must admit that you might have no alternative. It might be true that, whatever you do, you will harm these people. In either case, the question is: Should I harm one of these people, if that would enable you not to harm the others? Or should I again be concerned only with what *I* do?

Suppose we take the second view. Consider *Case Four*. Through no fault of ours, it has become true that each must harm three innocent people. We cannot communicate. But each could now improve our moral situation. Each could either (1) enable himself to harm one fewer or (2) enable the other to harm two fewer. The outcomes would be these:

	You do (1)	You do (2)
I do (1)	Each must harm two innocent people	I must harm none, you three
I do (2)	I must harm three, you none	Each must harm one

If the aim of each should be that *he* does not harm innocent people, each should again do (1) rather than (2). Each would thus, whatever the other does, enable himself to harm fewer. But if both do (1) rather than (2) each must harm more. This case is again unlikely to occur. But its many-person version has some practical importance.

III

We can now ask what, if anything, such cases show. We believe that each should have certain moral aims. We successfully obey our moral theory when each succeeds in doing what, of the acts available, best achieves his moral aims. In my cases it is certain that, if both rather than neither successfully obey our moral theory, we will thereby cause the moral aims of each to be worse achieved. Our moral theory is here directly collectively self-defeating. Is this an objection?

Let us start with a smaller question. Could we revise our theory, so that it would not be self-defeating? If there is no such revision, ours may be the best possible theory. Since we believe our theory, we should ask what is the smallest such revision. So we should first identify the part of our theory which is self-defeating.

It will help to bring together two of the distinctions drawn above. One part of a moral theory may cover successful acts on the assumption of full compliance. Call this part *ideal act theory*. This says what we should all try to do, on the assumptions that we all try and all succeed. Call this *what we should all ideally do*. Note next that, in my examples, what is true is this. If *all* of us *successfully* obey our moral theory, it will be self-defeating. It is our ideal act theory which is self-defeating. If we ought to revise our theory, this is the part that must certainly be revised.

The revision would be this. Call our theory M. In such cases we should all ideally do what will cause the M-given aims of each to be better achieved. Thus in my examples we should both ideally do (2) rather than (1). That will make the outcome better for both our children, and will enable each both to benefit his child more and to harm fewer innocent people.

Call this revision R. Note first that R applies only to those cases where M is self-defeating. If we decide to adopt R, we will need to consider how such cases can be recognized. I believe that they are common. But I have no space to discuss this here.

Note next that R is restricted to ideal act theory. It does not say what we ought to do when there are some who do not obey R. Nor does it say what our aims should be when there is a serious chance that our attempts will fail. Nor does it say what dispositions we should have. Since these are the questions with most practical importance, it may seem that adopting R would make little difference. But this does not follow. If we revise this part of our theory, we may be led to revise the rest. Return, for instance, to the public good that would benefit our children. According to R, we should all ideally contribute. If some do not contribute, R ceases to apply. But it would be natural to make this further claim: each should still contribute provided that enough others do so too. We would need to decide what counts as enough. But, whatever we decide, adopting R would have made a difference. We would now regard non-contribution as at most a defensive second-best. Consider next the relation between acts and dispositions. In Case One each could either (1) save his own child from a lesser harm or

(2) save the other's child from a greater harm. According to R, we should both ideally do (2). Should we be *disposed* to do (2)? If the lesser harm would itself be great, such a disposition might be incompatible with love for our children. This may lead us to decide that we should remain disposed to do (1). This would mean that, if the case arose, our children would be harmed more; but, if we are to love them, this is a risk they must run. These remarks cannot be plausibly extended to all other cases where M is self-defeating. It would be possible to love one's children and contribute to most public goods. Nor would the remarks apply to all similar obligations—such as those to pupils, patients, those whom we represent, or our fellow-countrymen. It therefore seems likely that, if we adopt R, we would be led to change our view about some dispositions.

We can now return to the main question. Ought we to adopt R? Is it an objection to our moral theory that, in certain cases, it is self-defeating? If it is, R is the obvious remedy. R revises M only where M is self-defeating. And the only difference is that R is not.

Remember first that, in these cases, M is *directly* self-defeating. The problem is not that our attempts are failing. That might be no objection. But in my examples all of us successfully obey M. Each succeeds in doing what, of the acts available, best achieves his M-given aim. This is what makes M self-defeating. And this would seem to be an objection. If there is any assumption on which a theory should *not* be self-defeating, it is the assumption that it is universally successfully obeyed.

Remember next that by 'aims' I mean substantive aims. I have ignored our formal aim: the avoidance of wrongdoing. This may seem to remove the objection. Thus consider those cases where, if we obey M, either the outcome will be worse for all our children, or each can benefit his children less. We might say: 'These results are, of course, unfortunate. But how could we avoid them? Only by failing to give priority to our own children. That would be wrong. So these cases cast no doubt on our moral theory. Even to achieve our other moral aims, we should never act wrongly.'

These remarks are confused. It is true that, in these cases, M is not formally self-defeating. If we obey M, we are not doing what we believe to be wrong. On the contrary, we think it wrong *not* to obey M. But M is substantively self-defeating. Unless we all do what we now think wrong, we will cause our M-given aims to be worse achieved. The question is: Might this show that we are mistaken? Ought we perhaps to do what we *now think* wrong? We cannot answer, 'No—we should never act wrongly.' If we are mistaken, we would *not* be acting wrongly. Nor can we simply say, 'But, even in these cases, we *ought* to give priority to our own children.' This just assumes that we are not mistaken. To defend our theory, we must claim more than this. We must claim that it is no objection to our theory that, in such cases, it is substantively self-defeating.

This would be no objection if it simply did not matter whether our M-given aims will be achieved. But this does matter. The sense in which it matters may be unclear. If we have not acted wrongly, it may not matter morally. But it matters in a way that has moral implications. Why should we try to achieve our M-given aims? Part of the reason must be that, in this other sense, their achievement matters.

Someone might say: 'You call M *self*-defeating. So your objection must appeal *to* M. You should not appeal to some rival theory. This is what you have now done. When you claim that it matters whether our M-given aims will be achieved, you are merely claiming that, if they are not, the outcome will be worse. This assumes consequentialism. So you beg the question.'

This is not so. It will help to introduce two more labels. When our aims are held in common, call them *agent-neutral*; when they are different for different agents call them *agent-relative*. Any aim may be concerned either with what happens or with what is done. So there are four kinds of aim. Here are some examples:

	Concerned with	
	what happens	what is done
agent-neutral	that no one starve	that no one steal
agent-relative	that my children do not starve	that I do not steal

When I claim that it matters whether our *M*-given aims will be achieved, I am not assuming consequentialism. Some of these aims are concerned with what we *do*. More important, I am not assuming agent-neutralism. Since our moral theory is, for the most part, agent-relative, this would beg the question. But it need not be begged.

There are here two points. First, I am not assuming that what matters is the achievement *of M-given aims*. Suppose that I could either (1) promote my *M*-given aims or (2) more effectively promote yours. According to *M*, I should here do (1) rather than (2). I will thereby cause *M*-given aims to be, on the whole, worse achieved. But this does not make *M* self-defeating. I will cause *my M*-given aims to be better achieved. In my examples the point is not that, if we both do (1) rather than (2), we will cause *M*-given aims to be worse achieved. The point is that we will cause *each of our own M*-given aims to be worse achieved. We will do worse not just in agent-neutral but in agent-relative terms.

The second point is that this can matter in an agent-relative way. This can be shown with a comparison. Consider the account of rationality which gives to each agent this overriding aim: that the outcome be better for himself. Call this theory *prudence*, or *P*. Suppose that *P* was indirectly self-defeating. Suppose that, when each tries to make the outcome better for himself, he fails. If we believe theory *P*, would we think this matters? Or does it only matter whether each achieves his formal aim: the avoidance of irrationality? The answer is clear. According to theory *P*, acting rationally is a mere means. All that matters is the achievement of our substantive *P*-given aims. But the important point is this. The achievement of these aims matters in an agent-relative way. To think it an objection that *P* is self-defeating, we need not appeal to the agent-neutral form of *P*: utilitarianism. *P* is not a moral theory. But the example shows that, in discussing *M*, we need not beg the question. If it matters whether our *M*-given aims will be achieved, this, too, can matter in an agent-relative way.

Does this matter? Note that I am not asking whether this is all that matters. I am not suggesting that the achievement of our formal aim—the avoidance of wrongdoing—is a mere means. Though assumed by consequentialists, this is not what most of us believe. We may even think that the achievement of our formal aim always matters most. But this is here irrelevant. We are asking whether it casts doubt on M that it is substantively self-defeating. Might this show that, in such cases, M is incorrect? It may be true that what matters most is that we avoid wrongdoing. But this truth cannot show M to be correct. It cannot help us to decide what *is* wrong.

Can we claim that *all* that matters is our formal aim? If that were so, my examples would show nothing. We could say, 'To be substantively self-defeating is, in the case of M, *not* to be self-defeating.' Can we defend our theory in this way? In the case of some M-given aims, perhaps we can. One example might involve trivial promises. We might believe both that we should try to keep such promises and that it would not matter if, through no fault of ours, we fail. But we do not believe this about all of our M-given aims. If we can benefit our children less, or must harm the innocent, this matters.

Remember finally that, in my examples, M is collectively *but not individually* self-defeating. Could this provide a defence?

This is the central question raised by these examples. It is because M is individually successful that, at the collective level, it is here *directly* self-defeating. Why is it true that, if we both do (1) rather than (2), we *successfully* obey M? Because *each* is doing what, of the acts available, *best* achieves his M-given aim. Is it perhaps no objection that *we* thereby cause the M-given aims of each to be *worse* achieved?

It will again help to remember prudence. In so-called 'Prisoner's Dilemmas' P is directly collectively self-defeating. If all rather than none successfully obey P, that will here be worse for everyone. The P-given aim of each will be worse achieved. If we were choosing a collective code, something that we will all follow, P would here tell us to reject itself. It would be prudent to vote against prudence. But someone who believes in P might call this irrelevant. He might say: 'P is not a collective code. To be collectively self-defeating is, in the case of prudence, *not* to be self-defeating.'

Can we defend our moral theory in this way? This depends upon our view about the nature of morality. On most views, the answer is 'No'. But I must here leave this question open.[3]

[3] It remains open in my 'Prudence, Morality, and the Prisoner's Dilemma'. But I there discuss certain other questions which I have ignored here. One is the question whether, if we could all communicate, M would still be self-defeating. Would it not tell us to promise to each other that, in return for the same promise, we will all do (2) rather than (1)? The answer is in theory 'Yes'. If we are all trustworthy, joining this conditional agreement would be the best way for each to promote his own M-given aims. In a two-person case, this solution could often be achieved. But in many-person cases, which are those with practical importance, this is not so. (We can now redefine my proposed revision. We should all ideally do what, if we could make this joint promise, we ought to promise to do. In this redefinition, R need not explicitly refer to those cases where M is self-defeating. Only here would M tell us that we ought to make this promise. And this redefinition makes R more plausible. We believe that, if we could, we ought to promise to each other that we will all do (2). Does this not suggest that, even when we cannot make this promise, this is what we should all ideally do?)

9

RIGHTS AND AGENCY

AMARTYA SEN

THIS paper is about three distinct but interrelated problems: (1) the role of rights in moral theory, (2) the characterization of agent-relative values and their admissibility in consequence-based evaluation, and (3) the nature of moral evaluation of states of affairs.

First, it is argued in Sections 1 to 3 that both welfarist consequentialism (such as utilitarianism) and constraint-based deontology are fundamentally inadequate because of their failure to deal with certain important types of interdependences present in moral problems. This leads to an alternative approach, called goal rights systems, which incorporates, among other things, some types of rights in the evaluation of states of affairs, and which gives these rights influence on the choice of actions through the evaluation of consequent states of affairs. The formulation of goal rights in the form of rights to certain 'capabilities' is explored and contrasted with other approaches in Section 4.

Goal rights systems require consequential analysis, though they may or may not be fully consequentialist. Recently, consequentialism has been sharply criticized by Williams, Nozick, Nagel, and others for, among other things, its failure to accommodate agent-relative values of the kind suggested by deontological reasons as well as reasons of autonomy and integrity. Different types of agent relativities (in particular, doer relativity, viewer relativity, and self-evaluation relativity) are distinguished in this paper, and their interrelations are analysed. Different kinds of agent-relative

Amartya Sen, 'Rights and Agency', *Philosophy and Public Affairs* 11, No. 1 (Winter 1982). Copyright © 1982 by Princeton University Press. Reprinted by permission of Princeton University Press and the author.

values are shown in Section 5 to involve different combinations of these agent relativity types.

Consequentialism is then shown in Section 6 to accommodate some agent-relative values, but not others. But even those agent relative values that are inconsistent with consequentialism are accommodated in consequence-based evaluation, admitting evaluator relativity in the evaluation of consequences themselves. Thus, goal rights, including capability rights, and other goals can be combined with deontological values (in the non-constraint form), along with other agent-relative considerations, in an integrated system.

The possibility of evaluator relativity in the evaluation of states of affairs raises a complex problem of second-order moral theory. Examining this problem using various interpretations of moral judgements of states, I present and explore the possibility of a 'positional interpretation' of such judgements in Section 7. In the last section I make some concluding remarks on positive and negative freedoms.

1. WELFARIST CONSEQUENTIALISM AND CONSTRAINT-BASED DEONTOLOGY

In the instrumental view rights are not valuable in themselves, but right-based rules, conventions, institutions, etc., are useful in pursuing other—right-independent—goals. The most commonly identified goals in the instrumental approach tend to be 'welfarist' goals,[1] with the goodness of states of affairs being judged entirely by the personal utility features of the respective states. One special case of welfarist evaluation is by far more common than others, and that is the case of utilitarian evaluation in which the goodness of a state of affairs is judged simply by the sum total of personal utilities in that state.[2] But other welfarist approaches exist, for example, judging states by the utility level of the worst-off

[1] For a discussion of the distinguishing features of welfarism, and a critique, see my 'Utilitarianism and Welfarism'.
[2] When the population is a variable, one has to make the further distinction between 'classical' and 'average' utilitarianism. In this paper I shall not go into that issue.

individual in that state, as under a variant of Rawls's 'Difference Principle',[3] or by some other method of distribution-sensitive aggregation of personal utilities.[4]

In contrast, in the constraint-based deontological view rights are treated as constraints on actions. These constraints must not be violated *even if* such violation would lead to better states of affairs. Violating rights is simply wrong. Unlike in the instrumental view, rights *are* given intrinsic importance, but unlike in 'goal rights systems', to be presented later in this paper, rights *directly* affect judgements of actions—and only of actions—rather than being embedded first in the evaluation of states of affairs and then affecting the evaluation of actions through consequential links between actions and states. As Robert Nozick puts it, 'Individuals have rights, and there are things no person or group may do to them (without violating their rights).'[5] Further, 'Rights do not determine a social ordering but instead set the constraints within which a social choice is to be made, by excluding certain alternatives, fixing others, and so on.'[6]

I shall now argue that both the welfarist instrumental approach (including, *inter alia*, the traditional utilitarian approach) and the deontological constraint-based approach are inadequate in important ways. Furthermore their respective inadequacies are related to a common ground shared by the two, despite sharp differences in other respects. The particular common ground is the *denial* that realization and failure of rights should enter into the evaluation of states of affairs themselves and could be used for consequential

---

[3] J. Rawls, *A Theory of Justice*. Rawls himself repudiates this *variant*, but it is nevertheless much used. See E. S. Phelps, ed., *Economic Justice* (Harmondsworth: Penguin Books, 1973); P. J. Hammond, 'Equity, Arrow's Conditions and Rawls's Difference Principle', *Econometrica* 42 (1976); and C. d'Aspremont and L. Gevers, 'Equity and Informational Basis of Collective Choice', *Review of Economic Studies* 46 (1977).

[4] See my *On Economic Inequality* (Oxford: Basil Blackwell, 1973). K. Roberts has provided an axiomatization of the class of distribution-sensitive, utility-based social welfare functionals, satisfying symmetry, homotheticity, and additive separability; see his 'Interpersonal Comparability and Social Choice Theory', *Review of Economic Studies* 47 (1980). See also C. Blackorby and D. Donaldson, 'Utility vs. Equity: Some Plausible Quasi-orderings', *Journal of Public Economics* 7 (1977).

[5] R. Nozick, *Anarchy, State, and Utopia*, p. ix.

[6] Nozick, *Anarchy, State, and Utopia*, p. 166.

analysis of actions. Nozick's view that 'rights do not determine a social ordering' is shared fully by welfarists in general and utilitarians in particular. Their ways part there, however, with the welfarist instrumentalist viewing rights in terms of their consequences for *right-independent* goals and the constraint-based deontologist reflecting rights *without consequential justification* as constraints on actions. State-evaluation independent of rights leaves a gap that cannot be adequately closed by either of these approaches.

Consider the constraint-based deontological approach first. It is of course obvious that this approach can hardly do justice to those rights associated with the so-called positive freedom.[7] But the problem is not confined to that, and is present even when the intrinsic value of positive freedom is disputed and the focus is chosen to be entirely on non-coercion and related issues of negative freedom. Even with negative freedom, *multilateral* interdependences can arise and undermine the rationale of the constraint-based deontological approach. The only way of stopping the violation of a very important liberty of one person by another may be for a third to violate some other, less important liberty of a fourth. To take a crude example, the only way of saving A from rape by B could be for C to arrive speedily at the spot in a car stolen from D, who is not a party to the rape but who does not want his car to be used for this purpose. The justification of C's action will require consequential analysis trading off the badness of violating D's right to the disposal of his own car against the badness of letting the rape occur. Since the constraint-based deontological view does not permit violation or realization of rights 'to determine the social ordering',[8] it is particularly

[7] For the classic statement of the distinction between 'positive' and 'negative' freedom, see I. Berlin, 'Two Concepts of Liberty', in his *Four Essays on Liberty* (Oxford: Clarendon Press, 1969).

[8] Nozick, p. 166. It is, however, possible to respond to problems of this kind by making the so-called 'constraints' non-constraining under particular circumstances, though there is obviously a danger here of resorting to *ad hoc* solutions. (For an illuminating critique of some possible reasons for overriding right-based constraints, see J. J. Thompson, 'Self-defense and Rights'.) For example, it can be specified that if the badness of the state of affairs resulting from obeying the constraint exceeds some 'threshold', then the constraint may be overridden. Such a threshold-based 'constraint' system must rest ultimately on consequential analysis, comparing one

inadequate in dealing with such cases of *multilateral* interdependences, which can be easily accommodated however in a system of consequential evaluation.

The instrumental welfarist approach is well armed with a consequential framework of moral evaluation. But since the evaluation of consequences is based ultimately on utility information only (non-utility information being valued just as a causal influence on—or as a surrogate for—utility information[9]), mental features (such as pleasures, happiness, desires, etc., depending on the particular interpretation of utility) rule the roost entirely. The losses of the victim and other sufferers are contrasted with the gains of the violators and other gainers entirely in terms of relative utility features. There might have been good utilitarian reasons for forcing men to fight wild animals in the Colosseum with the utility gain of the thousands of spectators outweighing the utility loss of the few forced men.

I shall return to these general issues later. In the next section, I illustrate the difficulties created by the two traditional approaches by taking up a particular example of a moral problem.

2. AN ILLUSTRATIVE MORAL PROBLEM

Ali is a successful shopkeeper, who has quickly built up a good business in London since immigrating from East Africa. He is, however, hated by a small group of local racists, and a particular gang of them—I shall call them bashers—are, it happens, planning to bash Ali that evening in some secluded spot to which Ali will go alone. Donna, a West Indian friend of Ali, has just come to know of the bashers' plan, and wants to warn Ali about it. But Ali has

set of consequences (badness resulting from obeying the constraint) with another (badness of violating the constraint itself, given by the threshold), and its distinguishing feature will be the particular *form* of the consequence-evaluation function. Compromises of this kind raise other problems, which I do not pursue here, but I should emphasize that I do not include such consequential analysis in the category of 'constraint-based deontological approach', against which my criticism here is directed.

[9] See my 'On Weights and Measures: Informational Constraints in Social Welfare Analysis', *Econometrica* 43 (1977), and 'Personal Utilities and Public Judgments: Or What's Wrong with Welfare Economics?' *Economic Journal* 89 (1979).

gone away for the day, and will go to that secluded spot without returning home. Donna does not know where Ali has gone nor the location of the planned bashing, but she does know that Ali has left a message on the desk of his business contact Charles about his movement. However, Charles is away for the day also, and cannot be contacted. Hence the only way of getting Ali's message is by breaking into Charles's room. Donna asked for the help of the police, who dismissed Donna's story as a piece of paranoiac fantasy. Donna knows that she can certainly frustrate the planned bashing by breaking into Charles's room, recovering the message, and warning Ali during the day. But she cannot do this without violating the privacy of Charles, who is, Donna also knows, a secretive man who will feel rather embarrassed at the thought of someone looking through his personal papers to find the message. Indeed, Donna also knows Charles, a self-centred egoist, well enough to be sure that he will be more disturbed by the violation of his own privacy than by the bashing of Ali. What should Donna do?

The long-term utilities of Ali and the ten people in the gang of bashers are given in Table 1.

TABLE 1. *Long-term utilities*

State of Affairs	Ali's Utility	Each Basher's Utility (10 Bashers)	Utility Sum Total	Minimum Utility	Inequality of Utilities
No bashing	15	5	65	5	more
Bashing	10	6	70	6	less

Notice that Ali will suffer a good deal more than any of the bashers will gain in utility terms, but the aggregate utility gain of the bashers exceeds the utility loss of Ali. In terms of these utilities, however, Ali remains better off than the gang of poor, unemployed bashers, even though his suffering is large enough to make a substantial impact on his long-term utility total.[10]

[10] Cardinal interpersonal comparability of utility is assumed in the table. None of the arguments will change if the numbers are all altered by applying some positive linear (affine) transformation, for example, multiplying each number by

Donna considers the utility information in viewing the problem first from the welfarist angle. In terms of the utilitarian objective, it is clear that the bashing up is doing more good than harm. There could be indirect effects, of course, but Donna finds that they won't be very serious in this case. There is so much fear of racial violence in that locality anyway, that one incident will not *add* significantly to the general sense of insecurity. Also, whether or not the bashing is prevented by warning Ali, the bashers will continue to go about their business as usual, and there will certainly not be any better chance of making the police take some action if Ali is *not* actually bashed up. Thus, there is nothing in these considerations to weaken the utility argument for the incident. Of course, there is Charles's utility also, but that will strengthen the case for no action by Donna, since breaking into his room to stop the bashing will reduce his utility.

Donna turns next to the welfarist version of Rawlsian difference principle. She finds that the utility level of the worst-off individuals will go up rather than down as a consequence of the bashing up. So this 'maximin' view also favours doing nothing to stop the bashing up. Indeed, so will every welfarist criterion that responds positively to a *larger utility total, more equally distributed*. So Donna moves to indirect utilitarian (and more generally, indirect welfarist) reasoning. She can well believe that among the class of 'uniform' rules dealing with bashing up, the rule of not treating anyone thus, in any situation whatever, may receive much support from the point of view of utilitarian evaluation of outcomes. But clearly from the same point of view that is, at most, a second best if choices are not necessarily confined to such uniform rules. Better still will be compliance with the no-bashing rule *except* in cases like this, in view of the net utility gain from this particular incident. Why should utilitarianism settle for such a second best by arbitrarily restricting choices to the class of rigid rules only?[11] Will

10, or adding 100 to each. On the framework for measurability and comparability assumptions, see my *Collective Choice and Social Welfare* (San Francisco: Holden-Day, 1970; distribution taken over by North Holland, Amsterdam); and L. Gevers, 'On Interpersonal Comparability and Social Welfare Orderings', *Econometrica* 45 (1979). Also K. Basu, *Revealed Preference of Governments* (Cambridge: Cambridge University Press, 1979).

[11] Cf. D. Lyons, 'Utility and Rights', *Nomos* 24 (1982).

it not be better from the utilitarian point of view to have a more flexible rule that permits bashing up in cases of the type described, thereby avoiding unnecessary sacrifice of utility? The justification of any policy—be it a rule, or an act, or something else—must rest ultimately on the ability to produce the best outcomes, judged by 'outcomes utilitarianism'.[12]

However, it is possible that following such flexible rules is not feasible, and this is quite possibly a case when we should deal with 'disposition' as a variable. Henry Sidgwick[13] had seen in this an argument for going against act-utilitarian reasoning, and recently this aspect of the problem has been thoroughly investigated from different perspectives in the works of Richard Hare, Robert Adams, John Harsanyi, and others.[14] Even if a particular act of bashing, or raping, or torturing improves the utility picture, given other things, this does not imply a utilitarian endorsement of that act if that act must go with a certain disposition that will typically cause harm.[15] The eschewal of that act will then be a necessary part of the suppression of that bad disposition.

Donna ponders over this indirect utilitarian reasoning, and becomes convinced that if she were to advise *the bashers* on what to do, from the utilitarian point of view, she would indeed argue for the removal of the disposition to bash up innocent people (including Ali). But Donna also recognizes that advising the bashers on what to do is not the exercise in which she is currently engaged, and her actions, whatever they are, are most unlikely to have any significant effect on the disposition of the bashers. Her moral problem concerns the issue of whether to break into Charles's room to collect the information that will permit her to warn Ali. There is no direct utilitarian case for her to break in, and it is not clear how bringing in the choice of dispositions is going to

---

[12] Cf. my 'Utilitarianism and Welfarism', pp. 464–7.

[13] H. Sigwick, *The Methods of Ethics*.

[14] See especially R. M. Hare, 'Ethical Theory and Utilitarianism', in *Contemporary British Philosophy*, ed. H. D. Lewis (London: Allen & Unwin, 1976); R. M. Adams, 'Motive Utilitarianism'; J. Harsanyi, 'Rule Utilitarianism and Decision Theory', in *Decision Theory and Social Ethics*, ed. H. W. Gottinger and W. Leinfellner (Dordrecht: Reidel, 1978).

[15] For a discussion of some of the difficulties with this general approach, see the 'Introduction' to *Utilitarianism and Beyond*, ed. A. Sen and B. Williams.

provide an argument for her to break in. Of course, if a disposition 'to break into other people's rooms' were found to be a good disposition to cultivate, this would give her, in terms of disposition utilitarianism, a reason to break in. But she can hardly believe that it is likely that such a general disposition to break in, or even a disposition to break in for a perceived excellent cause, will be a good one to cultivate in terms of utilitarian evaluation of consequences. Clearly, what is needed in this particular case and in cases like this is a *discriminating* defence of breaking in that balances pros and cons, rather than a general disposition to break down the door. And in this case such a calculating defence of the act of breaking in is yet to be found within the utilitarian (and more generally, welfarist) approach.

Of course, a strong argument for breaking into Charles's room could have emerged if the violation of Ali's bodily integrity were given a force strong enough for it not to be outweighed by the countervailing utility advantage of the bashers. But the utilitarian and other welfarist methods of outcome evaluation do not permit this, as they insist on judging the strength of claims exclusively in terms of utility information only.

Despite this failure of welfarism (including utilitarianism) to give Donna a good ground for doing what her moral conviction tells her she should do, to wit, break into Charles's room and save Ali, she decides that she must stick by her conviction. How can a person's bodily integrity, his freedom to move about without harm, be outweighed by mere pleasure or desire-fulfilment of the bashers? By not stopping the bashers, she would rob Ali of one of his most elementary rights. With this thought in mind, Donna decides to turn now to constraint-based deontological approaches. And yes, she sees that there is indeed an inflexible 'side constraint', in Nozick's terms, which is morally imposed on the bashers not to bash up Ali. However, this constraint does not affect Donna directly since she is not one of the bashers! There is nothing in that constraint-based deontological perspective that would require Donna to do anything at all.

The more Donna thinks about it, however, the more she feels convinced that she must really break into Charles's room and save Ali from bodily injury. Maybe she is not *required* to do anything, but surely she is *free* to? But, no, she isn't free to break into Charles's room since that deontological perspective also imposes a side constraint against the violation of *Charles's* rights. Since right violations and realizations do not enter the evaluation of states of affairs ('do not', as Nozick puts it, 'determine a social ordering') and the violation of Ali's more important right cannot be used for consequential justification of infringing Charles's less important right, Donna's hands are tied. Indeed, Nozick repudiates such trade-offs (what he calls 'utilitarianism of rights'[16]), and the constraint-based deontological approach, free from consequential analysis, offers nothing else.

To summarize the position, at the risk of some over-simplification, Donna can have a good case for breaking into Charles's room to save Ali if she can use a consequential analysis with non-welfarist evaluation of consequences. Constraint-based deontology does not permit the former (namely, consequential analysis), while welfarist instrumentalism does not permit the latter (namely, non-welfarist evaluation of consequences). It appears that to make room for her deeply held and resilient conviction that she must save Ali by breaking into Charles's room, Donna must reject both these traditional approaches and look for a new approach that is at once consequentialist and non-welfarist.

3. GENERAL PROBLEMS AND SPECIAL EXAMPLES

The example illustrating the moral issues in the last section might be considered to be rather a special one, and so indeed it is. Does this undermine the whole line of my criticism of the two traditional approaches? I shall argue that it does not.

First, while the chosen example illustrates the problem, the nature of it could be anticipated on the basis of the general arguments presented in Section 1. The failure to introduce fulfilment and non-realization of rights in the evaluation of states of affairs produces a lacuna that can scarcely be made good either by inflexible deontological constraints used without consequential

---

[16] Nozick, *Anarchy, State, and Utopia*, pp. 28–9. [Reprinted in this volume, pp. 136–7—Ed.] On this question see H. Hart, 'Between Utility and Rights', 828–46.

evaluation or by trying to catch the importance of rights in terms of the metric of utilities.[17] It is not so much that we stumbled on some peculiar intuition that we did not expect and then proceeded to argue against the two traditional approaches; the example merely served the purpose of *illustrating* a difficulty diagnosed in general terms.

The idea of incorporating realization of rights in the evaluation of states of affairs themselves might also appear to be an *ad hoc* device to take care of problems of the kind illustrated by the chosen example. Further, it may be asked whether statements about states of affairs in terms of rights realization really make sense.

In fact, as it happens, statements about states of affairs involving such incorporation are perfectly natural in other contexts as well. Consider the remark that the period of Emergency Rule in India was a bad one because so many rights of so many people were violated. This *is* a statement about a state of affairs, and it does include the violation of rights directly in the evaluation of the state. Statements like this can be used in a consequential analysis of actions, and this will translate the importance of fulfilment and violation of rights from the evaluation of states of affairs to that of actions.

Second, I don't think the example is in any sense peculiar, but even if it were, this would not imply that the intuition from it should be dismissed. Indeed, in many of the common cases, intuitions based on quite different principles tend to run in the same direction, so that it is impossible to be sure of the basis of an overall judgement. The problem is comparable to that in statistical inference when different explanatory variables corresponding to alternative models move together (and are 'multicollinear'),

---

[17] However, it is possible to go some distance in filling this lacuna by the approach of discounting, ignoring, or even disvaluing 'bad' pleasures or desires, for example, those related to sadism (see Harsanyi, 'Rule Utilitarianism and Decision Theory', p. 8). Although I shall not examine this alternative approach here, I believe it to be inadequate fundamentally; for example, the contrast between sadomasochistic fantasies (involving private reading) and cruel actions (involving right violations) may involve similar types of pleasures, but require quite different moral perspectives. Further, violation of rights need not necessarily involve 'bad' pleasures or desires.

making discrimination impossible. In order to do the discrimination, we choose examples such that different principles (for example, utilitarianism and the approach of incorporating rights in the evaluation of states of affairs) push us in different directions, even if such examples are somewhat less common than the ones in which either approach will recommend the same answer. It is methodologically wrong, therefore, to ignore the relevance of our intuitions regarding rather unusual examples which are brought for this reason into moral arguments. Hare's dismissal of what he sees as the 'commonest trick'[18] and even Rawls's decision to postpone discussing 'hard cases'[19] are on reflection rather less justified than they might first appear.

Third, although the example involving Ali, bashers, Charles, and Donna is a rather elaborate one, it had to be finely tuned to be usable *simultaneously* against welfarist instrumentalism and constraint-based deontology. It is, in fact, much easier to find different examples in which each of the two traditional approaches fails respectively to account for our deeply held moral convictions.

All this does not, of course, dispute the need to test one's intuition by seeking what John Rawls has called a reflective equilibrium.[20] Nor to dispute the importance of assessing moral beliefs at the 'critical' level, seeking principles that 'would be arrived at by leisured moral thought in completely adequate knowledge of facts'.[21] But there is nothing particularly illegitimate in illustrating difficulties with specific moral approaches by referring to resilient moral intuitions dealing with comparatively unusual cases, when these cases provide scope for discrimination the more 'usual' cases lack.[22]

---

[18] See Hare, 'Ethical Theory and Utilitarianism', p. 123. See also K. Ng, 'Welfarism: A Defence against Sen's Attack', *Economic Journal* 91 (1981).

[19] See J. Rawls, 'A Kantian Concept of Equality,' *Cambridge Review* (Feb. 1975), p. 96.

[20] Rawls, *A Theory of Justice*, p. 20. Nor to subjecting them to what B. Ackerman calls 'dialogic test' (*Social Justice in the Liberal State* (New Haven: Yale University Press, 1980), p. 353).

[21] Hare, 'Ethical Theory and Utilitarianism', p. 123.

[22] See also my 'Utilitarianism and Welfarism', pp. 475–9, and 'Equality of What?' in *The Tanner Lectures on Human Values*, I, ed. S. McMurrin (Cambridge: Cambridge University Press, 1980).

4. GOAL RIGHTS SYSTEMS AND CAPABILITIES

A moral system in which fulfilment and non-realization of rights are included among the goals, incorporated in the evaluation of states of affairs, and then applied to the choice of actions through consequential links will be called a goal rights system. A few preliminary warnings may be called for to avoid misunderstanding.

First, the goal rights systems form a wide *class* rather than represent some unique moral position. There are many sources of difference, for example, what rights to include among the goals, in what form they are to be included, what non-right values (if any) are to be admitted, what weights to use, how should choice of actions be related to the evaluation of outcomes.

Second, although rights are included within the evaluation of states of affairs, there could be other things to which the evaluation of states of affairs is sensitive in a goal rights system. The crucial issue is the inclusion of fulfilment and non-fulfilment of rights—rather than the exclusion of non-right considerations—in the evaluation of states of affairs.

Third, while *sensitivity* of action-evaluation to consequences is essential for a rights-consequence system, such a system need not be fully consequentialist. This question is further pursued in Section 6.

Fourth, it may be worth emphasizing that, although a goal rights system incorporates a goal-included view of rights, it does not reject the instrumental relevance of rights either.[23] Indeed, the violation of a right, say, freedom of speech, might be seen as making the outcome worse *both* because of the violation of that right itself and because of the negative effect it has on other objectives, including quite possibly other right-based goals, for example, making it more difficult for the economically deprived to make claims on the state for corrective action.[24] Furthermore, even in a goal rights system there can be rights that are justified

---

[23] See T. Scanlon, 'Rights, Goals, and Fairness' [reprinted as Chapter 4 above], on the essentiality of the instrumental role of rights. See also P. Dasgupta, 'Decentralization and Rights', *Economica* 47 (1980).

[24] The suppression of the freedom of speech in India during the Emergency Rule was widely criticized—in my judgement correctly—on *both* types of grounds.

entirely in instrumental terms, for example the ticket checker's right to see your ticket during a train journey. The important point is that a goal rights system permits the inclusion of right-based considerations in the goals themselves (and thus permits its direct use in the evaluation of outcomes and consequences), but it does not deny the use of instrumental considerations as well.

I turn now to the question of how to incorporate goal rights in the evaluation of states of affairs. It is not unusual to think of rights as a relation between two parties i and j, for example, person i having the claim on j that he will do some particular thing for i.[25] There is, however, some advantage in characterizing goal rights as a relation not primarily between two parties but between one person and some 'capability' to which he has a right, for example, the capability of person i to move about without harm.[26] This rather blurs the distinction between rights that relate to so-called positive freedoms and those related to negative freedoms such as liberty and non-coercion. If all goal rights take the form of rights to certain capabilities, then a goal rights system may be conveniently called a capability rights system.

The capability perspective has some distinctive advantages. An important advantage over the two-person (or two-agent) relationship can be illustrated even in terms of the type of problem encountered in the earlier example involving Donna's dilemma. Consider two different variations of that case. Denoting the original case as case A, consider variant B, in which the so-called bashers are not in fact planning to bash up Ali, but to injure him by planting a small explosive device on the spot where Ali is going to be that evening. After planting that bomb, the so-called bashers

---

[25] See, for example, W. N. Hohfeld, *Fundamental Legal Conceptions* (New Haven: Yale University Press, 1923); S. Kanger 'New Foundations for Ethical Theory' in *Deontic Logic: Introductory and Systematic Readings*, ed. R. Hilpinen (Dordrecht: Reidel, 1971); and the helpful critical account given by L. Lindahl, *Position and Change* (Dordrecht: Reidel, 1977). See also J. Raz, *The Concept of a Legal System* (Oxford: Clarendon Press, 1970; 2nd ed., 1980).

[26] Cf. my 'Equality of What?' pp. 215–20. The focus on capabilities also differs fundamentally from that on utilities in being concerned with (i) achievements rather than their mental assessments, and (ii) the opportunity sets and not only the chosen position. See also J. Mackie, 'Can There Be a Right-Based Moral Theory', *Midwest Studies in Philosophy* 3 (1978), and J. Bennett, 'Goods, Needs, and Social Theory', mimeographed (Cornell University, 1978).

have actually disappeared—in fact emigrated from 'rotting' England—and they will never really find out what happened; it is agreed that the bashers' utilities are independent of the success of the plot.[27] Donna can, as before, save Ali by warning him about this danger, but given the garbled message she has received (without any locations specified), she can only do this by breaking into Charles's room and finding that note from Ali about his own movements. The consequences on Ali and Charles are the same as in the original version of the problem.

In variant C, there are no bashers. But there is, in fact, an explosive device surviving from the last war at the spot where Ali is planning to be that evening. Donna has come to know of this without being able to decipher from the message where that spot is. Again, Donna can save Ali in exactly the same way as before, that is, by breaking into Charles's room and finding out about Ali's current whereabouts and warning him. The utility consequences on Ali and Charles are just as in variants A and B.

Now the question. If it is all right for Donna to break into Charles's room in variant B, is it all right for her to break into Charles's room in variant C? If we look at the violation of the right of Ali *vis-à-vis* the bashers, the two cases are quite different. In variant B, Ali's right of 'immunity' against the bashers is violated by them, whereas in variant C no such violation is involved. If, however, one takes the view—as seems plausible—that the bad outcomes Donna may be trying to prevent are equally bad in the two cases, then that view seems to undermine the consequential relevance of the particular perspective of *right violation by someone else*. It is the harm to Ali that one is concerned with in the two variants, and that harm is the same. If the important issue is Ali's safety, his 'general right' to the capability of moving about without harm, then variants B and C must be taken to be exactly comparable.

It might, however, appear that in asserting this close moral similarity of Donna's decision problems in variants B and C we

---

[27] This need not be so in some variant of the desire fulfilment version of utility without an 'awareness requirement', on which see J. Glover, *Causing Death and Saving Lives*, p. 63. See also J. Griffin, 'The Concept of Utility', mimeographed (Keble College, Oxford, n.d.).

have over-proved our case. While, on the one hand, that argument does push us in at least one respect further from the deontological constraint-based perspective (the formulation of rights is not only not in terms of constraints, it may not even be related to *violation* by other persons), but, on the other hand, it might seem to push us closer to the utilitarian (or, more generally, welfarist conse-quentialist) position. In terms of utility consequences, variants B and C are not distinguishable, and by treating them as involving closely similar moral problems for Donna, we might appear to be back in the welfarist ballpark. Indeed, in the particular contrast between variants B and C there is not a lot to choose between the capability framework and the welfarist framework. However, contrasting variants B and C is not the only thing of interest. In dealing with case A, welfarism seemed particularly inadequate, and that inadequacy remains despite the congruence of the general rights position and the welfarist positions in contrasting B and C.

In fact, the issues can be brought out more sharply by considering, in addition, a further contrast. Corresponding to case A, we now have a case D in which the utility picture is just as in case A, but the non-utility features involving rights are quite different. In particular, the so-called bashers aren't bashers really; in fact they work in Ali's shop. (Ali calls them bashers since he is liable to complain that they handle the merchandise clumsily.) The bashers suspect that they have been given a more dismal picture about the firm's financial position than is justified by the accounts, and they want to examine the accounts without Ali's permission in Ali's absence. Donna has come to know of this, and is considering warning Ali about this likely occurrence, which will have, Donna knows, bad consequences for Ali's business plans. But she can warn Ali only by breaking into Charles's room, and the utilities are all as in case A (with 'bashing up' being replaced by 'examining Ali's business accounts without permission'). If it is all right for Donna to break into Charles's room to warn Ali in case A, is it all right for her to do the same in case D? Since *all* the utility consequences are taken to be exactly the same, all welfarist moralities (including the utilitarian one) must treat cases A and D in exactly similar ways. On the other hand, the general right not to be bashed up is hardly matched in terms of seriousness by the right of not having one's financial accounts examined and one's business affected, even when the utility consequences are just the same. The ability to retain bodily safety is quite a different type of right from the ability to keep one's financial accounts private. Donna could very well decide to break into Charles's room in case *A* but not in case *D* if she is to be guided by some capability rights systems of the type being explored in this paper.

The constraint-based deontological view will, of course, treat cases *A* and *D* as similar, since *Charles's* right must not be violated in either case. On the other hand, a consequentialist system with goal rights being specified in the traditional two-party form may well discriminate between *A* and *D* since the 'immunity' right of Ali against the bashers may be given much greater weight in case *A* (when bodily injury is involved) than in case *D* (when only privacy of accounts is at issue).

The contrasting positions of the four approaches are shown in Table 2. To simplify matters, the two-person goal rights systems and capability rights systems are considered in their 'exclusive' form, with no goals other than fulfilment of the respective rights and with full consequentialism.

TABLE 2. *Moral correspondences*

Can Donna Justifiably Intervene?	Direct Utilitarian Systems	Constraint based De-ontological Systems	Pure Two-person Goal Rights Systems	Pure Capability Rights Systems
Case *A*	No	No	Yes	Yes
Case *B*	Yes	No	Yes	Yes
Case *C*	Yes	No	No	Yes
Case *D*	No	No	Depends on specification	Depends on specification
Same answer in cases *A* and *D*?	Yes	Yes	No	No
Same answer in cases *B* and *C*?	Yes	Yes	No	Yes

5. AGENT RELATIVITY

I turn now to the issue that Derek Parfit[28] and Thomas Nagel[29] have called agent relativity of values. 'Agent-relative values' are 'specified by reference to the agent for whom they provide reasons'.[30] The question of agent relativity is an important one in moral philosophy,[31] and it is of obvious relevance to the contrast between characterizing rights and duties in terms of deontological constraints and doing that through a consequential system. Indeed, Nagel has argued that 'certain ethical positions, those sometimes called consequentialist, admit only agent-neutral values'.[32]

I would like to examine how agent relativity might fit into a goal rights system, but before getting on to that question, two preliminary issues have to be sorted out. First, what *is* agent relativity? In this section I shall argue that agent relativity can be of very different types, which—for many purposes—require a discriminating analysis rather than being lumped together to be dealt with similarly. Second, what are the restrictions on admitting agent-relative values that are imposed by consequence-based evaluation in general and consequentialism in particular? That question is taken up in Section 6.

An agent *does* things and also *views* actions and outcomes. Agent neutrality can be characterized in terms of the switching of the 'doer' role or of the 'viewer' role or of both together. The corresponding invariance requirements are quite different though, obviously, not independent. These yield three different conditions of neutrality.

---

[28] D. Parfit, 'Prudence, Morality, and the Prisoner's Dilemma'.

[29] T. Nagel, 'The Limits of Objectivity'.

[30] Nagel, 'The Limits of Objectivity', p. 119; also pp. 101–4, and 120–1.

[31] See also B. Williams, 'A Critique of Utilitarianism', in *Utilitarianism: For and Against*, ed. J. J. C. Smart and B. Williams [reprinted in part as Chapter 2 in this collection—Ed.] and his 'Persons, Character and Morality', in *The Identities of Persons*, ed. A. Rorty (Berkeley: University of California Press, 1976); J. Glover, *Causing Death and Saving Lives*; J. Mackie, *Ethics: Inventing Right and Wrong* (Harmondsworth: Penguin Books, 1977); S. Hampshire, ed., *Public and Private Morality* (Cambridge: Cambridge University Press, 1978); C. Fried, *Right and Wrong*; N. Davis, 'Utilitarianism and Responsibility'.

[32] Nagel, 'The Limits of Objectivity', p. 119.

The analysis presented here concentrates on a very simple case, which is not only easy to investigate but is also adequate for bringing out the distinctions and for categorizing the agent relative values examined by Nagel, Parfit, Williams, and others. There are two persons sharing the same, possibly agent-relative, morality. and at most one of them can do some act. But it can be either. *provided* he is not stopped by the other. The consequences—other than the identity of the agent doing the act—depend only on whether or not the action is performed, and not on who does the act or whether either has been stopped by the other.[33]

> *Doer neutrality (DN)*: person i may do this act if and only if person i may permit person j to do this act.
> *Viewer neutrality (VN)*: person i may do this act if and only if person j may permit person i to do this act.
> *Self-evaluation neutrality (SN)*: person i may do this act if and only if person j may do this act.

Denoting $A_i(i)$ as the assertion that person i may do the act himself, and denoting $A_i(j)$ as the assertion that person i may permit j to do the act, we get the following entailment relations, with the appropriate universal quantifiers (for all i and j, for all acts and the corresponding consequences with the characteristics specified).

> *Doer neutrality* $A_i(i) \Leftrightarrow A_i(j)$.
> *Viewer neutrality* $A_i(i) \Leftrightarrow A_j(i)$.
> *Self-evaluation neutrality* $A_i(i) \Leftrightarrow A_j(j)$.

How do these neutralities relate to each other? Two results are straightforward.

> DN, VN, and SN are bilaterally independent of each other (that is, none of them alone entails any of the others);   (1)
> any two of DN, VN, and SN together entail the third.[34]   (2)

Doer relativity (DR), viewer relativity (VR), and self-evaluation relativity (SR) are defined as negations of DN, VN, and SN

---

[33] These are exacting requirements, but tend to be typically implicit in discussions on agent relativity.

[34] To check (2), the following will do. From SN and DN: $A_i(i) \Leftrightarrow A_j(j) \Leftrightarrow A_j(i)$; thus VN. From SN and VN: $A_i(i) \Leftrightarrow A_j(j) \Leftrightarrow A_i(j)$; thus DN. Finally, from DN and VN: $A_i(i) \Leftrightarrow A_i(j) \Leftrightarrow A_j(j)$; thus SN.

respectively. Taking '*may permit*' as '*has no obligation to prevent*', these conditions can be stated thus:

> *Doer relativity (DR)*: it is not the case that *i* may do this act if and only if he has no obligation to prevent *j* from doing this act.
>
> *Viewer relativity (VR)*: it is not the case that *i* may do this act if and only if *j* has no obligation to prevent *i* from doing this act.
>
> *Self-evaluation relativity (SR)*: it is not the case that *i* may do this act if and only if *j* may do this act.

In view of (1) and (2) above:

two of *DR*, *VR*, and *SR can* hold with or without
the third;   (1*)
exactly *one* of *DR*, *VR*, and *SR cannot* hold.   (2*)

Hence, if any one type of relativity is satisfied, at least one other type of relativity will also obtain.

I turn now to the agent-relative values discussed in the literature. Thomas Nagel identifies 'two broad types of reasons that appear to be agent-relative in form':

The first type of reason stems from the desires, projects, commitments, and personal ties of the individual agent, all of which give him reasons to act in the pursuit of ends that are his own. These I shall collect under the general heading of reasons of *autonomy*.

The second type of reason stems from the claims of other persons not to be maltreated in certain ways. What I have in mind are not agent-neutral reasons for everyone to want it to be *the case* that no one is maltreated, but agent-relative reasons for each individual not to *maltreat others himself*, in his dealings with them (e.g., by violating their rights, breaking his promises to them, etc.). These I shall collect under the general, ugly, and familiar heading of deontology.[35]

I start with deontology. The agent relativity of this value is brought out nicely by Nagel's example, the analysis of which from the deontological point of view leads to the following conclusion:

. . . it seems that you shouldn't twist the arm of a small child to get its grandmother to do something, even if the thing is quite important—

---

[35] Nagel, 'The Limits of Objectivity', pp. 119–20.

important enough so that it would not be reasonable to forego a comparable benefit in order to prevent someone else from twisting a child's arm.[36]

Notice that this involves only one *viewer* (namely, *you*) and two *doers* (namely, *you* and *someone else*). Thus directly this invokes *doer relativity* (*DR*). For reasons of consistency—see (2*)—it must also lead to at least one other type of relativity. The reasoning makes it clear that the obvious candidate for this is *viewer relativity* (*VR*). Although that 'someone else'—if he or she shared that deontological morality—could not think it OK to twist a child's arm (despite the stated benefits), he or she need not accept the obligation to stop another person (say, *you*) from doing the arm twisting (with similar other consequences).

Self-evaluation relativity is *not*, however, a part of this 'deontological view', and *SN* can indeed hold. It is *not* OK for you to do the twisting of the child's arm, and it is also *not* OK for someone else to do that.

Although the deontological argument is presented by Nagel in the form of requiring a *constraint* (to wit: '*shouldn't* twist the arm of a small child'), this is, of course, much stronger than negating doer neutrality, and his arguments really amount to a defence of doer relativity (negating *DN*) rather than a justification for doing this through the extremism of a constraint.[37] I have already argued against a constraint-based deontological morality in Sections 1 to 3, but that was not an argument against doer relativity. In fact, deontological morality in the weak form of denying doer neutrality— and correspondingly viewer neutrality—can be accommodated *within* a goal rights system. The point will be further pursued in Sections 6 and 7.

I turn now to what Nagel calls autonomy. This is a very broad category and includes rather different types of agent-relative

---

[36] Nagel, 'The Limits of Objectivity', p. 127.

[37] Similarly, B. Williams's analysis of the deontological issue in the form of Jim's dilemma ('A Critique of Utilitarianism', pp. 98–118) [pp. 34–50 in this volume—Ed.] does not lead to treating deontological grounds as sufficient for imposing a constraint that *must be* met, but to treating them as important in moral calculation. Indeed, Williams comes to the conclusion, after balancing the pros and cons in Jim's decision problem, that overriding the deontological consideration is 'probably right in this case' (p. 117) [p. 50 in this volume—Ed.].

AMARTYA SEN

arguments, based on 'desires, projects, commitments and personal ties'. One type of argument relates to Bernard Williams's analysis of 'integrity' applies to cases like the following:

> George, who has taken his Ph.D. in chemistry, finds it extremely difficult to get a job . . . An older chemist, who knows about this situation, says that he can get George a decently paid job in a certain laboratory, which pursues research into chemical and biological warfare. George says that he cannot accept this, since he is opposed to chemical and biological warfare. The older man replies that he is not too keen on it himself, come to that, but after all George's refusal is not going to make the job or the laboratory go away; what is more, he happens to know that if George refuses the job, it will certainly go to a contemporary of George's who is not inhibited by any such scruples and is likely if appointed to push along the research with greater zeal than George would . . . What should he do?[38]

Williams argues that for George to be persuaded by the older chemist's argument 'is to neglect the extent to which *his* actions and *his* decisions have to be seen as the actions and decisions which flow from the projects and attitudes with which he is most closely identified', and it 'is thus, in the most literal sense, an attack on his integrity' (pp. 116–17).

I am not concerned here with assessing the force of this example, or of Williams's arguments.[39] My concern here is solely with the types of agent relativity that follow from Williams's arguments if they are accepted. This connection might look more immediate than it, in fact, is. It is, of course, true that although Williams's arguments will tend to support George's judgement that it will be wrong of him to take the job, they will not suggest a similar case—based on integrity—for his contemporary to refuse that employment. But this does not imply that self-evaluation relativity is involved in this example, since George and his contemporary do *not* share the same morality. Indeed, the

[38] Williams, 'A Critique of Utilitarianism', pp. 97–8 [pp. 33–4 in this volume—Ed.].

[39] An important issue is raised by J. Glover, 'It Makes No Difference Whether Or Not I Do It', *Proceedings of the Aristotelian Society*, Supplement (1975); on this see also B. Williams, 'Utilitarianism and Moral Self-indulgence', in *Contemporary British Philosophy*, ed. H. D. Lewis (London: Allen & Unwin, 1976).

consequences of George's taking the job can be seen to be quite different from those resulting from his contemporary's taking the job, if the violation of George's moral attitude is directly counted in, abandoning the rather limited system of consequence-accounting on which utilitarianism happens to rely. While this feature of the example can be modified by making George and his contemporary share the same morality, this will alter the nature of the example altogether, possibly affecting the moral judgements related to it.

On the other hand, there is nothing especially problematic about making the older chemist—call him Harry—share George's morality (he is not, we know, 'too keen' on chemical and biological warfare anyway). With this modification, and further altering the story in such a way that the other consequences of Harry taking the job are identical with those of George taking it, we can now ask:

(1) *Viewer relativity*: is it not the case that George may take the job if and only if Harry has no obligation to stop George from taking it?

(2) *Doer relativity*: is it not the case that Harry may take the job if and only if he has no obligation to stop George from taking it?

The answers to these questions will depend on how integrity is treated.

I shall distinguish between 'integrity respect', a general respect for integrity no matter whose, and 'integrity responsibility', a personal responsibility for one's own integrity. With general integrity respect featuring in the shared morality of George and Harry, there is no need to require viewer relativity or doer relativity. No matter who takes the job and who views it, the same unfavourable picture of involvement in chemical and biological warfare, by someone who believes such involvement to be wrong, comes through. On the other hand, with integrity responsibility viewer relativity *is* involved: George must not take the job even though Harry has no obligation to stop him. And so is doer relativity: Harry must not take the job even though he has no obligation to stop George from taking it ('It's *your* decision,

210 AMARTYA SEN

George').[40] Notice that in neither case is self-evaluation relativity involved, since George and Harry sharing the same morality and circumstances must evaluate their own respective acts of taking the job in the same way.

A somewhat similar interpretational dichotomy can be found in the other cases covered under the broad heading of 'autonomy'. Take the case of 'personal ties'.[41] It may be the case that parents should be specially concerned with their own children's welfare, and this will immediately entail self-evaluation relativity. It may be OK for me to do some act differentially benefiting my children over yours without it being OK for you to do this (benefiting my children over yours), given your responsibility to your own children. We know from the analytical result presented earlier (see (2*)) that self-evaluation relativity must go with *at least one* of doer relativity and viewer relativity, and indeed it can be either.

Consider the distinction between (1) people having different aims related to their own kith and kin, for example, parents aiming differentially to further benefits to their own children ('tie aims', for short), and (2) everyone having the same aims but valuing acts directly responsive to ties, for example, everyone valuing the acts of parents helping their respective children ('tie respect', for short). In the former case there can be viewer relativity: i may do something favouring his own children *vis-à-vis* j's children, but j—sharing the same tie-aimed morality—must try to stop i from doing this. This can go with doer *neutrality*, since it need not matter *how* the benefits to one's children are brought about, whether by one's own actions or by those of others.

In contrast, what is important in the case of tie respect is the

---

[40] The concern with one's own integrity does not imply that the person must take integrity as a virtue on its own rights. As B. Williams argues, integrity is not 'a disposition which itself yields motivations'; 'it is rather that one who displays integrity acts from those dispositions and motives which are most deeply his' ('Utilitarianism and Moral Self-indulgence', p. 316).

[41] See Parfit, 'Prudence, Morality, and the Prisoner's Dilemma'. Parfit links up the discussion with issues of 'co-ordination', on which see also H. Herzberger, 'Coordination Theory', in *Foundations and Applications of Decision Theory*, I, ed. C. Hooker, J. Leach, and E. McClennen (Dordrecht: Reidel, 1978); and D. Regan, *Utilitarianism and Co-operation*. The characteristic of being 'collectively self-defeating' is associated with viewer relativity without necessarily involving doer relativity.

belief that parents themselves should respond by taking actions benefiting their own children, and it is not so good if the same benefits were brought about by helpful actions of strangers. This implies doer relativity, and it can go with viewer neutrality, since in this case no one need specially value benefits going to one's own children. It can also involve self-evaluation relativity: Ed may do something helping his own children at the cost of Bill's children, while Bill may not do that thing helping Ed's children (not because Bill values benefits to Ed's children differently from the way Ed does, but both value the action of someone helping his own children *himself*).

It is, of course, possible to have a 'mixed' case, that of 'aimed tie respect', in which people have different aims favouring, say, their own children, but also value that the benefits to their own children are brought about by their own actions.[42] In this case *VR*, *DR*, and *SR* may all be involved. Ed may do something favouring his own children, while it could be the case that (1) Bill must try to stop Ed (viewer relativity), (2) Ed must try to stop Bill from doing the same thing helping Ed's children (doer relativity), and (3) Bill may refuse to do the same thing helping Ed's children (self-evaluation relativity).

This discussion has not, of course, begun to exhaust different types of agent relative reasons, but even with the few types

TABLE 3. *Moral reasons and agent-relativity types*

	Deontology	Tie Aims	Tie Respect	Aimed Tie Respect	Integrity Respect	Integrity Responsi- bility
Doer Relativity	Yes	No	Yes	Yes	No	Yes
Viewer Relativity	Yes	Yes	No	Yes	No	Yes
Self- evaluation Relativity	No	Yes	Yes	Yes	No	No

[42] Cf. Parfit, 'Prudence, Morality, and the Prisoner's Dilemma', p. 562.

considered here, quite a rich variety of contrasts have been found. Before moving in the next section to the question of how these different types of agent relativity relate to the discipline of consequence-based evaluation, I present a summary picture of the different agent relative reasons in terms of DR, VR, and SR (see Table 3).

<h6>6. CONSEQUENCE-BASED EVALUATION
AND CONSEQUENTIALISM</h6>

An outcome morality is a morality dealing with judging states of affairs. Consequentialism requires the hegemony of outcome morality over moral judgements concerning other variables as well, for example, actions. There are various strategic issues involved in the use of control variables to achieve the best consequences taking everything into account, and it is possible to show that no consequentialist strategy can be fully successful in getting the best possible outcomes if it concentrates only on a 'single influence', whether it be acts, rules, motives.[43] However, in this paper I shall abstract from these issues, and concentrate on act consequentialism only, in situations in which act-based calculations are adequate for serving overall *consequentialist* goals.

Whether consequentialism can accommodate agent-relative values will depend on the way outcome morality is characterized. In especially narrow formulations, consequences are defined *excluding* the actions that bring them about, and in this case agent relativity of the 'doer relative' kind would be impossible to accommodate. But this is an arbitrary exclusion, and it is not imposed in broader characterizations of consequentialism.[44]

[43] On the relationship between outcome morality and various types of consequentialism (depending on the 'control' variables), see my 'Utilitarianism and Welfarism', pp. 464–8. The internal difficulties of act consequentialism are brought out by the classic paper of A. Gibbard, 'Rule Utilitarianism: A Merely Illusory Alternative?' *Australasian Journal of Philosophy* 43 (1965). See also T. Schelling, *The Strategy of Conflict* (Cambridge, Mass.: Harvard University Press, 1960); Herzberger, 'Coordination Theory'; J. Harsanyi, 'Rule Utilitarianism and Decision Theory', *Erkenntnis* 11 (1977); Regan, *Utilitarianism and Co-operation*; and Parfit, 'Prudence, Morality, and the Prisoner's Dilemma'.

[44] See, for example, Williams, 'A Critique of Utilitarianism', pp. 86–8. [pp. 23–5 in this volume—Ed.]

Another important issue concerns the nature of the outcome evaluation function. Within a *given* moral approach, must every person have the same outcome evaluation function $G(x)$ irrespective of differences in their positions *vis-à-vis* actions, beneficiaries, and the like? That is indeed the standard assumption in the consequentialist literature, but it is worth enquiring whether that feature is essential or accidental, for example owing to the historical association of consequentialism with utilitarianism, which certainly does impose an evaluator-neutral perspective on outcome evaluation. There is, it seems to me, no compelling reason why a morality that is sensitive to the differences in the position of people *vis-à-vis* states (including actions that bring the states about) should not permit—indeed require—that different people evaluate the same state differently. A morality that insists that after killing his wife Desdemona Othello must regard that *state of affairs* to be morally exactly as good or as bad as others would—and no worse than that—would seem to miss something about the nature of moral evaluation of states.[45] I would, therefore, not rule out evaluator-relative forms of outcome morality, with $G_i(x)$ being the moral value of state x from the point of view of person i. This raises some serious interpretational problems, given the traditional wisdom on the nature of outcome morality,[46] which I shall consider in Section 7.

The term consequentialism is, however, strongly associated with a characterization of morality that would not permit evaluator relativity in the evaluation of outcomes, and must insist on $G_i(x) = G_j(x)$ for all i and j, for all x. When that restriction is relaxed but otherwise the hegemony of outcome morality is maintained, I shall call the approach 'consequence-based evaluation'. Consequentialism, then, is the special case of consequence-based evaluation in which the outcome morality is evaluator neutral. It requires not

[45] One aspect, among others, of the issue relates to what B. Williams describes as 'moral philosophy's habit . . . of treating person in abstraction from character' ('Persons, Character and Morality', in *The Identities of Persons*, ed. A. Rorty (Berkeley: University of California Press, 1976), p. 215).

[46] There are also problems of linguistic convention since 'morally good' is used in the form of a one-place predicate (for example, 'a morally good state'), not a two-place one (for example, 'a morally good state from the point of view of person i'). The case for two-place formulations is discussed in Section 7.

only that each person should judge his control variables (such as acts) ultimately in terms of their effects on the goodness of outcomes, but also that each person must judge the goodness of any given outcome in exactly the same way.

Consequentialism, thus characterized, cannot at all accommodate *viewer relativity* of action judgements, and thus cannot reflect 'deontology', 'tie aims', 'aimed tie respect', and 'integrity responsibility' (see Table 3). However, viewer relativity can be admitted within consequentialism by dropping the assumption stated earlier (and which is typically implicit in the treatment of consequentialism in the literature on agent-relative values) that 'the consequences—other than the identity of the agent doing the act—depend only on whether or not the action is performed, and not on . . . whether either has been stopped by the other'.[47] While this distinction is important in some cases and is worth introducing anyway, it provides a rather limited way of accommodating viewer relativity of action judgements (in the absence of evaluator relativity of outcome judgements).

However, 'tie respect' and 'integrity respect' do not at all require viewer relativity of action judgements. Are these types of moral reasons consistent with consequentialism? There is no difficulty in answering in the affirmative in the case of integrity respect, which—as we have already seen (in Table 3)—does not even involve any of the specified types of agent relativity. Although that is not the case with tie respect, which involves doer relativity and self-evaluation relativity, consistency with consequentialism does, in fact, hold.

Consider state x as involving some benefit to i's children and not to j's children, brought about by i's action, and state y as the same benefit's to i's children and not to j's children brought about by j's action. A tie-respecting evaluation function $G(.)$ will value these states differently, with $G(x) > G(y)$. A consequentialist morality

---

[47] As was noted earlier in footnote 33 these are 'exacting requirements'. There are often good reasons to distinguish between a state in which person i did not do act A because he did not *try* to, and a state in which person i did not do act A because he was *stopped* by person j. Even with evaluator-relative outcome judgements, which—as will be presently discussed—gives much scope for viewer relativity of action judgements, the distinction between 'not trying' and 'being stopped' will retain its relevance.

can, consistently with this, make it OK for i to take this action, but not for j (self-evaluation relativity). Further, it can make it not right for j to take that action but fine for him to let i take it (doer relativity). Thus, agent relativity associated with tie respect is consistent with consequentialism.

Consequentialism cannot, however, make much room for agent-relative action judgements associated with deontology, tie aims, aimed tie respect, and integrity responsibility. However, with evaluator-relative outcome evaluation function $G_i(.)$, consequence-based evaluation can cover agent relativity of these types. To understand how this would work, it may be useful to consider the outcome evaluation function $G_i(.)$ in the 'separable' form, related to the evaluation of the goodness of the actions a and the evaluation of the goodness of the 'rest of the state of affairs' b brought about by those actions: $G_i(x) = V(z_i(a), y_i (b))$, when $x = (a, b)$.[48]

When we are exclusively concerned with relativities based on *deontological* values, it is natural to think of $y_i(b)$ as evaluator-neutral, but the part dealing with action evaluation $z_i(a)$ has to be evaluator-relative, depending on whether or not the evaluator is himself the agent. This will lead to doer relativity and viewer relativity. Self-evaluation relativity will, however, be avoided since z_i will have the same value when the evaluator—no matter who—is *himself* the relevant agent.

With integrity *responsibility* of the kind illustrated by the case of George and Harry, in which the action and the agency are crucial, z_i will be clearly evaluator relative, but y_i can be, consistently with that illustration, evaluator neutral. This will lead to doer relativity and viewer relativity of action judgements in much the same way as in the case of deontological values.

[48] Separability is an exacting requirement and many functions do not have separable representations. For the issues involved in separability, see the helpful paper of W. M. Gorman, 'Tricks with Utility Functions', in *Essays in Economic Analysis*, ed. M. J. Artis and A. R. Nobay (Cambridge: Cambridge University Press, 1976). It is worth emphasizing that the ability of evaluator-relative, consequence-based evaluation to accommodate these different types of agent relativities does *not* depend on whether or not G_i is separable. Separability is assumed here for expositional purpose only to make the exercise transparent. Also note that an additional 'degree of freedom' can be introduced in the evaluator-relative form $G_i(x)$ by permitting an i-variant V function, that is $V_i(z_i(a), y_i(b))$.

In the pure case of *tie aims* illustrated by the situation in which the benefits to one's own children have to be specially valued but not the agency of the action that brings about these benefits, z_i will be evaluator neutral whereas y_i will be evaluator relative. Doer neutrality of action judgements will follow from the irrelevance of the agency of the relevant actions ('I *may do this* to help my children if and only if I *may permit you to do this* to help my children'), but viewer relativity and self-evaluation relativity will be produced by the evaluator-relative character of y_i. In the case of *aimed tie respect*, z_i and y_i are both evaluator relative, and all the three types of agent relativity can be induced by consequence-based evaluation.

7. EVALUATOR RELATIVITY AND THE POSITIONAL INTERPRETATION

The possibility of using consequence-based evaluation combined with an evaluator-relative outcome morality was entertained in the last section, distinguishing that package from consequentialism. But the notion of an evaluator-relative outcome morality may appear to be deeply problematic, and it certainly requires scrutiny.

Evaluator relativity of a given outcome morality must not be confused with interpersonal differences of moralities. Indeed insofar as a particular person k entertains an evaluator-relative morality, we can represent that morality in the form $G_i^k(x)$, reflecting the moral value that in the opinion of person k (parameter) should be appropriately attached to state x (variable) by person i (variable). This could, of course, include the moral value that k himself should attach to state x: $G_k^k(x)$.[49] Since I am not concerned currently with contrasting different outcome moralities but with interpreting any given one, the *super*script k is eschewed, and an outcome morality is represented in the two-variable form $G_i(x)$. This could stand for the moral beliefs of a

---

[49] Charles Taylor has pointed out to me the importance of clarifying that while $G_i^k(x)$ is called the 'outcome morality' of k, it is doing two quite distinct jobs: (i) the specification of k's *own* moral evaluation of states, and (ii) the specification of k's views of *appropriate correspondences* between different people's moral evaluations of states.

particular person k or a *possible* moral theory (to be compared with, say, the utilitarian outcome morality).

It is easy to entertain the suspicion that an evaluator-relative outcome morality must be an internally contradictory one: how can i and j morally value a given state x differently *within* one consistent moral theory? The inadmissability of evaluator relativity within one moral theory can be based on two propositions:

> interpersonal differences of moral valuations of the same states must indicate contradictory moral beliefs; (1)
> no moral theory should endorse the holding of contradictory moral beliefs. (2)

Evaluator relativity can be defended by denying either (1) or (2). or—of course—both.

Before disputing (1), which is my primary target, I should briefly comment on the possibility of justifying evaluator relativity via denying (2). There could be good *instrumental* reasons for a moral theory to require inconsistent moral beliefs. For example, in 'two-level' moral theories, which have been extensively explored by Hare,[50] instrumental use of an evaluator-relative morality (for example, parents valuing especially highly the benefits to their own children) can be justified quite possibly by results evaluated from the point of view of a higher-level, evaluator-neutral moral theory (in Hare's own case, utilitarianism). Another possibility arises from the higher-level morality valuing people's working moralities and valuational methods themselves. The higher-level moral values might judge favourably the evaluator relativity shown by people with warm concern, say, for their own families.[51] Thus an essentially evaluator-neutral higher-level moral theory could directly encourage evaluator-relativity in less reflective valuations.[52]

[50] See Hare, 'Ethical Theory and Utilitarianism'.

[51] I am grateful to Ronald Dworkin for helpful discussion of this possibility and for pointing out the relevance of valuational methods in judgements of 'character', which could figure prominently in the higher-level morality. Some related issues have been explored by B. Williams in 'Persons, Character and Morality' even though his own approach is rather different. It should be added that there are some interesting consistency problems in valuation-valuing evaluations, but I shall not pursue them here.

[52] See, however, the 'Introduction' to *Utilitarianism and Beyond*, ed. A. Sen and B. Williams, on some difficulties with two-level moral theories.

Neither of these two lines of reasoning need dispute that evaluator-relativity involves contradictory beliefs, that is, (1) need not be disputed. But contradictory beliefs are taken to be fruitful either—directly—because of 'valued valuations', or—indirectly—because of instrumental use, in each case disputing (2). I shall not pursue these possible lines here.

I turn now to (1). Much depends here on the *nature* of the exercise of morally evaluating states of affairs. One interpretation, which again, I shall not pursue here, but which potentially can accommodate evaluator relativity, is the 'preference' interpretation. John Harsanyi's concept of 'ethical preferences' defined over social states is an example of the preference interpretation of moral valuation.[53] Different preferences about the same states need not involve contradictory beliefs. Of course, it might well be taken to be appropriate to impose evaluator neutrality as a second-level moral condition. (Indeed, in the definition of 'ethical preferences' Harsanyi incorporates something that may push us in that direction, to wit: ethical preferences must 'express what he prefers in those possibly rare moments when he forces a special impartial and impersonal attitude upon himself'.) But once moral valuations are seen as preferences of some kind, the door to evaluator relativity is wide open, e.g., *you* must disprefer a state in which you *yourself* twist a child's arm (corresponding to Nagel's example of deontology).

One feature of the preference interpretation of moral valuation of states of affairs is that it is very close to judging *actions* themselves, since preferences can be interpreted in terms of hypothetical acts of choosing between alternative states. Contradictory beliefs on values of states are replaced, on this interpretation of moral evaluation, with disparate attitudes to action choice. I leave the preference interpretation here and pursue other interpretations.

If moral valuations of a state by different persons are seen as alternative statements about the same characteristic of the state, then clearly evaluator relativity must involve *contradictory* state-

---

[53] J. C. Harsanyi, 'Cardinal Welfare, Individualistic Ethics, and Interpersonal Comparisons of Utility', *Journal of Political Economy* 63 (1955). See also K. J. Arrow, *Social Choice and Individual Values* (New York: Wiley, 1951).

ments. But *are they* really about the same characteristic despite that appearance? I would like to explore the possibility that they are coherently interpretable as 'positional' statements, reflecting the view of the state from the position of the evaluator.

An analogy might be useful to bring out the distinction. Contrast the two following statements:

'Mount Everest is beautiful.' (*a*)

'From here, Mount Everest is beautiful.' (*b*)

Although an assertion and a denial of (*a*) by two persons respectively—taken literally—must be seen as contradicting each other, this is not necessarily the case with (*b*), since the two persons may be occupying different positions. If moral judgements about states of affairs are like aesthetic judgements of type (*b*), evaluator relativity of outcome morality need not imply holding contradictory views.

I would like to emphasize that the distinction between (*a*) and (*b*) does not correspond to the objective–subjective dichotomy. On the objective interpretation of values, anyone standing at the same position (say, fifty miles due north of Mount Everest, or—in the moral case—being opposed to chemical and biological warfare) may well be facing the same objective value. There are many such objective 'positional' judgements, for example regarding the relative brightness of stars or relativities of movements of bodies, which need not have anything to do with morals, values, or aesthetics. The issue of objectivity of values is left completely *open* in moving from interpretation (*a*) to interpretation (*b*).

Certainly (*b*) should not be interpreted as endorsing the view that beauty or moral value lies in the eyes of the beholder. Given the viewers occupying the same position regarding the states, the viewers may well be required by the given evaluator-relative morality to take the same view of the state. Being Desdemona's husband, lover, and killer—whether or not Othello—or being the person twisting the child's arm, may determine a person's position in regard to the state with sufficient definiteness to admit little or no variation of the evaluation of the corresponding states within that moral theory, irrespective of the exact identity of the person.

It follows that some types of evaluator relativity would indeed be contradictory for an outcome morality related to a certain identification of distinct positions. For example, if the position of being the twister of the child's arm is a crucial one for a particular moral theory, then two persons, differing in other respects but both *jointly* twisting the child's arm, are not free to judge quite differently the resulting state by virtue of their being *different evaluators*. If evaluator relativity is derived from the 'positional interpretation', then it is really *position relativity* that is admitted, which entails evaluator relativity only to the extent that evaluators differ from each other in their respective positions.

It should be noted that the aesthetic analogy in terms of which the positional concept of morality was explained is misleading in at least one respect. In the case of aesthetics it is possible in a natural way to move from statements of type (*b*) to those of type (*a*), since one can typically vary one's position in pursuing aesthetic appreciation. Statement (*a*), that is, 'Mount Everest is beautiful', can be interpreted as: 'there *exists* a position' (or perhaps 'there exist many positions') 'from which statement (*b*) is correct.' When it is asserted that Renoir's *La Loge* is beautiful, the claim isn't that statement (*b*) is correct no matter what one's position is *vis-à-vis* the painting (it *isn't*, I suspect, beautiful from a distance of 2 inches, nor of 200 yards), but that one *can* choose positions from which (*b*) can be emphatically affirmed. (*a*) is obtained, in the aesthetic case, from 'existential' use of (*b*).

In the case of moral evaluation of states the position of the evaluator may not be left open in a similar way. Othello cannot cease to be Desdemona's husband, lover, and killer for the purpose of the evaluation of *that* state. Nor can George admire the state in which he, the pacifist, works for the war machine by evaluating the state as a no-nonsense hawk. And if you are actually twisting the child's arm, you have to evaluate *that* state from that position. It is not that you must lack the *ability* to imagine what it would be like to evaluate the state from a different position—indeed $G_i^k(x)$ expresses just that for person k—but that one of the positions in that state is peculiarly *your own*. This contrasts with the aesthetic case, in which there is nothing to tie you to a certain spot in evaluating a picture.[54] It is this *positional fixity given the state* that makes translation of statements of type

[54] One is, as it were, a part of the 'picture' in the moral case.

(b) into statements of type (a), through 'existential' search, that much less admissible in moral theory than in aesthetic theory.

Thus, moral evaluation of states is more firmly anchored in the positional interpretation than aesthetic evaluation is. And evaluator relativity need not involve any contradictory beliefs under the positional interpretation so long as it is subsumed by position relativity.

This does not, of course, deny the substantive possibility that some things may be valuable or disvaluable from every position (starvation or acute suffering no matter to whom it occurs, for example, being a moral disvalue for every evaluator). The positional interpretation of moral judgements of states *permits* categories of moral thoughts not admissible in more traditional formats. How divergent, substantively, the positional valuations may be is a different question. Indeed, the exact scopes of both agent-relative *action* judgements and position-relative *state* judgements remain open issues. However, although some scope for agent-relative action judgements is widely accepted, there has been no corresponding acceptance of the admissibility of position-relative state judgements. My main concern in this section has been to assert that admissibility.

8. NEGATIVE AND POSITIVE FREEDOMS

The necessity of goal rights was argued in Sections 1 to 3 on the basis of the inadequacy of moral systems that do not give right-based considerations any role in outcome judgements. These goal rights may or may not be formulated in terms of two-person right-duty correspondences, and they can take the form of capability rights and corresponding duties (Section 4).

Of the more traditional approaches to rights, there is no particular difficulty in accommodating 'instrumental' rights in consequence-based evaluation, giving them a status *through* consequential reasoning despite non-inclusion in the goals (Section 4). Issues of co-ordination and co-operation can, of course, be both important and complex, but they are really concerned with how to *use* consequence-based evaluation, bringing in strategic considerations in the assessment of consequences.

It is the deontological approach—important especially for consideration of 'negative freedom'—that appear to be difficult to accommodate within consequence-based evaluation. However, deontological values can, in fact, be accommodated within consequence-based evaluation through evaluator-relative outcome moralities (Sections 6 and 7). This would yield doer relativity and viewer relativity of *action* judgements of the kind imposed by deontology, but will operate through consequence-based reasoning.

In a goal rights system with consequence-based evaluation,[55] negative freedom can figure in at least three distinct ways:

(1) *as parts of goal rights* (for example, as capability rights considered jointly with positive freedoms or as negative rights incorporated in the goals in the form of, say, non-coercion, though the merit of the latter approach was disputed in Section 4);

(2) *for instrumental reasons* (through the influence of negative freedom on the fulfilment and non-fulfilment of other goals);

(3) *through evaluator-relative values in the outcome morality* (for example, 'deontological' disvalue to an evaluator of a state in which he has done some 'bad' act).

This differs from the deontological constraint-based approach in at least two respects:

(i) admitting the possibility of these rights being *overridden* for other benefits—related to other rights or non-right goals—if they are sufficiently strong; and

(ii) entailing duties of 'third parties', who can help or hinder, requiring the evaluation of duties through consequential analysis of interdependences (possibly in an evaluator-relative form).

Positive freedoms can receive support through reasons of types (1) and (2). They can also receive support through reasons of type (3) in some cases, for example, through tie aims of i, giving a

---

[55] A goal rights system may or may not be consequence-based, since the dividing line is merely sensitivity to consequences (see Section 4) rather than the hegemony of outcome evaluation on the judgement of control variables. However, *consequence-based* goal rights systems form an important subclass, with a defined structure.

special weight on j's positive freedoms (connected with 'autonomy' reasons). However, the particular case of 'deontological' reasons working against 'bad' acts by the evaluator will apply to negative freedoms in a way that it would not to positive freedoms.

In this sense, negative freedom may well be valued in 'one more way' than positive freedom. However, that does not, of course, imply that negative freedoms on balance will be more important than positive freedoms. On the approach outlined in this paper, the relative importance of different types of rights and duties must depend ultimately on the comparative analysis of consequences and their evaluations.

10

UTILITARIANISM AND THE VIRTUES

PHILIPPA FOOT

IT is remarkable how utilitarianism tends to haunt even those of us who will not believe in it. It is as if we for ever feel that it must be right, although we insist that it is wrong. T. M. Scanlon hits the nail on the head when he observes, in his article 'Contractualism and Utilitarianism', that the theory occupies a central place in the moral philosophy of our time in spite of the fact that, as he puts it, 'the implications of act utilitarianism are wildly at variance with firmly held moral convictions, while rule utilitarianism . . . strikes most people as an unstable compromise'.[1] He suggests that what we need to break this spell is to find a better alternative to utilitarian theories, and I am sure that that is right. But what I want to do is to approach the business of exorcism more directly. Obviously something drives us towards utilitarianism, and must it not be an assumption or thought which is in some way mistaken? For otherwise why is the theory unacceptable? We must be going wrong somewhere and should find out where it is.

I want to argue that what is most radically wrong with utilitarianism is its consequentialism, but I also want to suggest that its consequentialist element is one of the main reasons why utilitarianism seems so compelling. I need therefore to say something about the relation between the two theory descriptions 'utilitarian' and 'consequentialist'. Consequentialism in its most general form simply says that it is by 'total outcome', that is, by the whole formed by an action and its consequences, that what is done is judged right or wrong. A consequentialist theory of ethics is one which identifies certain states of affairs as *good* states of affairs and

Philippa Foot, 'Utilitarianism and the Virtues', *Mind* 94 (1985), 196–209. An earlier version appeared in the Proceedings and Addresses of the American Philosophical Association 57 (1983). Copyright: Philippa Foot.

[1] T. M. Scanlon, 'Contractualism and Utilitarianism', pp. 103–28.

says that the rightness or goodness of actions (or of other subjects of moral judgement) consists in their positive productive relationship to these states of affairs. Utilitarianism as it is usually defined consists of consequentialism together with the identification of the best state of affairs with the state of affairs in which there is most happiness, most pleasure, or the maximum satisfaction of desire. Strictly speaking utilitarianism—taken here as welfare utilitarianism—is left behind when the distribution of welfare is said in itself to affect the goodness of states of affairs; or when anything other than welfare is allowed as part of the good. But it is of course possible also to count a theory as utilitarian if right action is taken to be that which produces 'good states of affairs', whatever these are supposed to be; and then 'utilitarianism' becomes synonymous with 'consequentialism'. By 'utilitarianism' I shall here mean 'welfare utilitarianism', though it is with consequentialism in one form or another that I shall be most concerned.

Although I believe that what is radically wrong with utilitarianism is its consequentialism, what has often seemed to be most wrong with it has been either welfarism or the sum ranking of welfare. So it has been suggested that 'the good' is not automatically increased by an increase in pleasure, but by non-malicious pleasure, or first-order pleasure, or something of the kind; in order to get over difficulties about the pleasures of watching a public execution or the pleasures and pains of the bigot or the prude.[2] Furthermore distribution principles have been introduced so that actions benefiting the rich more than they harm the poor no longer have to be judged morally worthy. Thus the criteria for the goodness of states of affairs have continually been modified to meet one objection after another; but it seems that the modifications have never been able to catch up with the objections. For the distribution principles and the discounting of certain pleasures and pains did nothing to help with problems about, e.g., the wrongness of inducing cancer in a few experimental subjects to make a substantial advance in finding a cure for the disease. If the theory was to give results at all in line with common moral opinion *rights* had to be looked after in a way that was so far impossible within even the modified versions of utilitarianism.

---

[2] See, e.g., A. Sen, 'Utilitarianism and Welfarism', pp. 463–89.

It was therefore suggested, by Amartya Sen, that 'goal rights' systems should be considered; the idea being that the respecting or violating of rights should be counted as itself a good or an evil in the evaluation of states of affairs.[3] This would help to solve some problems because if the respecting of the rights of the subject were weighted heavily enough the cancer experiment could not turn out to be 'optimific' after all. Yet this seems rather a strange suggestion, because as Samuel Scheffler has remarked, it is not clear why, in the measurement of the goodness of states of affairs or total outcomes, killings for instance should count so much more heavily than deaths.[4] But what is more important is that this 'goal rights' system fails to deal with certain other examples of actions that most of us would want to call wrong. Suppose, for instance, that some evil person threatens to kill or torture a number of victims unless we kill or torture one, and suppose that we have every reason to believe that he will do as he says. Then in terms of their total outcomes (again consisting of the states of affairs made up of an action and its consequences) we have the choice between more killings or torturings and less, and a consequentialist will have to say that we are justified in killing or torturing the one person, and indeed that we are morally obliged to do it, always supposing that no indirect consequences have tipped the balance of good and evil. There will in fact be nothing that it will not be right to do to a perfectly innocent individual if that is the only way of preventing another agent from doing more things of the same kind.

Now I find this a totally unacceptable conclusion and note that it is a conclusion not of utilitarianism in particular but rather of consequentialism in any form. So it is the spellbinding force of consequentialism that we have to think about. Welfarism has its own peculiar attraction, which has to do with the fact that pleasure, happiness, and the satisfaction of desire are things seen as in some way good. But this attraction becomes less powerful as distribution principles are added and pleasures discounted on an *ad hoc* basis to destroy the case for such things as public executions.

[3] A. Sen, 'Rights and Agency', [reprinted in this collection as Chapter 9—Ed.].
[4] S. Scheffler, *The Rejection of Consequentialism*, pp. 108–12.

If having left welfarist utilitarianism behind we still find ourselves unable, in spite of its difficulties, to get away from consequentialism, there must be a reason for this. What is it, let us now ask, that is so compelling about consequentialism? It is, I think, the rather simple thought that it can never be right to prefer a worse state of affairs to a better.[5] It is this thought that haunts us and, incidentally, this thought that makes the move to rule utilitarianism an unsatisfactory answer to the problem of reconciling utilitarianism with common moral opinion. For surely it will be irrational, we feel, to obey even the most useful rule if in a particular instance we clearly see that such obedience will not *have the best results*. Again following Scheffler we ask if it is not paradoxical that it should ever be morally objectionable to act in such a way as to minimize morally objectionable acts of just the same type.[6] If it is a bad state of affairs in which one of these actions is done it will presumably be a worse state of affairs in which several are. And must it not be irrational to prefer the worse to the better state of affairs?

This thought does indeed seem compelling. And yet it leads to an apparently unacceptable conclusion about what it is right to do. So we ought, as I said, to wonder whether we have not gone wrong somewhere. And I think that indeed we have. I believe (and this is the main thesis of the paper) that we go wrong in accepting the idea that there *are* better and worse states of affairs in the sense that consequentialism requires. As Wittgenstein says in a different context, 'The decisive movement in the conjuring trick has been made, and it was the very one that we thought quite innocent'.[7]

---

[5] The original version continued 'How could it ever be right, we think, to produce less good rather than more good?'. I have excised this sentence because in the context the use of the expression 'doing more good' suggested an identification which I was at pains to deny. At all times I have allowed *doing good* as an unproblematic notion, because although it does raise many problems, e.g. about different distributions of benefits, it does not raise the particular problems with which I am concerned. I want to insist that however well we might understand what it was to 'do as much good as possible' in the sense of producing maximum benefit, it would not follow that we knew what we meant by expressions such as 'the best outcome' or 'the best state of affairs' as these are used by moral philosophers. Cf. the discussion on page 231 of the present version of this paper.

[6] Scheffler, *The Rejection of Consequentialism*, p. 121.

[7] L. Wittgenstein, *Philosophical Investigations* (Macmillan 1953, and Blackwell 1958), § 308.

Let us therefore look into the idea of a good state of affairs, as this appears in the thought that we can judge certain states of affairs to be better than others and then go on to give moral descriptions to actions related productively to these states of affairs.

We should begin by asking why we are so sure that we even understand expressions such as 'a good state of affairs' or 'a good outcome'; for as Peter Geach pointed out years ago there are phrases with the word 'good' in them, as, e.g., 'a good event', that do *not* at least as they stand have a sense.[8] Following this line one might suggest that philosophers are a bit hasty in using expressions such as 'a better world'. One may *perhaps* understand this when it is taken to mean a 'deontically better world' defined as one in which fewer duties are left unfulfilled; but obviously this will not help to give a sense to 'better state of affairs' as the consequentialist needs to use this expression, since he is wanting to fix our obligations not to refer to their fulfilment.

Nevertheless it may seem that combinations of words such as 'a good state of affairs' are beyond reproach or question, for such expressions are extremely familiar. Do we not use them every day? We say that it is a good thing that something or other happened; what difficulty can there be in constructing from such elements anything we want in the way of aggregates such as total outcomes which (in principle) take into account all the elements of a possible world and so constitute good states of affairs? Surely no one can seriously suggest that 'good state of affairs' is an expression that we do not understand?'

It would, of course, be ridiculous to query the sense of the ordinary things that we say about its being 'a good thing' that something or other happened, or about a certain state of affairs being good or bad. The doubt is not about whether there is some way of using the words, but rather about the way they appear in the exposition of utilitarian and other consequentialist moral theories. It is important readily to accept the fact that we talk in a natural and familiar way about good states of affairs, and that there is nothing problematic about such usage. But it is also important to see how such expressions actually work in the

[8] P. Geach, 'Good and Evil', *Analysis* 17 (1956), pp. 33–42.

contexts in which they are at home, and in particular to ask about the status of a good state of affairs. Is it something impersonal to be recognized (we hope) by all reasonable men? It seems, surprisingly, that this is not the case at least in many contexts of utterance of the relevant expressions. Suppose, for instance, that the supporters of different teams have gathered in the stadium and that the members of each group are discussing the game; or that two racegoers have backed different horses in a race. Remarking on the course of events one or the other may say that things are going well or badly, and when a certain situation has developed may say that it is a good or a bad state of affairs. More commonly they will welcome some developments and deplore others, saying 'Oh good!' or 'That's bad!', calling some news good news and some news bad, sometimes describing what has happened as 'a good thing' and sometimes not. We could develop plenty of other examples of this kind, thinking for instance of the conversations about the invention of a new burglar alarm that might take place in the police headquarters and in the robbers' den.

At least two types of utterance are here discernible. For 'good' and its cognates may be used to signal the speaker's attitude to a result judged as an end result, and then he says 'Good!' or 'I'm glad' or 'That's good' where what he is glad about is something welcomed in itself and not for any good it will bring. But a state of affairs may rather be judged by its connection with other things called good. And even what is counted as in itself good may be said to be bad when it brings enough evil in its train.

Now what shall we say about the truth or falsity of these utterances? It certainly seems that they can be straightforwardly true or false. For perhaps what appears to be going to turn out well is really going to turn out badly: what seemed to be a good thing was really a bad thing, and an apparently good state of affairs was the prelude to disaster. 'You are quite wrong' one person may say to another and events may show that he *was* wrong. Nevertheless we can see that this quasi-objectivity, which is not to be questioned when people with similar aims, interests, or desires are speaking together, flies out of the window if we try to set the utterances of those in one group against the utterances of those in another. One will say 'a good thing' where another says 'a bad thing', and it is the same for states of affairs. It would be bizarre to suggest that at the races it really *is* a good thing that one horse or the other is gaining (perhaps because of the pleasure it will bring to the majority, or the good effect on the future of racing) and so that the utterance of one particular punter, intent only on making a packet, will be the one that is true.

This is not to say, however, that what a given person says to be a good thing or a good state of affairs must relate to his own advantage. For anyone may be *interested in* the future of racing, and people commonly are *interested in*, e.g., the success of their friends, saying 'that's a good thing' if one of them looks like winning a prize or getting a job; incidentally without worrying much about whether he is the very best candidate for it.

Now it may be thought that these must be rather special uses of expressions such as 'good state of affairs', because we surely must speak quite differently when we are talking about public matters, as when for instance we react to news of some far-away disaster. We say that the news is bad because a lot of people have lost their lives in an earthquake. Later we may say that things are not as bad as we feared and someone may remark 'that's a good thing'. 'A bad state of affairs', we might remark on hearing the original news about people dead or homeless, and this will usually have nothing to do with harm to us or to our friends.

In this way the case is different from that of the racegoers or the cops and robbers, but this is not of course to imply that what we say on such occasions has a different status from the utterances we have considered so far. For why should its truth not be 'speaker-relative' too, also depending on what the speakers and their group are *interested in* though not now on the good or harm that will come to them themselves? Is it not more plausible to think this than to try to distinguish two kinds of uses of these expressions, one speaker-relative and the other not? For are there really two ways in which the police for instance might speak? And two ways in which the robbers could speak as well? Are we really to say that although when they are both speaking in the speaker-relative way they do not contradict each other, and may both speak truly, when speaking in the 'objective' way one group will speak truly and the other not? What shows that the second way of speaking exists?

What thoughts, one may ask, can we really be supposed to have which must be expressed in the disputed mode? Considering examples such as that of the far-away earthquake we may think that we believe the best state of affairs to be the one in which there is most happiness and least misery, or something of the sort. But considering other examples we may come to wonder whether any such thought can really be attributed to us.

Suppose for instance that when walking in a poor district one of us should lose a fairly considerable sum of money which we had intended to spend on something rather nice. Arriving home we discover the loss and telephone the police on the off chance that our wad of notes has been found and turned in. To our delight we find that it was picked up by a passing honest policeman, and that we shall get it back. 'What a good thing' we say 'that an officer happened to be there.' What seemed to be a bad state of affairs has turned out not to be bad after all: things are much better than we thought they were. And all's well that ends well. But how, it may now be asked, *can* we say that things have turned out better than we thought? Were we not supposed to believe that the best state of affairs was the one in which there was most happiness and least misery? So surely it would have been *better* if the money had not been returned to us but rather found and kept as treasure trove by some poor inhabitant of the region? We simply had not considered that because most of us do not actually *have* the thought that the best state of affairs is the one in which we lose and they gain. Perhaps we should have had this thought if it had been a small amount of money, but this was rather a lot.

No doubt it will seem to many that there must be non-speaker-relative uses of words evaluating states of affairs because moral judgements cannot have speaker-relative status. But if one is inclined, as I am, to doubt whether propositions of this form play any part in the fundamentals of ethical theory there is no objection on this score. It is important however that the preceding discussion has been about propositions of a particular form and nothing has been said to suggest that all judgements about what is good and bad have speaker-relative status. I have not for instance made this suggestion for what Geach called 'attributive' judgements concerning things good or bad of a kind—good knives and houses and essays, or even good actions, motives, or men. If there is some reason for calling these 'speaker-relative' the reason has not been given here. Nor has anything been said about the status of propositions about what is *good for* anyone or anything, or about that in which their good consists.

What has I hope now been shown is that we should not take it for granted that we even know what we are talking about if we enter into a discussion with the consequentialist about whether it can ever be right to produce something other than 'the best state of affairs'.

It might be suggested by way of reply that what is in question in these debates is not just the best state of affairs without qualification but rather *the best state of affairs from an impersonal point of view.* But what does this mean? A good state of affairs from an impersonal point of view is presumably opposed to a good state of affairs from *my* point of view or from *your* point of view. and as a good state of affairs from my point of view is a state of affairs which is advantageous to me, and a good state of affairs from your point of view is a state of affairs that is advantageous to you, a good state of affairs from an impersonal point of view presumably means a state of affairs which is generally advantageous. or advantageous to most people, or something like that. About the idea of maximum welfare we are not (or so we are supposing for the sake of the argument) in any difficulty.[9] But an account of the idea of a good state of affairs which simply defines it in terms of maximum welfare is no help to us here. For our problem is that something is supposed to be being said *about* maximum welfare and we cannot figure out what this is.

In a second reply, more to the point, the consequentialist might say that what we should really be dealing with in this discussion is states of affairs which are good or bad, not simply, but *from the moral point of view.* The qualification is, it will be suggested. tacitly understood in moral contexts, where no individual speaker gives his own private interests or allegiances a special place in any debate, the speaker-relativity found in other contexts thus being left behind. This seems to be a pattern familiar from other cases,

---

[9] Cf. footnote 5.

as, e.g., from discussions in meetings of the governors of public institutions. Why should it not be in a similar way that we talk of a good and a bad thing to happen 'from a moral point of view'? And is it not hard to reject the conclusion that right action is action producing *this* 'best state of affairs'?

That special contexts can create special uses of the expressions we are discussing is indeed true. But before we proceed to draw conclusions about moral judgements we should ask why we think that it makes sense to talk about morally good and bad states of affairs, or to say that it is a good thing (or is good that) something happened 'from a moral point of view'. For after all we cannot concoct a meaningful sentence by adding just any qualification of this verbal form to expressions such as these. What would it mean, for instance, to say that a state of affairs was good or bad 'from a legal point of view' or 'from the point of view of etiquette'? Or that it was a good thing that a certain thing happened from these same 'points of view'? Certain interpretations that suggest themselves are obviously irrelevant, as, for instance, that it is a good state of affairs from a legal point of view when the laws are clearly stated, or a good state of affairs from the point of view of etiquette when everyone follows the rules.

It seems, therefore, that we do not solve the problem of the meaning of 'best state of affairs' when supposed to be used in a non-speaker-relative way simply by tacking on 'from a moral point of view'; since it cannot be assumed that the resulting expression has any sense. Nevertheless it would be wrong to suggest that 'good state of affairs from a moral point of view' is a concatenation of words which in fact has no meaning in *any* of the contexts in which it appears, and to see this we have only to look at utilitarian theories of the type put forward by John C. Harsanyi and R. M. Hare, in which a certain interpretation is implicitly provided for such expressions.[10]

Harsanyi for instance argues that the only *rational* morality is one in which the rightness or wrongness of an action is judged by its relation to a certain outcome, i.e. the maximization of social

[10] See, e.g., J. C. Harsanyi, 'Morality and the Theory of Rational Behavior'. *Social Research* 44 (1977), reprinted in Sen and Williams, *Utilitarianism and Beyond*, pp. 39–62; and R. M. Hare, *Moral Thinking*.

utility. The details of this theory, which defines social utility in terms of individual preferences, do not concern us here. The relevant point is that within it there appears the idea of an end which is the goal of moral action, and therefore the idea of a best state of affairs from a moral point of view. (It does not of course matter whether Harsanyi uses these words.)

Similarly Hare, by a more elaborate argument from the universalizability and prescriptivity of moral judgements, tries to establish the proposition that one who takes the moral point of view must have as his aim the maximization of utility, reflecting this in one way in his day-to-day prescriptions and in another in 'critical' moral judgements. So here too a clear sense can be given to the idea of a best state of affairs from a moral point of view: it is the state of affairs which a man aims at when he takes the moral point of view and which in one way or another determines the truth of moral judgements.

Within these theories there is, then, no problem about the meaning of expressions such as 'the best state of affairs from the moral point of view'. It does not follow, however, that those who reject the theories should be ready to discuss the pros and cons of consequentialism in these terms. For unless the arguments given by Hare and Harsanyi are acceptable it will not have been shown that there is any reference for expressions such as 'the aim which each man has in so far as he takes up the moral point of view' or *a fortiori* 'the best state of affairs from the moral point of view'.

If my main thesis is correct this is a point of the first importance. For I am arguing that where non-consequentialists commonly go wrong is in accepting from their opponents questions such as 'Is it ever right to act in such a way as to produce something less than the best state of affairs that is within one's reach?'[11] Summing up the results reached so far we may say that if taken in one way, with no special reference to morality, talk about good states of affairs

[11] See, e.g., T. Nagel, 'The Limits of Objectivity', p. 131, where he says that '. . . things would be better, what *happened* would be better' if I twisted a child's arm in circumstances where (by Nagel's hypothesis) this was the only way to get medical help for the victims of an accident. He supposes that I might have done something worse if I hurt the child than if I did not do it, but that the total outcome would have been better. It does not, I think, occur to him to question the idea of *things* being better—or *things* being worse.

seems to be speaker-relative. But if the qualification 'from a moral point of view' is added the resulting expression may mean nothing; and it may lack a reference when a special consequentialist theory has given it a sense.

In the light of this discussion we should find it significant that many people who do not find any particular consequentialist theory compelling nevertheless feel themselves driven towards consequentialism by a thought which turns on the idea that there are states of affairs which are better or worse from a moral point of view. What is it that seems to make this an inescapable idea?

Tracing the assumption back in my own mind I find that what seems preposterous is to deny that there are some things that a moral person must want and aim at in so far as he is a moral person and that he will count it 'a good thing' when these things happen and 'a good state of affairs' either when they are happening or when things are disposed in their favour. For surely he must want others to be happy. To deny this would be to deny that benevolence is a virtue—and who wants to deny that?

Let us see where this line of thought will take us, accepting without any reservation that benevolence is a virtue and that a benevolent person must often aim at the good of others and call it 'a good thing' when for instance a far-away disaster turns out to have been less serious than was feared. Here we do indeed have the words 'a good thing' (and just as obviously a 'good state of affairs') necessarily appearing in moral contexts. And the use is explained not by a piece of utilitarian theory but by a simple observation about benevolence.

This, then, seems to be the way in which seeing states of affairs in which people are happy as good states of affairs really is an essential part of morality. But it is very important that we have found this end *within* morality, and forming part of it, not standing outside it as the 'good state of affairs' by which moral action in general is to be judged. For benevolence is only one of the virtues, and we shall have to look at the others before we can pronounce on any question about good or bad action in particular circumstances. Off-hand we have no reason to think that whatever is done with the aim of improving the lot of other people will be morally required or even morally permissible. For firstly there are virtues such as friendship which play their part in determining the requirements of benevolence, e.g., by making it consistent with benevolence to give service to friends rather than to strangers or acquaintances. And secondly there is the virtue of justice, taken in the old wide sense in which it had to do with everything *owed*. In our common moral code we find numerous examples of limitations which justice places on the pursuit of welfare. In the first place there are principles of distributive justice which forbid, on grounds of fairness, the kind of 'doing good' which increases the wealth of rich people at the cost of misery to the poor. Secondly, rules such as truth telling are not to be broken wherever and whenever welfare would thereby be increased. Thirdly, considerations about rights, both positive and negative, limit the action which can be taken for the sake of welfare. Justice is primarily concerned with the following of certain rules of fairness and honest dealing and with respecting prohibitions on interference with others rather than with attachment to any end. It is true that the just man must also fight injustice, and here justice like benevolence is a matter of ends, but of course the end is not the same end as the one that benevolence seeks and need not be coincident with it.

I do not mean to go into these matters in detail here, but simply to point out that we find in our ordinary moral code many requirements and prohibitions inconsistent with the idea that benevolence is the whole of morality. From the point of view of the present discussion it would be acceptable to describe the situation in terms of a tension between, for instance, justice and benevolence. But it is not strictly accurate to think of it like this, because that would suggest that someone who does an unjust act for the sake of increasing total happiness has a higher degree of benevolence than one who refuses to do it. Since someone who refuses to sacrifice an innocent life for the sake of increasing happiness is not to be counted as less benevolent than someone who is ready to do it, this cannot be right. We might be tempted to think that the latter would be acting 'out of benevolence' because his aim is the happiness of others, but this seems a bad way of talking. Certainly benevolence does not require unjust action, and we should not call an act which violated rights an act of benevolence. It would not, for instance, be an act of benevolence to induce cancer in one person (or deliberately to let it run its course) even for the sake of alleviating much suffering.

What we should say therefore is that even perfection in benevolence does not imply a readiness to do anything and everything of which it can be said that it is highly probable that it will increase the sum of human happiness. And this, incidentally, throws some light on a certain type of utilitarian theory which identifies the moral assessment of a situation with that of a sympathetic impartial observer whose benevolence extends equally to all mankind.[12] For what, we may ask, are we to suppose about this person's *other* characteristics? Is he to be guided simply and solely by a desire to relieve suffering and increase happiness; or is he also just? If it is said that for him the telling of truth, keeping of promises, and respecting of individual autonomy are to be recommended only in so far as these serve to maximize welfare then we see that the 'impartial sympathetic observer' is by definition one with a utilitarian point of view. So the utilitarians are defining moral assessment in their own terms.

Returning to the main line of our argument we now find ourselves in a better position to see that there indeed is a place *within* morality for the idea of better and worse states of affairs. That there is such a place is true if only because the proper end of benevolence is the good of others, and because in many situations the person who has this virtue will be able to think of good and bad states of affairs, in terms of the general good. It does not, however, follow that he will always be able to do so. For sometimes justice will forbid a certain action, as it forbids the harmful experiment designed to further cancer research; and then it will not be possible to ask whether 'the state of affairs' containing the action and its results will be better or worse than one in which the action is not done. The action is one that *cannot* be done, because justice forbids it, and nothing that has this moral character comes within the scope of the kind of comparison of total outcomes that benevolence may sometimes require. Picking up at this point the example discussed earlier about the morality of

---

[12] See Harsanyi, 'Morality and the Theory of Rational Behavior', Sen and Williams, *Utilitarianism and Beyond*, p. 39.

killing or torturing to prevent more killings or torturings we see the same principle operating here. If it were a question of riding out to rescue a small number or a large number then benevolence would, we may suppose, urge that the larger number be saved. But if it is a matter of preventing the killing *by* killing (or conniving at a killing) the case will be quite different. One does not have to believe that all rights to non-interference are absolute to believe that *this* is an unjust action, and if it is unjust the moral man says to himself that he cannot do it and does not include it in an assessment he may be making about the good and bad states of affairs that he can bring about.

What has been said in the last few paragraphs is, I suggest, a sketch of what can truly be said about the important place that the idea of maximum welfare has in morality. It is not that in the guise of 'the best outcome' it stands *outside* morality as its foundation and arbiter, but rather that it appears *within* morality as the end of one of the virtues.

When we see it like this, and give expressions such as 'best outcome' and 'good state of affairs' no special meaning in moral contexts other than the one that the virtues give them, we shall no longer think the paradoxical thought that it is sometimes right to act in such a way that the total outcome, consisting of one's action and its results, is less good than some other accessible at the time. In the abstract a benevolent person must wish that loss and harm should be minimized. He does not, however, wish that the whole consisting of a killing to minimize killings should be actualized either by his agency or that of anyone else. So there is no reason on this score to think that he must regard it as 'the better state of affairs'.[13] And therefore there is no reason for the non-consequentialist, whose thought of good and bad states of affairs in moral contexts comes only from the virtues themselves, to describe the refusal as a choice of a worse total outcome. If he does so describe it he will be giving the words the sense they have in his opponents' theories, and it is not surprising that he should find himself in their hands.

---

[13] I have discussed examples of this kind in more detail in 'Morality, Action, and Outcome', in T. Honderich, ed., *Morality and Objectivity: A Tribute to J. L. Mackie*.

We may also remind ourselves at this point that benevolence is not the only virtue which has to do, at least in part, with ends rather than with the observance of rules. As mentioned earlier there belongs to the virtue of justice the readiness to fight for justice as well as to observe its laws; and there belongs to truthfulness not only the avoidance of lying but also that other kind of attachment to truth which has to do with its preservation and pursuit. A man of virtue must be a lover of justice and a lover of truth. Furthermore he will seek the special good of his family and friends. Thus there will be many things which he will want and will welcome, sometimes sharing these aims with others and sometimes opposing them, as when working differentially for his own children or his own friends.[14] Similarly someone who is judging a competition and is a fair judge must try to see to it that the best man wins. The existence of these 'moral aims' will of course give opportunity for the use, in moral contexts, of such expressions as 'a good thing' or 'the best state of affairs'. But nothing of a consequentialist nature follows from such pieces of usage, found here and there within morality.

An analogy will perhaps help to make my point. Thinking about good manners we might decide that someone who has good manners tries to avoid embarrassing others in social situations. This must, let us suppose, be one of his aims; and we might even decide that so far as manners is concerned this, or something like it, is the only prescribed *end*. But of course this does not mean that what good manners require of anyone is universally determined by this end. A consequentialist theory of good manners would presumably be mistaken; because good manners, not being solely a matter of purposes, also require that certain things be done or not done: e.g. that hospitality not be abused by frank discussion of the deficiencies of one's host as soon as he leaves the room.[15] So if invited to take part in such discussions a well-mannered person will, if necessary, maintain a silence embarrassing to an interlocutor, because the rule here takes precedence over the aim prescribed. Assuming that this is a correct account of good manners—and it

[14] See D. Parfit, 'Prudence, Morality, and the Prisoner's Dilemma', and A. Sen, 'Rights and Agency'.
[15] It is customary to wait until later.

does not of course matter whether it is or not—we can now see the difficulty that arises if we try to say which choice open to the agent results in the best state of affairs from the point of view of manners. In certain contexts the state of affairs containing no embarrassment will be referred to as a good state of affairs, because avoiding embarrassment is by our hypothesis the one *end* prescribed by good manners. But we should not be surprised if the right action from the point of view of good manners is sometimes the one that produces something *other* than this good state of affairs. We have no right to take an end from within the whole that makes up good manners and turn it, just because it is an *end*, into the single guide to action to be used by the well-mannered man.

This analogy serves to illustrate my point about the illegitimacy of moving what is found within morality to a criterial position outside it. But it may also bring to the surface a reason many will be ready to give for being dissatisfied with my thesis. For surely a morality is unlike a code of manners in claiming rational justification for its ordinances? It cannot be enough to say that we *do* have such things as rules of justice in our present system of virtues: the question is whether we should have them, and if so why we should. And the reason this is crucial in the present context is that the justification of a moral code may seem inevitably to involve the very idea that has been called in question in this paper.

This is a very important objection. In its most persuasive form it involves a picture of morality as a rational device developed to serve certain purposes, and therefore answerable to these purposes. Morality, it will be suggested, is a device with a certain object, having to do with the harmonizing of ends or the securing of the greatest possible general good, or perhaps one of these things plus the safeguarding of rights. And the content of morality—what really is right and wrong—will be thought to be determined by what it is rational to require in the way of conduct given that these are our aims. Thus morality is thought of as a kind of tacit legislation by the community, and it is, of course, significant that the early Utilitarians, who were much interested in the rationalizing of actual Parliamentary legislation, were ready to talk in these terms.[16] In moral legislation our aim is, they thought, the general good. With this way of looking at morality there reappears the idea of better and worse states of affairs from the moral point of view. Moreover consequentialism *in some form* is necessarily reinstated. For while there is room on such a model for rational moral codes which enjoin something other than the pursuit of 'the best state of affairs from the moral point of view' this will be only in so far as it is by means of such ordinances that the object of a moral code is best achieved.[17]

Thus it may seem that we must after all allow that the idea of a good state of affairs appears at the most basic level in the critical appraisal of any moral code. This would, however, be too hasty a conclusion. Consequentialism in some form follows from the premiss that morality is a device for achieving a certain shared end. But why should we accept this view of what morality is and how it is to be judged? Why should we not rather see that as itself a consequentialist assumption, which has come to seem neutral and inevitable only in so far as utilitarianism and other forms of consequentialism now dominate moral philosophy?

To counter this bewitchment let us ask awkard questions about who is supposed to *have* the end which morality is supposed to be in aid of. J. S. Mill notoriously found it hard to pass from the premiss that the end of each is the good of each to the proposition that the end of all is the good of all.[18] Perhaps no such *shared end* appears in the foundations of ethics, where we may rather find individual ends and rational compromises between those who have them. Or perhaps at the most basic level lie facts about the way individual human beings can find the greatest goods which they are capable of possessing. The truth is, I think, that we simply do not have a satisfactory theory of morality, and need to look for it. Scanlon was indeed right in saying that the real answer to utilitarianism depends on progress in the development of alternatives. Meanwhile, however, we have no reason to think that we

---

[16] See, e.g., J. Bentham, *An Introduction to the Principles of Legislation* (1789), ch. 3, Section 1.

[17] For discussions of this possibility see, e.g., R. Adams, 'Motive Utilitarianism', and D. Parfit, *Reasons and Persons*, pp. 24–8.

[18] J. S. Mill, *Utilitarianism*, ch. 4.

must accept consequentialism in any form. If the thesis of this paper is correct we should be more alert than we usually are to the possibility that we may unwittingly, and unnecessarily, surrender to consequentialism by uncritically accepting its key idea. Let us remind ourselves that the idea of the goodness of total states of affairs played no part in Aristotle's moral philosophy, and that in modern times it plays no part either in Rawls's account of justice or in the theories of more thoroughgoing contractualists such as Scanlon.[19] If we accustom ourselves to the thought that there is simply a blank where consequentialists see 'the best state of affairs' we may be better able to give other theories the hearing they deserve.

[19] J. Rawls, *A Theory of Justice*; T. M. Scanlon, 'Contractualism and Utilitarianism'.

11

AGENT-CENTRED RESTRICTIONS, RATIONALITY, AND THE VIRTUES

SAMUEL SCHEFFLER

THERE is no substantive moral theory that is obviously correct. All such theories stand in need of some defence. However, in my book *The Rejection of Consequentialism*,[1] I argued that the need is particularly acute in the case of typical deontological theories. For although the common-sense morality of our culture is substantially deontological in content, and although many moral philosophers find themselves drawn toward some version of deontology, I maintained that there is a distinct air of paradox surrounding such views. And this mixture of real appeal and apparent paradox—always a potent combination in philosophy—lends a special urgency to the defence of deontology.

That typical deontological views are apparently paradoxical, I argued, is to be explained by their inclusion of what I call 'agent-centred restrictions'. An agent-centred restriction is, roughly, a restriction which it is at least sometimes impermissible to violate in circumstances where a violation would serve to minimize total overall violations of the very same restriction, and would have no other morally relevant consequences. Thus, for example, a prohibition against killing one innocent person even in order to minimize the total number of innocent people killed would ordinarily count as an agent-centred restriction. The inclusion of agent-centred restrictions gives traditional deontological views considerable anti-consequentialist force, and also considerable intuitive appeal. Despite their congeniality to moral common

Samuel Scheffler, 'Agent-Centred Restrictions, Rationality, and the Virtues', *Mind* 94 (1985), 409–19. Reprinted by permission of Oxford University Press.

[1] Oxford, Clarendon Press, 1982.

sense, however, agent-centred restrictions are puzzling. For how can it be rational to forbid the performance of a morally objectionable action that would have the effect of minimizing the total number of comparably objectionable actions that were performed and would have no other morally relevant consequences? How can the minimization of morally objectionable conduct be morally unacceptable?

In the two published versions of her Presidential Address to the Pacific Division of the American Philosophical Association,[2] Philippa Foot attempts 'to show that there is no paradox at the heart of non-consequentialist morality'.[3] Foot agrees that agent-centred restrictions *appear* paradoxical. And she believes that consequentialism, which first gives some principle for ranking overall states of affairs from best to worst from an impersonal or agent-neutral standpoint, and then says that the right act in a given situation is the one that will produce the best overall outcome of any act available, has a 'spellbinding force'.[4] But she also believes that a certain kind of non-consequentialist moral view can in the end be shown to be free of paradox despite the fact that it includes agent-centred restrictions, and that the spell of consequentialism can thus be broken. The kind of moral view she has in mind is one in which a conception of the virtues plays a central role. Now many of what I have been calling traditional deontological views do not assign this kind of role to the virtues. Indeed, so-called 'virtue theories' are often thought to represent an alternative to both

---

[2] The reference for the first version is 'Utilitarianism and the Virtues', *Proceedings and Addresses of the American Philosophical Association* (abbreviated hereafter as *PAAPA*) 57 (1983), 273–83. The second version appeared, with the same title, in *Mind* 94 (1985), pp. 196–209. [The *Mind* version is reprinted in this collection as Chapter 10—Ed.] Foot described it as 'an expanded version'. She added: 'Much of the text is unaltered and all the ideas are the same, but I hope to have explained myself more clearly this time around.' See *Mind*, p. 196. When quoting, I will always indicate whether or not the passage as quoted appears in both versions of Foot's paper. Where it does, I will give both page references. Where it does not, I will give the page reference for the version in which it does appear, and I will also compare the quoted passage with the corresponding passage in the other version, if there is one. If there is no corresponding passage, I will so indicate.

[3] *PAAPA*, p. 282. These words have been eliminated from the second version, but the description they provide of the aim of the paper fits both versions equally well.

[4] *PAAPA*, p. 274; *Mind*, p. 198 [p. 226 above].

consequentialist and deontological moral conceptions. For the purposes of this discussion, therefore, it is important to remember that Foot's claim is, in effect, that agent-centred restrictions are not paradoxical when they are set in the context of a non-consequentialist view of a certain kind. There will be occasion later in this paper to consider the extent to which assignment of a central role to the virtues really is essential to the sort of defence of agent-centred restrictions that Foot wants to give.

Foot says that what seems compelling about consequentialism is 'the rather simple thought that it can never be right to prefer a worse state of affairs to a better'.[5] And what seems paradoxical about those non-consequentialist views that include agent-centred restrictions is that they appear to claim that it is sometimes morally impermissible to produce the best state of affairs that one is in a position to produce. Sometimes, they seem to say, we must do less good, or prevent less evil, than we could. Perhaps, for example, we must refrain from harming one innocent person even if harming that person would result in the minimization of the total number of innocent people comparably harmed. That consequentialism should seem compelling, and that agent-centred restrictions should seem paradoxical, Foot believes, is inevitable once we grant the apparently innocent idea 'that there *are* better or worse states of affairs in the sense that consequentialism requires'.[6] But, she maintains, this idea is really not so innocent; it can be challenged, and it is through such a challenge that she hopes to break the spell of consequentialism and dissolve the air of paradox surrounding agent-centred restrictions.

Foot does not claim, as some others have, that evaluations of states of affairs never make sense in moral contexts. On the contrary, she thinks it is important 'to see the place that there indeed is *within* morality for the idea of better and worse states of affairs'.[7] 'That there is such a place', she adds, 'follows from the fact that the proper end of benevolence is the good of others, and

---

[5] *PAAPA*, p. 275; *Mind*, p. 198 [p. 227 above].

[6] *PAAPA*, p. 275; *Mind*, p. 199 [p. 227 above].

[7] *PAAPA*, p. 281. In the *Mind* version, the quoted material has been slightly altered: 'to see that there indeed is a place *within* morality for the idea of better and worse states of affairs' (*Mind*, p. 206) [p. 237 above].

that in many situations the person who has this virtue will be able to think of good and bad states of affairs in terms of the general good.'[8] Thus, for example, if there is 'a question of riding out to rescue a small number or a large number then benevolence would urge that the larger number be saved'.[9] What Foot wants to argue, however, is the following. Although someone who possesses the virtue of benevolence will indeed be disposed to promote good states of affairs in certain circumstances, benevolence is not the only virtue. Justice, for example, is also a virtue. And there are various rules and requirements that the person who possesses the virtue of justice must observe: rules of distributive justice, truth telling, respect for rights, and so on. Rules and requirements such as these restrict the area 'in which benevolence is free to pursue its ends';[10] for 'sometimes justice will forbid a certain action, . . . and then it will not be possible to ask whether "the state of affairs" containing the action and its result will be better or worse than the one in which the action is not done. The action is one that *cannot* be done because justice forbids it, and nothing that has this moral character comes within the scope of the kind of comparison of total outcomes that benevolence may sometimes require.'[11]

Now by itself the claim that an unjust action falls outside 'the scope of the kind of comparison of total outcomes that benevolence may sometimes require' is not entirely unambiguous. One might wonder whether it means that no meaningful comparison of outcomes is *possible* in cases where one of the outcomes would

---

[8] *PAAPA*, pp. 281–2. In *Mind*, the corresponding passage reads: 'That there is such a place is true if only because the proper end of benevolence is the good of others, and because in many situations the person who has this virtue will be able to think of good and bad states of affairs, in terms of the general good' (*Mind*, p. 206) [p. 237 above].

[9] *PAAPA*, p. 282. In the *Mind* version, the phrase 'we may suppose' has been inserted between 'would' and 'urge'. See *Mind*, p. 206 [p. 238 above].

[10] *PAAPA*, p. 282. This phrase does not appear in the *Mind* version, but the view I am describing surely does.

[11] *PAAPA*, p. 282. In *Mind*, the corresponding passage reads: 'sometimes justice will forbid a certain action, . . . and then it will not be possible to ask whether "the state of affairs" containing the action and its result will be better or worse than one in which the action is not done. The action is one that *cannot* be done, because justice forbids it, and nothing that has this moral character comes within the scope of the kind of comparison of total outcomes that benevolence may sometimes require' (*Mind*, p. 206) [p. 237 above].

result from an unjust action, or whether it means instead that since one must not perform the unjust action in any case, it is inappropriate actually to *carry out* the relevant comparison of overall outcomes. However, the following passage from the earlier version of Foot's paper suggests that it is the first interpretation that more nearly reflects her thinking:

When we . . . give expressions such as 'best outcome' and 'good state of affairs' no special meaning in moral contexts other than the one that the virtues give them, we shall no longer think the paradoxical thought that it is sometimes right to act in such a way that the total outcome, consisting of one's action and its results, is less good than some other accessible at the time. What the non-consequentialist should say is that 'good state of affairs' is an expression which has a very limited use in these contexts. It belongs in cases in which benevolence is free to pursue its ends, and chooses among possibilities . . . But the expression has no meaning when we try to use it to say something about a whole consisting of what we would illicitly do, allow, or wish for, together with its consequences. In the abstract a benevolent person must wish that loss and harm should be minimized. He does not, however, wish that the whole consisting of a killing to minimize killings should be actualized either by his own agency or that of anyone else. So there is no reason on this score to say that he must regard it as the 'better state of affairs'. And therefore there is no reason for the non-consequentialist, whose thought of good and bad states of affairs in moral contexts comes only from the virtues themselves, to describe the refusal as a choice of a worse state of affairs. If he does so describe it he will be giving the words the sense they have in his opponents' theories, and it is not surprising that he should find himself in their hands.[12]

The view expressed in this passage seems to be that comparisons of overall states of affairs in moral contexts can only be meaningfully made when action aimed at promoting the good of others is called for, that such action is forbidden in cases where it would transgress some rule of justice, and that in cases of this kind it is not possible meaningfully to say that the prohibited action would produce a better overall state of affairs than the alternative. Now in the later version of her paper, Foot has eliminated that portion of the passage just quoted which begins with the words

[12] *PAAPA*, p. 282.

'What the non-consequentialist should say' and ends with the words 'together with its consequences', thus withdrawing the explicit claim that the expression 'good state of affairs' has no meaning when the outcome of an unjust act is in question. Nevertheless, the broad outlines of her position remain unchanged. She continues to maintain that while comparisons of states of affairs in moral contexts can meaningfully be made when benevolent action is called for, the claim that some unjust act would result in a better overall state of affairs than any of the available alternatives lacks any clear sense in ordinary non-consequentialist moral thought. And, she argues, while consequentialist theories may *give* it a sense, someone who has not already accepted one of those theories has no reason to believe that there *are* better and worse states of affairs in the consequentialist's sense.[13] Thus, Foot believes, the air of paradox surrounding non-consequentialist views that include agent-centred restrictions can be dispelled. For what seems paradoxical about those views, according to Foot, is that they appear to claim that we must sometimes produce a worse overall outcome instead of a better one. And if she is right, this appearance can be shown to be illusory. There will of course be situations in which the *consequentialist will describe the non-consequentialist* as insisting that we must produce a worse overall outcome rather than a better one. But the non-consequentialist can, if Foot is right, deny that that description has any ordinary meaning in such situations. The non-consequentialist can thus maintain that either the consequentialist is talking nonsense, or else he is supplying his words with some special meaning derived from his own theory, in which case he is begging the question against the non-consequentialist.

There seem to me, however, to be three reasons for doubting whether Foot has really succeeded in dispelling the air of paradox surrounding agent-centred restrictions. First, I am sceptical of the idea that, in ordinary non-consequentialist moral discourse, evaluations of overall states of affairs are meaningful when

---

[13] The expression 'good state of affairs from a moral point of view', she writes in the second version of her paper, 'may mean nothing; and it may lack a reference when a special consequentialist theory has given it a sense' (*Mind*, p. 204) [p. 235 above].

benevolent action is called for, but meaningless when the outcome of an unjust action is in question. People who deny that such evaluations *ever* make sense typically do so because they do not believe that the benefits and harms of different human beings can be meaningfully summed. But this worry about aggregation does not seem to be what concerns Foot, since she is happy to speak, for example, of 'the important place that the idea of maximum welfare has in morality'.[14] And, as we have seen, she wants to claim, not that evaluations of states of affairs never make sense in moral contexts, but only that they may lose their sense whenever the candidate for assessment is the outcome of an unjust act. But do we really cease to understand what is meant by 'a better state of affairs' if the question is raised whether infringing a right or telling a lie or treating a particular individual unfairly might perhaps produce a better state of affairs than failing to do so? I do not think so. Many moral dilemmas take the form of conflicts between considerations of justice, rights, or fairness on the one hand, and considerations of aggregate well-being on the other. And it seems to me quite natural to characterize the dilemmatic feature of a situation of this kind by saying, for example, that one is faced with a problem because violating someone's rights would in this case produce better results on the whole than would respecting them. I do not think that it is only consequentialists who think of matters in these terms, and unless it can be shown that there is something incoherent about *any* interpersonal aggregation of benefits and burdens, I see no reason to deny us this way of speaking and conceiving of the matter.

Second, in order for Foot's attempt to dissolve the apparent paradox surrounding agent-centred restrictions to be successful, it must be the case that the alleged paradox cannot be formulated without using the idea of one overall state of affairs being better than another. But, as my initial characterization of the paradox at the beginning of this paper was meant to suggest, it can in fact be formulated without using the notion of an 'overall state of affairs' at all. How, I asked, can it be rational to forbid the performance of a morally objectionable action that will have the effect of

---

[14] *PAAPA*, p. 282; *Mind*, p. 206 [p. 238 above].

minimizing the total number of comparably objectionable actions that are performed and will have no other morally relevant consequences? How can the minimization of morally objectionable conduct itself be morally unacceptable? Even if, for the sake of argument, we grant Foot's claim that the idea of one overall state of affairs being better than another lacks any clear non-consequentialist sense in cases of injustice, *these* questions can still be formulated and understood, and the answers to them still do not seem obvious. Even if Foot's claim is granted, the defender of agent-centred restrictions can hardly say that it is meaningless to assert that circumstances can arise in which a certain moral rule will be violated several times unless I violate it once. And while he can, if Foot's claim is granted, deny that it is meaningful to say that the state of affairs containing several violations is worse than the state of affairs containing just one violation, I do not believe that we need the latter claim in order to see the agent-centred prohibition as puzzling. All we need is the recognition that fewer violations will occur if I act one way rather than another, together with the idea that such violations are morally objectionable, in the rather unambitious sense that it is morally preferable that no such violations should occur than that any should. And while Foot may in fact want to reject even this weaker idea, I believe, as I shall argue in a few pages, that the costs of doing so are prohibitive.

Third, although Foot begins her paper by acknowledging that 'utilitarianism tends to haunt even those of us who will not believe in it',[15] and although her paper is meant as an 'exorcism',[16] an attempt to rid consequentialism of its 'spellbinding force', the way in which she ultimately tries to do this is such as to make it seem mysterious how consequentialism was ever taken seriously in the first place, let alone viewed as spellbinding. For if, in asking how it can ever be right 'to prefer a worse state of affairs to a better',[17] the consequentialist is either talking nonsense or else using the language of his own theory instead of the language that the rest of us speak, how is it that we find his question troubling, haunting? After all, if Foot is right, it is not clear that we even understand the

[15] *PAAPA*, p. 273; *Mind*, p. 196 [p. 224 above].
[16] *PAAPA*, p. 273; *Mind*, p. 196 [p. 224 above].
[17] *PAAPA*, p. 275; *Mind*, p. 198 [p. 227 above].

question. So wherein lies its power to haunt us? I do not believe that Foot's view allows any adequate answer to this question, and for this reason if for no other her position seems to me worrisome.

Although I do not agree with the idea that attempts to make agent-centred restrictions seem paradoxical are question-begging, or with the idea that we will find views that include such restrictions paradoxical only if we have already conceded the truth of consequentialism in accepting the description of those views that is supposed to generate the difficulty, I think I understand one reason why these ideas seem tempting. Moreover, although I do not agree with them, I think that there is *something* right about them, and that in an appreciation of what is right about them lies the key to any adequate defence of agent-centred restrictions. These ideas seem tempting partly, I believe, because we have the sense that in finding the restrictions paradoxical, we are relying on a conception of rationality that seems to lie at the heart of consequentialism, and that if accepted seems inevitably to make the restrictions look problematic. And there is a way in which this is right. The reason that it is nevertheless not question-begging to say that the restrictions seem paradoxical is that although the conception of rationality that generates the appearance of paradox lies at the heart of consequentialism, it is not peculiar to consequentialism. On the contrary, it is a fundamental and familiar conception of rationality that we accept and operate with in a very wide and varied range of contexts. The fact that this powerful conception of rationality seems both to lie at the heart of consequentialism and to generate the sense that agent-centred restrictions are paradoxical does not show that the restrictions will only seem paradoxical to us if we have already, wittingly or unwittingly, accepted consequentialism. It shows rather that the 'spellbinding force' of consequentialism, its capacity to haunt even those who do not accept it, derives from the fact that it appears to embody a notion of rationality which we recognize from myriad diverse contexts, and whose power we have good independent reason to respect. It also shows that the seeming paradox of agent-centred restrictions goes deep; no questions need be begged to find the apparent clash between the morality of common sense and the rationality of common sense troubling, haunting, difficult to ignore or dismiss. At the same time it suggests that a fully satisfying defence of agent-centred restrictions could take one of two forms. It might, first, consist in showing that the conflict between such restrictions and the kind of rationality they seem to defy is only apparent: that, appearances to the contrary notwithstanding, the restrictions can be reconciled with that familiar form of rationality. Or it might, alternatively, consist in showing that the restrictions embody a limitation on the scope of that form of rationality, and give expression to a different form of rationality which we also recognize and which also has its place in our lives.

The kind of rationality that consequentialism seems so clearly to embody, and which makes so much trouble for views that incorporate agent-centred restrictions, is what we may call *maximizing* rationality. The core of this conception of rationality is the idea that if one accepts the desirability of a certain goal being achieved, and if one has a choice between two options, one of which is certain to accomplish the goal better than the other, then it is, *ceteris paribus*, rational to choose the former over the latter. Consequentialism seems to embody this kind of rationality because it starts from a conception of what is desirable (the overall good) and then tells us always to promote as much of it as we can. Views that incorporate agent-centred restrictions, by contrast, seem troubling, relative to this notion of rationality. For they appear to identify certain kinds of actions as morally objectionable or undesirable, in the sense that it is morally preferable that no such actions should occur than that any should. but then tell us that there are situations in which we must act in such a way that a greater rather than a lesser number of these actions are actually performed.

There is, of course, nothing within maximizing rationality itself that requires us to accept the consequentialist's choice of goals. and so although consequentialism embodies that form of rationality, it is not the only normative theory of action that does so. For example egoism, construed here as the view that one ought always to pursue one's *own* greatest advantage, also embodies maximizing rationality. Indeed common-sense deontological morality, standing between egoism and consequentialism, sometimes seems to be caught in a kind of normative squeeze, with its rationality challenged in parallel ways by (as it were) the maximizers of the right and of the left: those who think that one ought always to pursue one's own good, and those who are convinced that one should promote the good of all.

I said a moment ago that a satisfying defence of agent-centred restrictions could take one of two forms. The first would be to show that, appearances to the contrary notwithstanding, there really is no conflict between such restrictions and maximizing rationality. Thus it might be denied, to start with, that views incorporating agent-centred restrictions actually do present as desirable any goal whose maximum accomplishment they then prohibit. They assign each person the agent-relative goal of not violating any restrictions himself, it might be said, but they do not present the overall non-occurrence of such violations as desirable. Thus in forbidding the minimization of overall violations, they are not in fact thwarting the achievement of any goal whose desirability they recognize.

Now I do not believe that defenders of standard *deontological* views are really in a position to make these claims. The difficulty is that such views do, as I have suggested, seem committed to the idea that violations of the restrictions are morally objectionable or undesirable, in the sense that there is a moral point of view from which it is preferable that no violations should occur than that any should. Defenders of deontological views are typically happy to say things like this, and with good reason. For on standard deontological views, morality evaluates actions from a vantage-point which is concerned with more than just the interests of the individual agent. In other words, an action will be right or wrong, on such a view, relative to a standard of assessment that takes into account a number of factors quite independent of the interests of the agent. And defenders of such views are unlikely to claim that the relevant standard of assessment includes agent-centred restrictions, but that it is a matter of indifference, from the vantage-point represented by that standard, whether or not those restrictions are violated. For if it is not the case that it is preferable, from *that* vantage-point, that no violations should occur than that any should, it is hard to see how individual agents could possibly be thought to have reason to observe the restrictions when doing so did not happen to coincide with their own interests or the interests of those they cared about. In other words, deontological views need the idea that violations of the restrictions are morally objectionable or undesirable if the claim that people ought not to commit such violations when doing so would be in their own interests is to be plausible. Yet if such views do regard violations as morally objectionable or undesirable, in the sense that it is morally preferable that none should occur than that any should, it does then seem paradoxical that they tell us there are times when we must act in such a way that a larger rather than a smaller number of violations actually takes place. Notice that egoism, by contrast, *does* seem committed exclusively to agent-relative goals. It assigns each person the agent-relative goal of maximizing his own advantage. And since it does not purport to assess actions from a point of view which is concerned with more than just the interests of the individual agent, it is not committed in the way deontology is to presenting as desirable any non-relative goal whose maximum accomplishment it then prohibits. That is why *it does not for a moment seem paradoxical for the egoist to say that one ought to maximize one's own advantage even if that means that fewer people overall will be able to maximize theirs.*

Thus defenders of standard deontological views do not appear to be in a position to make the claim that, in forbidding us to minimize the violation of those restrictions they insist on, they are not thwarting the achievement of any goal whose desirability they recognize. The situation may be different, however, with other kinds of non-consequentialist views. In particular, someone who accepts a view like Foot's may be in a position to make this claim more plausibly. For if agent-centred restrictions are seen as restrictions that those who possess certain virtues will be disposed to observe, and if these virtues are thought of as traits of character whose possession enables a person to live the kind of life that is good for him,[18] then it may perhaps be denied that the commitment to agent-centred restrictions involves any commit-

----

[18] I am not in fact sure that Foot herself would be prepared to say this. (See footnote 20 below.) But the argument I am imagining in defence of agent-centred restrictions depends on a willingness to say it. And as indicated in footnote 19 below, that argument seems in obvious respects to be rather in the spirit of Foot's overall position.

ment to assessing actions from a 'moral point of view' which is concerned with something more than just the interests of the individual agent.[19] Such a denial would reveal a significant difference between this kind of view and standard deontological views, and it would make the assignment of a central role to the virtues essential to the defence of agent-centred restrictions; but it would also carry with it a commitment to the idea that actions are right or wrong—if at all—relative to a standard of assessment that does not ultimately take anything but the well-being of the agent into account. Thus, perhaps, what would be wrong with injustice, lying, and the like would be, roughly, that the disposition to engage in such activities does not contribute to a good life for the agent, and that the disposition not to does. But this, it seems to me, rather glaringly fails to capture our actual sense of what is ordinarily wrong with these things. Even if we agree that the disposition to behave unjustly does not in fact contribute to the agent's ability to live a life that is good for him, we are unlikely to agree that that is the only reason injustice is wrong. It may be objected that the kind of view under discussion is best understood as claiming, not that certain kinds of actions are wrong because the disposition to perform them does not contribute to the living of a good life by the agent, but rather that the disposition to perform them does not contribute to the living of a good life by the agent because they are wrong (by some independent standard).[20]

[19] Such a denial would of course be entirely consistent with Foot's general scepticism, expressed in both versions of her paper, about the phrase 'the moral point of view'. It would, I think, also be in keeping with the spirit of the following passage from the second version: 'Perhaps no . . . *shared end* appears in the foundations of ethics, where we may rather find individual ends and rational compromises between those who have them. Or perhaps at the most basic level lie facts about the way individual human beings can find the greatest goods which they are capable of possessing' (*Mind*, p. 209) [p. 241 above].

[20] Judging from various of Foot's other published works, it is not clear that *she* would want to make *either* of these claims. For in some of her more recent writings she has expressed increasing doubts about the closeness of the connection between one's possession of the virtues and one's good. (See, for example, her introduction to *Virtues and Vices*, her paper 'Morality as a System of Hypothetical Imperatives' (reprinted in *Virtues and Vices*), and the final footnote in the version of 'Moral Beliefs' that appears in the same volume.) Without something like the first claim, however, the defence of agent-centred restrictions that I have been sketching does not get off the ground. And as I indicated in the preceding note, Foot does seem to have more than a little sympathy for at least some elements of that defence.

Understood in this way, however, the view loses its ability to avoid the deontologist's predicament. For it no longer claims that the standard relative to which actions are right or wrong is one that takes nothing but the well-being of those who perform them into account. It thus loses its ability to disclaim any commitment to the idea of assessing actions from a point of view which is concerned with more than just the interests of the individual agent, and hence to the idea that there is a moral point of view from which it is preferable that no violations of the restrictions should occur than that any should. And so it loses its ability to make the claim that, in forbidding the minimization of overall violations, it is not thwarting the achievement of any goal whose desirability it recognizes.

As an alternative to trying to make that claim, someone who wanted to show that there was no conflict between agent-centred restrictions and maximizing rationality might point out that, if the *ceteris paribus* clause in the formulation of maximizing rationality were fully cashed out, one of its main features would be a provision to the effect that it can sometimes be rational to act in such a way as to worse achieve one goal if that will make it possible to better achieve another. Since that is so, it might be said, views that include agent-centred restrictions need not come into conflict with maximizing rationality when they tell us to further the agent-relative goal of not violating the restrictions ourselves at the expense of the non-relative goal of minimizing violations of the restrictions. By itself, however, this claim is not fully persuasive. The problem is that the agent-relative goal and the non-relative goal appear to be related to each other in such a way as to make the insistence on giving priority to the relative goal puzzling, from the standpoint of maximizing rationality. Since, as our earlier discussion suggested, the fact that violations of the restrictions are objectionable from a moral point of view constitutes at least part of the basis for claiming that individual agents ought not ordinarily to commit such violations, the agent-relative goal looks as if it is derivative from, and given life by, the non-relative objection, and does not appear to represent something independently desirable. Rather, the desirability of achieving the agent-relative goal seems contingent on its serving to advance the non-relative goal of minimizing the morally objectionable. And if that is so, then the insistence that one must satisfy the agent-relative goal even when doing so will inhibit achievement of the non-relative goal is incompatible with considerations of maximization.

The project of reconciling agent-centred restrictions with maximizing rationality thus faces the following difficulty. On the one hand, as I have already argued, the compatibility of such restrictions with that form of rationality cannot be satisfactorily established by dispensing altogether with the idea of a moral point of view. For if one dispenses with that idea, one cannot do justice to our sense of what is ordinarily wrong with the conduct that the restrictions prohibit. Nor, as I have also argued, can the compatibility of the restrictions with maximizing rationality be established by accepting the notion that morality evaluates actions from a point of view that is concerned with more than just the interests of the individual agent, but denying that violations of the restrictions are objectionable or undesirable from that point of view. For if one accepts the former notion, then one needs the claim that violations are morally objectionable or undesirable in order to explain why individuals ought not to commit such violations when doing so would be in their own interests. On the other hand, however, the argument of the preceding paragraph suggests that, if the compatibility of agent-centred restrictions and maximizing rationality is to be established, neither can it be conceded that the *entire basis* for the restrictions is the objectionableness from the moral point of view of the behaviour they prohibit. For if one makes that concession, then the requirement that the agent-relative goal be given priority over the non-relative goal cannot be reconciled with considerations of maximization. To show that agent-centred restrictions are compatible with maximizing rationality, therefore, one must agree that the behaviour they rule out is morally objectionable or undesirable, but deny that that very objectionableness constitutes the entire rationale for the restrictions. And then, of course, one must supply the remainder of the rationale.

One idea, along these lines, would be to argue that agent-centred restrictions serve some independent maximizing purpose. Thus it might be said, for example, that the inclusion of such restrictions enables a moral conception to give more weight than consequentialism does to some important fact or consideration: some natural feature of persons, perhaps. In *The Rejection of Consequentialism* I tried to use a strategy of roughly this kind to motivate an 'agent-centred prerogative', a prerogative allowing each agent to devote energy and attention to his own projects and commitments out of proportion to the weight in any impersonal calculus of his doing so. If my argument there was correct, such a strategy can thus be used to explain why one is not always *required* to give the non-relative goal of minimizing overall violations priority over the agent-relative goal of avoiding violations oneself. At the same time, I indicated that I myself do not see how, specifically, to deploy such a strategy in defence of agent-centred restrictions: in defence of the view that one is not always *permitted* to give the non-relative goal priority over the relative one. I do not, in other words, see how to make a convincing case that there is some particular important fact or consideration to which a moral theory gives sufficient weight only if it includes agent-centred restrictions. Obviously, however, that is hardly conclusive, and this strategy continues to represent a means by which it might be possible to reconcile agent-centred restrictions and maximizing rationality, thereby dispelling the apparent paradox attached to the restrictions.

Of course, even if no reconciliation were possible, that would not show that agent-centred restrictions are indefensible. As I said earlier, a satisfying defence of the restrictions could take either of two forms. Reconciliation with maximizing rationality would be one sort of defence. But it is, after all, not obvious that maximizing rationality constitutes the whole of rationality. And if in fact there were no way to defend agent-centred restrictions while remaining within the framework of maximizing rationality, then the alternative for a defender of the restrictions would be to try to show that they embody a departure from maximization which is licensed by the more comprehensive tapestry of full human rationality. In other words, the task would be to try to set the restrictions convincingly within the broad contours of practical rationality as we understand it.

Now it might be thought that this task could be easily

dispatched. After all, if it really is true that, as I said earlier, agent-centred restrictions are congenial to the common-sense morality of our culture, and if the restrictions thus embody constraints on practical reasoning that seem to us natural and intuitively appealing, then that might be thought sufficient to show that they do in fact have their place within what we are prepared to recognize as human practical rationality, even if they represent a departure from maximization. This idea may not in fact be so very different from what Foot wishes to maintain. The difficulty with this quick solution is that the appearance that the restrictions are *irrational* is generated by an apparently appropriate application of a very powerful form of thought which itself occupies a central place within what we recognize as human practical rationality. The seeming paradox arises out of a process of reasoning that itself seems natural and intuitively compelling, and not through the introduction of some theoretically attractive but humanly unrecognizable model of rationality. Thus to dispel the paradox and give a satisfying account of the place of the restrictions within full human rationality, more must be done than simply to call attention to their naturalness and appeal. For to do no more than that is to leave in place all of those elements which combine to create the impression that, in so far as it is drawn to agent-centred restrictions, human practical reason may be at war with itself.

Viewed from one perspective, it may seem odd that agent-centred restrictions should be thought to have a specially insecure relationship to considerations of practical rationality. For such restrictions are often thought of as broadly Kantian in spirit, and it is Kant, along with Aristotle, who is most closely associated with the idea that moral norms are rooted in the structure of practical reason. The oddity may be lessened somewhat if we remember that the normative view whose rationality is in question, although standardly referred to as Kantian, represents at most one aspect of Kant's own view. Roughly speaking, we can distinguish the following elements, among others, in Kant's moral thought: a view about the nature of moral motivation (an act done purely from inclination lacks any genuine moral worth), a view about the constraints imposed by reason on the maxim of an action (the categorical imperative procedure), and a view about the substantive moral norms derivable from the categorical imperative. If there is a genuinely Kantian view being challenged here, it is this: that it is possible to interpret the categorical imperative in such a way that it is plausibly thought of both as a requirement of practical reason and as supporting agent-centred restrictions in particular. This leaves much of what Kant thought about the relation of morality and rationality untouched. At the same time, the question it does raise is one to which the answer, I think, is not at all clear.

12

THE AUTHORITY OF THE
MORAL AGENT

CONRAD D. JOHNSON

RECENT moral philosophy shows much interest in the problem of how deontological constraints are to be reconciled with consequentialism.[1] On the other hand, there is the intuition that there are certain things it is simply wrong for an individual to do, even if violating the prohibitions would produce better consequences. On the other hand, moral prohibitions themselves are not above critical scrutiny, and, when we turn to this enterprise, consequentialism broadly conceived has a powerful claim; for how else are we to evaluate and possibly revise our conception of morally right behaviour if not by reflecting on the consequences?

Trouble develops when we try to reconcile deontological intuitions with consequentialist insights. Some versions of rule utilitarianism have seemed promising at first, but dissatisfaction returns when we try to give a careful explanation of the relationship between the rules that are utilitarianly justified and the particular actions that one is called upon to do. When it is absolutely clear to the agent in a particular case that following the rule will have worse consequences than breaking it, even though the rule is in general the best, is it morally right to break the rule? If the rule is conceived as merely cautionary and simplifying, then there is no argument against bypassing it in a particular case in

Conrad D. Johnson, 'The Authority of the Moral Agent', *Journal of Philosophy* 82, No. 8 (August 1985), pp. 391–413. Reprinted by permission of the Editors of the Journal of Philosophy and the author.

[1] See, for example, the recent book by S. Scheffler, *The Rejection of Consequentialism*. See also T. Nagel, *Mortal Questions* (New York: Cambridge, 1979), Ch. 14; and 'The Limits of Objectivity'; and R. M. Hare, *Moral Thinking*, esp. chs. 1–3. Parenthetic references to these authors will refer to these books.

which the situation is wholly clear and the calculation has already taken place or was unnecessary. On the other hand, if the rule is conceived as having some independent authority, then what is the nature of this independent authority? The rule-bound or super-stitious person might adhere to the rule for its own sake, but the rational person would not.[2]

If we follow the usual deontological conception, there are also well-known difficulties. If it is simply wrong to kill the innocent, the wrongness must in some way be connected to the consequences. *That* an innocent person is killed must be a consequence that has some important bearing on the wrongness of the action; else why be so concerned about the killing of an innocent? Further, if it is wrong in certain cases for the agent to weigh the consequences in deciding whether to kill or to break a promise, it is hard to deny that this has some connection to the consequences. Following one line of thought, it is consequentialist considerations of mistrust that stand behind such restrictions on what the agent may take into account.[3] But then again it is hard to deal with that rare case in which the agent can truly claim that his judgement about the consequences is accurate, or, in that last resort of the philosophical thought experiment, has been verified by the Infallible Optimizer

[2] Even a very recent and sophisticated rule utilitarianism like Richard Brandt's is open to this objection. Brandt defines 'is morally wrong' as 'would be prohibited by any moral code which all fully rational persons would tend to support, in preference to all others or to none at all, for the society of the agent, if they expected to spend a life-time in that society'. (See *A Theory of the Good and the Right*, p. 194.) Though it is indeed important to take into account the various costs of teaching a moral code and getting it suitably internalized, the individual agent in a particular case is still faced with the question, 'Ought I to go for the best consequences in this case even though to do so would violate the Brandtian-best moral *code*? Given that the consequences are the ultimate determinant of right and wrong, and the moral code is only "an instrument" (p. 196) to this end, why not?' The *definition* (as Brandt regards it) of right as linked to rules of a hypothetical ideal code still leaves unexplained why, if at all, the agent's practical reasoning in particular cases must exclude direct appeal to the consequences.

On the general problem for traditional rule-utilitarian accounts, see J. Raz, 'Promises and Obligations', in P. M. S. Hacker and Raz, eds., *Law, Morality, and Society* (New York: Oxford, 1977), esp. pp. 200–1.

[3] See T. Scanlon, 'Rights, Goals, and Fairness', in S. Hampshire, ed., *Public and Private Morality* (New York: Cambridge, 1978), pp. 93–111 [reprinted in this volume as Chapter 4—Ed.].

(Scheffler, ch. 3). These counter-examples are a challenge, not because they are at all likely, but because they test our intuitions. The deontological conviction in even the more hard-bitten consequentialists among us seeks a deeper foundation than any prevailing and sufficiently consequentialist account is able to give.

In the following, I attempt to construct an alternative model on which we can conceptualize the deontological limits on the moral agent's authority while at the same time allowing for a fundamentally consequentialist account even of the rationale standing behind those very constraints. However, it is no part of my purpose to defend consequentialism as such, but rather to remove what is thought to be a major objection to the reconciliation of consequentialism with agent-constraints. The main idea is to pursue further a legal analogy already used by others (most notably John Rawls[4]): the distinction between the roles of judge and of legislator.

I

Thomas Nagel and Samuel Scheffler take up the following kind of challenge, as raised by Robert Nozick. Suppose that an agent, A_1 is confronted with the choice either (i) to violate a restriction R, thus causing some disvalue N_1 or (ii) *not* to violate the restriction, thus causing some greater disvalue of the same kind $N_1 + N_2$. For example, A_1 must choose between killing an innocent person or, as a consequence of inaction, allowing five other equally innocent persons to be killed. Notice that the problem can be formulated using whatever you wish as an account of good and bad consequences. If killing someone is bad because unfair, or a violation of their rights, then the problem emerges when the alternative is that so many more people are unfairly killed, or have their rights violated. If the evil is that someone is killed by the *action* of an agent A_1, then the problem arises again if the alternative is that five people are killed by the actions of agents $A_2, \ldots A_6$. Like Scheffler, we can also conceive of consequen-

[4] 'Two Concepts of Rules', *Philosophical Review* 64, 1 (Jan. 1955), 3–32, reprinted in M. D. Bayles, ed., *Contemporary Utilitarianism* (Garden City, NY: Anchor, 1968), p. 59; parenthetical page references to this article will be to Bayles.

tialism as involving an impersonal ranking of states of affairs, and it does not really matter for our purposes if we rank states of affairs using a distribution-sensitive theory of the good. So by consequentialism we are not restricted to any ordinary utilitarianism. But the problem of providing a rationale for the agent-centred restriction remains (see Scheffler, ch. 4).

One kind of levels conception of moral thinking (see Hare, *Moral Thinking*) proceeds by explaining that there are good consequentialist reasons for developing a deeply engrained *compunction* against violating the restriction, and that it is entirely proper for a moral agent to hesitate, to think long and hard before acting, and then to feel guilty on violating the restriction, even though the action might in retrospect be accounted right. Yet this observation, interesting and important as it is for some purposes, does not speak precisely to the question that the deontologist poses. For the deontological intuition is that there is something (at least *something*—we leave open how absolute and conclusive it is) wrong about this action itself, and it is not simply that moral agents do or ought to *feel* some way or other before or after such an action.

Another approach is to distinguish, as Nagel does, between the 'subjective' and the 'objective', the first being the agent-centred, deontological point of view, and the second being the impersonal, consequentialist point of view. We cannot reduce the deontological point of view to the consequentialist, Nagel thinks; nor can we properly eliminate the one or the other. Nagel's preferred alternative is 'to resist the voracity of the objective appetite, and to stop assuming that understanding of the world and our position in it can always be advanced by detaching from that position and subsuming whatever appears from there under a single more comprehensive conception' (211). But this approach, though I am in no position here to do it full justice, seems to me to be unnecessarily mysterious. There is a more plausible model available which provides for the reconciliation.

This model is provided by the law. In the moral analogue, the agent-centred restriction operates as a kind of limitation on the *authority* of the agent, and there is an important clue in the way that our deontological side is apt to react to the individual who chooses to kill one innocent person in order to save five other innocents: such a person is 'playing God'. This complaint is often metaphorical, to be sure. But the core idea is that the agent in question does not have the *authority* to do what he or she has done; the agent is illegitimately taking another role or office. The focus is not on the result that the agent has brought about. Indeed, the result may be the best given that unfortunate situation. The focus, rather, is on the illegitimacy of exercising an authority that one does not have.

One familiar understanding of the judge's role is that the judge decides cases only in accordance with pre-existing law. The legislator properly enacts law by reflecting on what legislation would best advance some complex of goals G. The judge, confronted with the necessity of making a decision in a dispute between two parties, must then follow the enacted legislation even if departing from the legislation would in this instance promote G better than strict adherence. There is, hence, at least a built-in presumptive exclusionary reason[5] for limiting the relevance of G-orientated reasons in reaching a decision. Depending on the authority we conceive a judge to have, however, this presumption may sometimes be outweighed if the G-orientated reasons are strong enough.

It would be mistaken to conceive of this restriction on judicial authority as *self*-imposed. It is not that, after taking into account all consequentialist considerations, judges conclude that they have an obligation to decide cases by applying the law rather than to depart from the law in order to advance G; it is rather that the office brings such restrictions with it, so that the very idea of acting in that capacity involves the understood limits. The imposition of restrictions has its source in an *external* authority, however that authority is to be conceived and however the judge's own ultimate participation in that external authority is to be understood. The matter would be very different if the obligation to decide in accordance with the law were wholly self-imposed. That would imply that the obligation (if it could be properly so called) is open

---

[5] I borrow the idea of an exclusionary reason from Raz, *Practical Reason and Norms* (London: Hutchinson, 1975), ch. 1, sec. 2.

to review and revision by the judge and for the same consequentialist reasons upon which it was grounded in the first place.

Another way of seeing the difference is to think of two quite different responses that a judge might give to the question, 'Why are you not completely free to depart from existing legislation in order to promote the goals for which that legislation was enacted?' Answer 1: 'Because the overall consequences of such a judicial freedom would be worse than a restriction.' Answer 2: 'Because, given the office I hold, it is not within my competence to do so.' Answer 1 invites reconsideration of the consequences in particular cases, on the supposition that, from the point of view of justification, the judicial obligation can always be cashed in *by the judge* for its consequential equivalent, then to be accepted or rejected according to the appropriate principles. Answer 1 thus presupposes that the judicial obligation is a matter for the judge to determine by a correct assessment of the consequences. Although both answers are consistent with a consequentialist conception of obligation, (1) supposes that the obligation is self-imposed, and (2) does not. One who gives the first answer reveals a different conception of the judge's relationship to fundamental justifying reasons than does one who gives the second answer.

The legal analogy has the advantage of making it abundantly clear how normative reasoning *can* take place according to a kind of division of labour, and thus be constrained. So even if consequentialist reasons are the only ultimate reasons that are valid, it does not, without more, follow that all individuals are free in all situations to employ those reasons in deciding how to act, even if their reasoning could be guaranteed to be in all other respects correct. (So, for example, even if we could guarantee the accuracy of the judge's assessment that failure to apply the law would better serve G, it would be wrong for the judge to act on that assessment.)

II

It may seem that this conception of restrictions on the moral agent's authority, when combined with a consequentialist account of the fundamental level, is merely a familiar form of rule consequentialism involving an unusually broad notion of what the utilities can be. But this is not so. Indeed, the residual problem in rule-utilitarian accounts has been the difficulty of explaining what independent status a rule can have for the moral agent, even if we assume that the utilitarian justification for the rule itself is beyond reproach. Thus even Rawls's account, though it uses the judge/legislator distinction, lacks an explanation of why the agent is to follow the rule when doing so in a particular instance conflicts with the very reason for the rule.

An example should help to illustrate the point. Discussing Rawls, David Lyons[6] considers the possibility that the *de facto* rules governing promising might be utilitarianly defective in some way:

> It is defective from a strictly utilitarian point of view: better results would flow from the observance (in general, or in particular cases) of a different set of rules. But if this is so, and if external assessments are based upon utility, then the criticism of the rules cannot be dismissed on logical grounds. Since the practice as a whole is subject to utilitarian criticism, what reason is there for observing the rules—at least in those cases in which observance of the rules conflicts with the directions of utility? (185)

Lyons is right in claiming that we cannot dismiss the criticism of rules on logical grounds alone. But the question ('what reason is there . . .?'), left begging for an answer, reflects a widely prevailing and false presupposition about the authority of the moral agent. The presupposition is that, in every decision and judgement the moral agent is to make, it is in principle permitted (and perhaps required) for the agent to go back to the most fundamental justifying basis of rules in order better to serve the fundamental ends, the only constraint being that the agent's reasoning be correct. Put in another way, it is the view that the set of considerations making an agent-restriction rational must also be an adequate set of considerations making it rational in any situation for the agent to adopt and act on that restriction. As Lyons puts it on the same page, in such cases following the rule does not have the best result, so the rules 'have no utilitarian backing'. Given this view, the whole foundation of right is at all

[6] *Forms and Limits of Utilitarianism.*

times within the agent's purview, and even constraints resting on that foundation are in principle always open to reconsideration.

Why is it so easy to make this assumption about the wide competence of the moral agent, even though a similar assumption about the authority of a judge in a legal system would be at least highly questionable? The answer, I think, lies in two directions. One motivation is the desire for simplicity and purity of moral theory. If one is going to embrace consequentialism, the thought runs, then the most consistent and pure form is an act consequentialism, or at least (and this seems to amount to the same thing) a rule consequentialism that allows for revisability whenever the consequences call for it.[7] Why purity in this sense is so frequently thought to be required is (to me at least) a mystery.

Another motivation appears in the most common of all objections to rule utilitarianism: to be committed to a rule even when the rule conflicts with its justifying principle is simply irrational rule worship. One might be able to explain the *psychological* fact that a rule becomes a sort of idol, but that does nothing to commend adherence to a philosopher.[8]

On the division-of-labour conception, properly and robustly construed, moral reasoning takes place within a framework in which the moral agent is confronted with a genuinely external authority which has the authority, within some bounds, to limit the competence[9] of moral agents. This framework is for the agent in such situations a *given*: It is not simply a new factor to be entered

---

[7] Lyons refers to S. Toulmin's view (in *An Examination of the Place of Reason in Ethics* (New York: Cambridge, 1950) as an 'early theory' that 'had impure second-order criteria, not strictly utilitarian' (12). See also Scanlon, 'Rights, Goals, and Fairness', p. 94 [p. 75 above], for a similar observation, noting that rule utilitarians are hard pressed to explain why direct appeals to consequences are not to be made.

The demand for simplicity and purity of moral theory, coming from at least some act consequentialism, rings especially hollow. The charge is that believers in a two-level system containing agent-constraints rely on mere unargued-for intuition. Yet to raise a presumption against agent-constraints merely on grounds that they complicate an otherwise clean, straight-line appeal to impersonal good seems to me to be yet another use of unargued-for intuition, if not prejudice.

[8] This charge of irrationality has frequently been made by J. J. C. Smart. See 'Extreme and Restricted Utilitarianism', in Bayles, *Contemporary Utilitarianism*, esp. pp. 107–9, and (with B. Williams) *Utilitarianism: For and Against*.

[9] Here I am using 'competence', of course, as a normative concept.

into a general weighing.[10] This does not entail that the framework of authority stands beyond evaluation or even revision. It is to say only that, for the kinds of normative conflicts that interest us here, its validity is not just one among other things to be weighed.

That this model is consistent with full publicity also needs emphasis. Some conceptions of moral theory—perhaps inspired by Henry Sidgwick—proceed by denying full publicity of moral theory to moral agents. The idea is that ordinary persons will adhere to non-consequentialist prohibitions because of a non-consequentialist moral education. Thus it is not supposed to occur to them to violate the prohibitions even where it would be optimific to do so. The élite would know more, but they are few in number. I do not wish to argue here for or against a publicity requirement; I wish merely to point out that the present rationale is consistent with full publicity. Just as a judge can adhere to the requirements of the office, while recognizing the different standards and points of view appropriate to the legislator's office, so too can the moral agent, embracing no logical inconsistency or irrationality, recognize the need to exclude certain kinds of reasons that in other situations would be appropriate. Whether denial of publicity would make adherence generally easier, and what would follow from this for moral education if true, represent. respectively, empirical and inferential questions on which I take no stand.

There are two related but different kinds of concern that are likely to arise with respect to the idea that there are limits on the moral agent's competence to act on wide-ranging normative reasons. Both of these spring from our regard for the moral agent's rationality and autonomy. First, how can it be rational to recognize externally imposed limits on one's own competence? A second question is, how can there be any place for the equal autonomy of all persons to evaluate and revise the structure of their moral rules when they in fact stand under limits placed by an external authority? For those very limits are limits on the

---

[10] On the role of exclusionary reasons and their connection to legitimate authority, see Raz, *The Authority of Law* (New York: Oxford 1979), ch. 1; and his 'Authority and Justification', *Philosophy and Public Affairs*, 14, 1 (Winter 1985). 3–29.

occasions on which fundamental revisions can be made, and to stand under an external authority seems to imply that the competence to make such fundamental revisions belongs to someone *else* (God, an élite, or the majority through the social conventions they establish).[11]

That certain kinds of reason should in some situations be put beyond the purview of the moral agent—excluded, as Joseph Raz would put it—is familiar from the case of promissory obligation. The obligation to do X puts beyond one's reach certain kinds of justificatory reason that otherwise would be quite appropriate: that doing X would be costly, inconvenient, or unappealing. Likewise, the existence of legitimate authority can be a source of exclusionary reasons which the rational person can acknowledge.[12] So the central question is the second one: how can the division-of-labour conception provide for the equal autonomy of all persons in the assessment and revision of their moral code?

Here I shall sketch the answer I develop more fully in the last section of the paper. Having taken our cue from legal and political philosophy in using the judge/legislator distinction, we can draw a bit further from this same source. In the political realm, the ideal of equal autonomy of citizens is unpacked as the equal right of participation in electoral processes—it is the idea that no citizen is more worthy of participation, nor has any right to a larger

---

[11] The robust division-of-labour conception defended here also provides for a robust moral constructivism—a more robust constructivism than that, say, outlined by Rawls in his Dewey Lectures 1980. Rawls's 'Kantian constructivism' emerges from the fact that the parties in the original position choose principles of justice under conditions of freedom and equality. (See *Journal of Philosophy* 77, 9 (Sept. 1980), 515–72.) Here the idea is rather that actual persons in the real world become (within limits) bound by moral legislation that may even be imperfect by the consequentialist standards appropriate to its evaluation. Freedom and equality of moral agents is then represented as the actual real-world freedom of moral agents equally to participate in evaluation and revision of an actual code.

[12] Raz's account of legitimate authority and the kind of justification appropriate to it is important here. (See 'Authority and Justification'.) But it should also be clear that Raz is talking primarily about authority as represented in particular other persons. Authority can also be embodied in collective entities, as defenders of participatory democracy (like Rousseau) would point out. If we are to make plausible the notion of moral-agent competence restricted by an external authority and do this is a way that is plausible to modern moral thinking, we must rely on the notion of collective authority rather than of individual authori*ties*.

influence on legislation and government, than does any other citizen. (It is well also to remember the importance of distinguishing the guiding ideal from the actual political and social circumstances.) Equal autonomy of citizens being protected by providing each with the freedom or fair opportunity to participate in a *collective* enterprise of legislation, the equal autonomy of moral agents is governed by the ideal that no person's moral opinions and judgements have greater standing simply because they emanate from that person. Each moral agent is thought to have equal access to the fundamental principles by which the moral code is evaluated. All are restricted in not always being free to revise the code; but all are equally restricted.

Linked to the concern about moral-agent autonomy is the thought that a division-of-labour conception will lead to a kind of psychological compartmentalization, either in individuals separately or in society generally. This is similar to the charge that Bernard Williams has levelled against utilitarianism, that is, that it would require either an unacceptable esoteric moral élite or an impracticable psychological compartmentalization (Smart and Williams, *Utilitarianism: For and Against*, 135–40).

The importance of such compartmentalization as there might be is easy to exaggerate. First, there is no mysterious intellectual compartmentalization necessary to one's understanding and acting on a division-of-labour conception of moral reasoning—nothing more mysterious than there is for the judge's acting within the constraints of legislation that may not have been the best. And psychological compartmentalization is not entailed by the division-of-labour conception, though admittedly it may make easier one's adherence to the limits of moral authority. Deciding to respect the restrictions on one's authority rather than to go directly for the impersonally best consequences may be hard for those with either a deeply engrained impersonal benevolence or an inclination to arrogate power to themselves. But it seems far too much to demand of a valid morality that it never produce anguish or bad feelings in dilemmatic situations.

There is a remaining point about the attractions of a robust division-of-labour conception of moral reasoning. When we take seriously the idea of individual moral agency as subordinate to an external authority that is literally a different entity, we have the framework for understanding a surprisingly broad set of different moral conceptions. Though the framework is consistent with a liberal conception of the equal autonomy of all moral agents, it has the advantage of allowing us to place quite different moral conceptions—for example, what might be called 'law conceptions of ethics'[13]—within it. This is so because different moral conceptions are in large part determined by different views about how extensive an authority the ordinary moral agent is understood to have; by the nature of that external authority (for example, whether a priestly class, God, or special representatives of the collective will); and by the nature of each individual agent's participation (if any) in the exercise of that authority.

III

In 'Two Concepts of Rules', Rawls emphasizes that the distinction between justifying a practice and justifying an action falling under it is a logical distinction. As he put it, 'One can be as radical as one likes but in the case of actions specified by practices the objects of one's radicalism must be the social practices and people's acceptance of them' (97). The notion that this is a logical distinction only and not a substantive one (i.e., one with conservative implications) needs examination and clarification. Rawls says, '[w]here a form of action is specified by a practice there is no justification possible of the particular action of a particular person save by reference to the practice' (97).

That the moral agent's authority is limited to justification under a practice is indeed a substantive limitation. Not being free to save innocent lives by killing an innocent is not a stricture imposed on us by logic. The advocacy of the stricture does reflect a substantively different attitude from that expressed by its denial. But the recognition of such a stricture in particular cases is

---

[13] The term 'law conception of ethics' I borrow from G. E. M. Anscombe's article 'Modern Moral Philosophy'. Anscombe's discussion usefully attracts attention to the contemporary problem of identifying a suitable legislator so to make sense of a law conception without divine sources and without worship of society's prevailing norms.

consistent with a wide spectrum of attitudes about how easy it should be for the rules to be restructured. It is perhaps this latter logical independence that Rawls had in mind when claiming that his was a logical point. The notion that a moral agent's authority is limited, however, requires philosophical argument, as does any other restriction with normative consequences. Neither it nor its negation should simply be imported into ethical theory as an unstated methodological assumption.

Here it does not add conviction to belabour the distinction between a summary conception of rules and a practice conception. Though the summary conception may, as Rawls suggests, miss the logical distinction between justifying a practice and justifying a particular action falling under it, it will hardly be enough, in explaining to a moral agent why he should adhere to the rule when doing so would admittedly not produce the best consequences, to claim that failure to do so would reflect lack of understanding of a logical distinction. It would thus be more to the point to tell such a moral agent: 'Your authority to do so is limited by the authority of society (or of God).' The account of why society or God has such authority can proceed from there, but it should proceed.

Two points about the 'derivation' of a deontological from a consequentialist point of view should be made. The division-of-labour conception defended here does explain how individual agent-restrictions can arise from broadly consequentialist considerations. In that sense, it provides a reconciliation of deontological and consequentialist insights. But is it deontological in the deeper sense of Kant and Rawls, i.e., of deriving the right without reference to any particular conception of the good?[14] The answer is not obvious. If a particular judgement of right is justified because it accords with a practice and if the most justified practice is in fact a *different* one which would generate a different result, then the agent's lack of authority to appeal directly to the consequences then and there constitutes a break in the chain from the good to the right: we cannot without qualification hold that the right has been derived from the good. It is perhaps this loose-

---

[14] For the distinction between the two kinds of deontology, I follow M. J. Sandel, *Liberalism and the Limits of Justice* (New York: Cambridge, 1982), pp. 2–3.

jointedness in the rule-utilitarian view that gives rise to uneasiness that it is not really pure utilitarianism. On the other hand, we cannot obtain any rules with which to operate unless we start from a conception of the good, and this conception of the good is also necessary to any evaluation and restructuring of the rules. In that sense, the right is derived from the good.

A second issue about derivation is that posed by Nagel. An advantage of the division-of-labour conception of moral authority is that it renders less mysterious the relationship between what Nagel calls the 'subjective' and 'objective' points of view. Nagel's three alternatives—reduction, elimination, and annexation (*Mortal Questions*, p. 210)—are indeed all unacceptable ways of reconciling deontological constraints of the subjective point of view with the impersonal evaluation of the consequentialist view. Hence elimination of the subjective viewpoint on grounds that it is an illusion simply does not do justice to the deeply engrained power that deontological intuitions exercise in our thinking. Their status seems as secure as those providing us with impersonal, consequentialist evaluations. Attempts at reduction create our initial problem: that if the wrongness of violating a restriction consists in creating some disvalue, then minimizing that kind of disvalue ought to be the goal, even if it sometimes means violating the restriction.

The reduction alternative is more plausible when cast in a different form, i.e., when reduction of the deontological view to the consequentialist is not expected in every agent-situation.[15] Rather, *this* agent in *this* situation must adhere to restriction *R* without allowing consequentialist considerations any full impact. But restriction *R* is open to full consequentialist evaluation in some different agent-situation. The reduction is thus a bona fide reduction, but via a more circuitous route, and without the implication that it can take place on each occasion. The two viewpoints are compartmentalized, but no more mysteriously than those of any other two offices that perform different functions and

[15] By this I mean only to allow for the possibility that limits on moral authority may attach to agent-situations rather than to agents as such or to 'situations' as such. An agent-situation S_1 is different from S_2 just when either the agent or the situation (loose as that notion may be) is different.

to which different structures of normative reasoning attach though the offices both belong to the same system.

What of an objection from the opposite direction? Instead of claiming that the first level is not really deontological, someone might object that the second level of the model is not really consequentialist, since there are 'impure' second-order criteria for determining when consequentialist considerations apply. In particular, pure consequentialist reasoning applies only to the evaluation and legislation of first-level rules, and *procedural* rules (or considerations) play a role in preventing some agent-situations from reducing to an instance of legislating. Thus procedural rules requiring, say, that legislation could never occur except prospectively for future situations, and not without some form of general acceptance, would prevent the reduction. (I do not claim that the procedural considerations for dividing the labour of moral reasoning would be quite this simple or quite so well defined.) But then the objector might hold that these procedural rules constitute an impurity in the putatively consequentialist theory.

In answer to this, several points must be made. Though there are procedural rules, the main consequentialist idea remains intact: the first-order moral rules are always to be evaluated by purely consequentialist considerations. No deontological elements get smuggled in here. The situation is analogous to that in which an organization is committed unanimously to a single abstract goal, and recognizes that *any* evaluation of the organization's rules—whether for idle philosophical purposes, for legislative deliberations, or from the standpoint of an individual making the ultimate decision that the organization has strayed so far from its goal that the rules are no longer to be respected[16]—must be made solely in light of that goal. In such an organization, there is typically still a need for procedural rules determining how the legislative process is carried out and who participates in it. First-order moral rules can in an analogous way be assessed by purely consequentialist criteria. It *would* embrace a covertly deontological

---

[16] To be precise, when the agent is in the position of having to judge the rules as so utilitarianly defective as to carry no authority, the deliberation involves weighing the quality of the rules (a purely goal-orientated evaluation) against the pull of authority, which may then be overridden.

view to claim that killing or lying is always wrong in every society regardless of the consequences of having such rules, that everyone making moral legislative deliberations must enact only legislation consistent with this, and that contrary legislation cannot be binding on the individual moral agent. That is not, however, the model I am trying to sketch. It should also be mentioned here that moral legislators might weigh in the balance such consequentialist considerations as how power would tend to be distributed in society given a certain set of rules—i.e., whether the clever would have more *de facto* power than the less clever, or whether an unequal distribution of agent discretion would be outweighed by some greater good. Given the possibility of a distribution-sensitive theory of the good, there would be no covert deontologism in this, either.

A final point about the impurity objection. Suppose that it is insisted: in order for a two-level moral theory to be consequentialist at its foundations, you must demonstrate (*a*) that it is rational in each and every situation to adhere to the procedural rules separating legislative- from individual agent-authority: *and* (*b*) that it is rational because it is optimific in each situation. The levels theory here proposes to demonstrate (*a*), but does not propose to demonstrate (*b*), which is almost certainly false. The demonstration of (*a*) uses the assumption that a rational moral agent can sometimes be subordinate to authority, and takes this assumption as part of the background framework *within* which the two-tiered account is presented. Those who still insist that a purely consequentialist account must also demonstrate (*b*) virtually guarantee that such an account will collapse into ordinary act consequentialism. But their argument begs the question. It is too redolent of tautology to be very interesting.

Scheffler (107) has rejected as failures various attempts to provide a rationale for agent-centred restrictions. The 'strongest kind of case', he thinks, is represented by the following sort of argument: the 'natural independence of the moral point of view', someone might claim, is rationally served by limiting standards of individual conduct to the personal perspective of the individual agent rather than tolerating the individual's pursuit of the best outcome as judged impersonally. Thus, the argument would run, agents are properly held to a standard of accountability that gives the 'intrinsic qualities' of an individual's acts moral priority over their impersonal optimality.

As Scheffler points out, this argument misconstrues the nature of the individual point of view in supposing that individuals are not permitted to form and act on intentions to do things having the (impersonally) best outcome. In short, why *require* that the agent not adopt the pursuit of impersonally best consequences, if that be the agent's choice?

The proffered defence of agent-centred restrictions is indeed weak, but other defences would be far more attractive than this is, resting as it does on the vague and one-sided notion of 'natural independence of the moral point of view'. The notion is one-sided because, as foundation for the attempt to derive restrictions on the agent's authority, it provides only the core idea of the *agent's* independence and the *agent's* perspective. The agent's perspective and independence, important as they may be, are not balanced by considerations taken from a social perspective, as represented by the external authority in which the agent participates but to which the agent is also subordinate. A related point is that the concept of the agent's perspective does not in itself bring any consideration of how *all* agent-orientated perspectives will fit together in a coherent system. This Kantian-sounding demand does not require an abandonment of consequentialism as the deeper foundation of theory; it requires only a more robust than usual conception of the distinction between legislative and judicial roles in moral thinking. But, most important, it is at least unpromising to seek the reasons for agent-*restrictions* in the notion of an agent's independence and perspective. The restrictions look more plausible when viewed from a legislative perspective that is separated from the judicial (i.e., deontological) by procedural rules. Taken together, the freedom of each must be limited, but this is a decision that is rational *on purely consequential grounds* only from the legislator's perspective. And even considerations of unfairness of consequences might enter here, if the account of good somehow weighs unfairness in the scales. But that would be different from taking unfairness as in itself a restriction on the individual's competence to weigh reasons.

What of the attempt to redescribe this situation in consequentialist terms? The objector might thus claim that here again we could have the familiar dilemma: violating the restriction R (forbidding self-arrogation of agent authority) which has the disvalue N_1, or not violating the restriction, which results in $N_1 + N_2$ (still more agents violating the restriction). Scheffler makes the point in connection with the evil mentioned by Charles Fried,[17] that of not respecting persons:

> It is obviously no answer to this question to simply claim that any minimizing harm must itself be a violation of respect for persons. For even if that is so (and it is far from obvious that it is), it is also the case that any such action must serve to minimize the total number of instances of comparable disrespect for persons. (Scheffler, 107)

Here the objection would exactly miss the mark. For the limits on the agent's authority to appeal to consequences may make it improper for the agent to take these consequences into account as well. It is not that the consequences here are unusual; it is that, again, the agent from the outset does not have authority to weigh them in reaching a decision. Considerations pointing to disvalues like N_1 and $N_1 + N_2$ are properly viewed as considerations showing the rationality of the restriction, but they are not considerations directed to this agent in this situation to adopt rather than reject the restriction. *That* question, though open on other occasions, is closed for this agent here and now.

If misunderstood, this conception of restrictions on agent authority can appear to be much weaker than it is, thus making the two-tiered system I am trying to sketch seem unstable. I shall therefore summarize and explain its main components, emphasizing in the process the differences from familiar rule utilitarianisms. The conception requires that we make sense of the following elements individually and that they together be consistent: (1) the rational person can sometimes stand under the authority of another (an individual or a collective entity), so that rules the other has adopted and imposed become moral reasons for action, and such that the usual full range of consequentialist reasons becomes restricted. (2) *When* the authority (whom we shall designate *moral legislator*) makes a decision about what rules to impose, no such restrictions on weighing consequences apply, and the decision is to be made on the basis of what rules are optimific. (3) The reasons why the moral agent is subordinate to the authority of the moral legislator, and what precisely determines the kinds of situation in which the agent is subordinate, is a question independent of (2), i.e., might, so far as (2) is concerned, be given either a deontological or a consequentialist treatment. (4) Though the moral legislator is required to impose rules that are optimific, a moral agent may nevertheless sometimes be bound by rules that are *not* optimific in general or in their application in particular situations. This is so because the moral legislator may have made a mistake, or the moral code may not have been revised recently enough. This springs directly from the fact that (5) the moral legislator and the moral agent are *literally* not the same entity in the same place and time.[18] (6) The moral autonomy of the individual, requiring the possibility of each agent's participation in unconstrained[19] consequentialist evaluation of

[18] This is very closely connected to Rousseau's problem and solution in Book 1, ch. 7 of *The Social Contract* when he seeks simultaneous reconciliation of three demands: (i) maximum equal autonomy of the individual to participate in sovereign decisions; (ii) the individual's obligation to live under the authority of that same sovereign; and (iii) the sovereign's collective *freedom* from any such restrictions. Thus he says: 'Here there can be no invoking the principle of civil law which says that no man is bound by a contract with himself, for there is a great difference between having an obligation to oneself and having an obligation to something of which one is a member.

'We must add that a public decision can impose an obligation on all the subjects towards the sovereign, by reason of the two aspects under which each can be seen, while, contrariwise, such decisions cannot impose an obligation on the sovereign towards itself' (M. Cranston, trans. (Middlesex, England: Penguin Books, 1968), p. 62).

[19] Unconstrained, that is, with respect to determining the best or most eligible rule for legislative enactment. However, there are constraints in the sense that, given the procedural rules requiring that other participants in the legislative process agree or that the issue can be taken up only on certain occasions, that which is best may not get enacted, or not get enacted immediately. But this kind of constraint leaves the second-tier consequentialist; for it remains true that the ultimate and only correct guide for evaluating hypothetical or actual moral legislation, whenever the question arises, is consequentialist. The only constraints are those which provide a robust demarcation between acting merely in the capacity of individual moral agent and acting in the capacity of moral legislator (or as member of a collective in the act of legislating). This is very different from pointing to such evils as unfairness or self-arrogation as additional consequences to be weighed or

moral rules, can be secured, among other possibilities, by guaranteeing equal participation of each agent in the process of moral legislation,[20] which in fact means *in part*, 'No person is more eligible to participate in second-order moral debate and criticism of first-order rules than any other.'

Feature (4) illustrates clearly the differences from usual forms of rule utilitarianism. Notice that if we are wedded to the idea that it is only *optimal* rules that can ever be binding on individual moral agents at any time, then even though the moral agent might still ask what that *hypothetical* authority *would* legislate, either this leaves open the question of why the individual moral agent should care about what a hypothetical authority would legislate, or it puts the moral agent in the position of that legislator, using the legislator's consequentialist reasoning to determine what must be done in the instant case (perhaps to fashion a sufficiently precise rule that provides for essentially the same result).

Feature (5) incorporates the procedural criteria for the evaluation and change of at least certain moral rules. These procedural considerations are constraints in some sense; but not such as to vitiate the consequentialist character of the second tier. They delineate only the circumstances and occasions for new or revised rules to come into being. As such, they allow that any and all evaluation, criticism, and definite judgement about the first-tier rules—whether hypothetical or as part of a binding judgement—are to be made on purely consequentialist grounds.

On the present model, the substance of the procedural considerations becomes the focus of the question, whether a particular version of the two-level conception is 'conservative' or not. On the one hand, it should be clear that acceptance of this two-level conception does not commit one to the view that moral right is defined simply by existing conventions. For example, how important a role is played by agreement or some form of

weighable in every agent's balance, whatever the situation. Having assumed that the appropriate person or group can have authority over the rational moral agent, thereby restricting the range of the agent's available reasons, we do not need to look for even more exotic consequences for the agent to take into account.

[20] Again, this is not to say that every moral decision is equivalent to a legislative question: the requirement is for equal, rather than unconstrained, participation.

acceptance as part of the legislation of new moral rules is a question about the nature of the procedural criteria. Obviously, the greater the role played by actual acceptance, the more a particular two-tiered conception would tend toward conservative worship of existing convention. The two-level model I have argued for requires only that *some* substantive distinction be made between legislative and individual agent's roles and has the virtue of leaving as a separate and open question what procedural criteria apply, and in what segments of morality.

Some words of caution are necessary regarding the (somewhat) metaphorical notions of the 'enactment' of moral legislation in accordance with 'procedural' considerations. This process has nothing like the definite and formal character that characterizes its analogue in law. Nor should we expect, especially in a pluralistic and shifting moral climate, that we can forge any clear consensus as to what these procedural criteria are, the extent (if any) to which we are subordinate to an external authority, or the degree of authority thus conferred on conventional rules. Indeed, we should expect that there will be inveterate disagreement about this in a society in which act utilitarians exist side by side with respecters of external moral authority. What I have attempted to do is to understand what I would regard as a family of moral conceptions and, thus, to understand the view that one can be under agent-constraints while simultaneously recognizing that those constraints can in the appropriate circumstances be evaluated on wholly consequentialist grounds.

Some may object to the model because they consider it simply inconsistent with rationality or with moral autonomy for any moral agent to stand under authority in this sense. Thus one might hold that there are occasionally reasons for following what society or another individual requires of us, but that these reasons are either prudential or open in every case to familiar consequentialist weighing (as distinguished, again, from consequentialist evaluation and revision only in some situations). I do not provide here any argument to convert such sceptics about moral authority. Such objectors then miss a promising possibility for accounting for deontological restrictions in a way cognizant of consequentialism's appeal, or they are from the outset simply not swayed by deontological conceptions or by ethical conceptions modelled on juridical ideas.

If the model so far sketched is adequate, it provides for a genuinely two-tiered conception of moral thinking, one that does not, on closer inspection, collapse into a single level. Given that it provides for more than one tier, we must bear in mind several points. Some of these belong to the category of likely misunderstandings to be avoided, and others constitute reminders of the genuine advantages obtainable from the multi-tiered conception.

The first point is that misunderstandings are especially likely if we forget the level on which the questions are being asked. (Perhaps nothing is more characteristic of levels conceptions, from Rawls to Hare, than the remainder to keep track of the level.) Thus consider again the notion of agent discretion and the self-arrogation of power. There are two quite different ways of looking at such self-arrogations, corresponding to the level from which they are viewed. From a legislative point of view, it may be thought that, for practical reasons as well as for reasons springing from the theory of the good, it may be necessary to limit agent discretion. A distribution-sensitive conception of the good might well take into account the way in which the good of agent-discretion is distributed, and take especially seriously the need that it be equally distributed (or roughly so). From the legislative point of view it would also be appropriate to take into account the extent to which temptation to engage in certain acts is deep and widespread, and also to take into account the degree of evil resulting from those acts. The moral code adopted from the legislative point of view will then reflect such considerations, but the agent acting within the code (in the 'deontological position') will be bound by the code and have reason to think of certain acts simply as wrong because a violation of the code. Self-arrogation as a wrong because a violation of the code is therefore one thing; self-arrogation as an evil in society for which we need a moral code as the remedy is another.

Further, it may seem that we as ordinary moral agents making judgements and decisions must take into account the seriousness of consequences when we decide how serious a wrong happens to be, and that this fact therefore vitiates the idea that agents in the deontological position must stick to the rules rather than focus on the consequences. Killing, for example, is a self-arrogation, just as telling a small lie is. But killing is far more serious than telling a small lie, and it seems that we can conclude this only by reflecting on the greater evil resulting from a killing.

There are several reasons why from the moral legislator's perspective human moral agents might be excluded from carrying out this weighing.[21] Human beings are subject to evil temptations; they will kill for the wrong reasons if not put under social pressure through a moral code; and the moral code's prohibitions must in some circumstances be especially simple, strict, and eminently teachable. But this is only the legislative perspective. The agent constraints must first be adopted and imposed from the legislative perspective, and then the agent is no longer permitted to reason by weighing evils. The constraints are then taken seriously by individual agents, though not because of the conception of good that is their rationale. The reason they are categorical for the individual agent is connected instead to the authority of the legislator over the individual agent. But at the same time, there is here, just as in the straightforwardly legal analogue, a place for the theory of the good within the grading of wrongs. Two different kinds of action—telling a minor lie and killing an innocent person—may both be wrong in the first instance because of the authority of the legislator. However, because the theory of the good places great weight on the value of innocent life, and great weight as well on the evil of conscious decisions to take innocent life, that kind of action would be graded a far more serious wrong by the legislator. The seriousness of the wrong would then be taken into account by moral agents when judging the character and the wrongs of wrongdoers. And what is especially important here is that, where the moral code is established and is within some

[21] T. Nagel has made a significant observation about the moral freedom of certain office holders, and this observation seems especially relevant here. The decisions of a President or Secretary of Defense may result in the foreseeable deaths of hundreds of innocents, and the decision maker is insulated from personal moral responsibility by the very office: restrictions that would otherwise apply in the pursuit of desirable end results are loosened significantly. See 'Ruthlessness in Public Life', in S. Hampshire, ed., *Public and Private Morality* (New York: Cambridge, 1978), pp. 75–91.

appropriate limits justified by the consequentialist rationale that is its normative foundation, moral agents do not need to engage in legislative reflections about ideal moral codes in order to make the needed judgements.

Two-level views have great advantages in answering perplexing questions in moral philosophy, and this gives them a certain initial credibility. One such question has been raised by Michael Slote. This he calls the 'self-other asymmetry' in common-sense morality.[22] He notes, in addition to the familiar problems about the reconciliation of agent-constraints with consequentialism, that there is the following perplexing fact about ordinary morality: it is permissible not to benefit oneself, and instead to favour others. even when this leads to less than optimific consequences (180). This, Slote suggests, 'appears odd and unmotivated'.[23]

Once we adopt a legislative point of view, an appealing explanation for the puzzle lies close at hand. We human beings are endowed with a fully adequate supply of self-love, indeed selfishness. It is hardly necessary for a social moral code to exert pressure on individuals to seek their own advancement and pleasure. Thus our moral thinking is full of obligations and other requirements to do good and avoid evil where others are concerned, but says little about the importance of pursuing our own good. This is just as we would expect it to be. Further, this *general* fact about human beings is only a general fact, and where particular persons may need the opposite kind of pressure, we are naturally bereft of the moral-code resources to ground special

[22] 'Morality and Self-other Asymmetry', *The Journal of Philosophy* 81, 4 (Apr. 1984), 179–92.

[23] 'Morality and Self-other Asymmetry', p. 185. In conversation, Slote has recalled the difficulties some might find in the whole notion of morality as a kind of public-policy and practical question of 'legislating' a moral code. Thus, what if we are to think of morality as a code of abstractly correct norms for behaviour, and that questions of practicality, simplicity, and other empirical facts about humans and their situation belong elsewhere, and not in our conception of what a valid morality is? Objections of this sort raise very deep and far-reaching issues which cannot be adequately addressed here. But, in view of the facts that morality is above all practical and action-guiding and that morality is something to be taught, remembered, and otherwise used by imperfect humans, it is this conception of the moral right as a kind of set of ideal forms—rather than the view of moral right as linked to the empirical and practical—that comes to us carrying a heavy presumption against it.

criticism in these special cases. We are left to the unusual but wholly explainable task of making appeals to a too-pale self-interest.

In the same way, we can obtain (or preserve) an illuminating perspective on the question of whether demonstrating the existence of agent-constraints in a two-level account brings with it a denial of agent *options* sometimes to do less than what would be impersonally optimific.[24] Failure to include in the code a strict requirement to sacrifice *oneself* in pursuit of impersonal good might be rational on several grounds: it might reasonably be judged better in the long run to allow people to direct attention in most cases to their own projects, on the assumption that that is where natural motivation lies and that doing private projects well contributes more to impersonal good than doing public projects rather badly. And though there are plenty of exceptions that the moral code could theoretically be made to reflect, considerations of simplicity, teachability, guilt feelings, and likelihood of mistake may militate against limiting agent options very much. If it be asked why the options left by the code are not eliminated by the direct application of impersonal consequentialist reasons, we would have to recall how *requirements* (as opposed to credit for supererogatory deeds) come into existence. They arise from some form of *collective* action or decision, and this is a function belonging to the whole. One does not impose *requirements* on *oneself* just for oneself, any more than one makes a binding promise to oneself; for in either case we are too free to release ourselves from the commitment for it to count as obligation.[25] And to think of requirements as directly imposed by a consequentialist principle is already to opt for a very different moral conception: it

[24] I draw this problem from 'The Limits of Morality', a Ph.D. dissertation by S. Kagan. Kagan's belief that the 'moderate' position (represented by familiar two-level accounts) is caught in the dilemma of establishing agent-constraints only if agent options are simultaneously denied is rendered less plausible when we think of the legislative perspective in the way I have suggested, i.e., as robustly distinguished from the individual agent's pespective.

[25] A corollary of the robust two-level conception is the possibility that not every existing agent-constraint or option is optimific. So long as it is not too far from being the best, it can still be binding on the agent until revised in a way that accords with proper procedure.

is to opt for a non-constructivist view that has no place for genuinely separate legislative and individual-agent functions.[26]

Some may find an extremely close similarity between the division-of-labour view I have defended here and the two-tier conception defended recently by Thomas Scanlon. Scanlon represents individual rights that must be respected as complexes of new (and important) goals to be weighed by the agent in deciding what is right. He holds that the new goals rest not so much on an idea of maximizing good consequences as on minimizing bad ones. In any case, they represent additional values to be weighed in the agent's balance, and in this way his view contains no real analogue to the central element of my own, that of a restriction on agent authority imposed from the point of view of an authority made distinct and external by something like procedural rules defining the legislative role.[27] My own view proceeds rather by taking Rawls's judge–legislator model more literally than even Rawls intended, making legislation something like an actual separate function and not just a conceptual or heuristic device for the moral agent.

Central to the robust judge–legislator model is the notion of external authority. Only something like the notion of external authority, I contend, captures the sense of subordination and the role of others in limiting one's own competence. This is characteristic of deontological ethical views, the force of which two-tier conceptions try to capture.

Without making any large claims about the history of ideas, it is possible to connect the modern problem of explaining agent restrictions to a particular route that the development of moral ideas might have taken. When people take seriously the idea of the authority of God over their lives, a law conception of ethics, with its notion of agent-constraints, lies close at hand. When the

---

[26] I suspect, but cannot here prove, that other well-entrenched though puzzling aspects of common-sense morality would appear less puzzling if the puzzled used and kept in mind a levels conception. For example, making a moral distinction between causing harm and allowing it to happen, even where this involves drawing some admittedly arbitrary lines, seems an eminently more plausible project for a legislator than for an individual agent who must decide, as it were, what to do in the absence of any binding code.

[27] See Scanlon, 'Rights, Goals, and Fairness', esp. pp. 104–7 [pp. 85–8 in this volume—Ed.].

authority of God is removed from the picture, either because of metaphysical doubts about God's existence or because the idea of God's authority in the moral sphere is thought inconsistent with the autonomy of the moral agent, there still remains the Rousseauian expedient of identifying authority with some sovereign collective social entity within which each moral agent plays an equally important role. Taken fairly literally, this idea yields the elements of authority; the external character of authority; the stability of the levels corresponding to the two roles; and the equal autonomy of each moral agent. But if we take a further step beyond this—a step which many contemporary moral philosophers appear to have taken whether they realize it or not—and insist that rational moral autonomy is inconsistent with the acceptance of any kind of authority that rests for the agent on a ground independent of the goals it is supposed to advance, then the path to act consequentialism is short and direct.

NOTES ON CONTRIBUTORS

PHILIPPA FOOT is Professor of Philosophy at the University of California, Los Angeles, and a Senior Research Fellow of Somerville College, Oxford.

CONRAD JOHNSON is Associate Professor of Philosophy at the University of Maryland.

THOMAS NAGEL is Professor of Philosophy at New York University.

ROBERT NOZICK is Professor of Philosophy at Harvard University.

DEREK PARFIT is a Fellow of All Souls College, Oxford.

PETER RAILTON is Associate Professor of Philosophy at the University of Michigan.

JOHN RAWLS is Professor of Philosophy at Harvard University.

T. M. SCANLON is Professor of Philosophy at Harvard University.

SAMUEL SCHEFFLER is Professor of Philosophy at the University of California, Berkeley.

AMARTYA SEN is Professor of Economics and Philosophy at Harvard University.

BERNARD WILLIAMS is Professor of Philosophy at the University of California, Berkeley.

SELECTED BIBLIOGRAPHY

Books

BRANDT, RICHARD, *A Theory of the Good and the Right* (Oxford: Clarendon Press, 1979).

DONAGAN, ALAN, *The Theory of Morality* (Chicago: University of Chicago Press, 1977).

FRIED, CHARLES, *Right and Wrong* (Cambridge, Mass.: Harvard University Press, 1978).

GLOVER, JONATHAN, *Causing Death and Saving Lives* (Harmondsworth: Penguin Books, 1977).

GRIFFIN, JAMES, *Well-being: Its Meaning, Measurement, and Moral Importance* (Oxford: Clarendon Press, 1986).

HARE, R. M., *Moral Thinking* (Oxford: Clarendon Press, 1981).

HODGSON, D. H., *Consequences of Utilitarianism* (Oxford: Clarendon Press, 1967).

LYONS, DAVID, *Forms and Limits of Utilitarianism* (Oxford: Clarendon Press, 1965).

MILL, JOHN STUART, *Utilitarianism* (London, 1863).

NAGEL, THOMAS, *The View from Nowhere* (New York: Oxford University Press, 1986).

NOZICK, ROBERT, *Anarchy, State, and Utopia* (New York: Basic Books, 1974).

PARFIT, DEREK, *Reasons and Persons* (Oxford: Clarendon Press, 1984).

RAWLS, JOHN, *A Theory of Justice* (Cambridge, Mass.: Harvard University Press, 1971).

RAZ, JOSEPH, *The Morality of Freedom* (Oxford: Clarendon Press, 1986).

REGAN, DONALD, *Utilitarianism and Co-operation* (Oxford: Clarendon Press, 1980).

ROSS, W. D., *The Right and the Good* (Oxford: Clarendon Press, 1930).

SCHEFFLER, SAMUEL, *The Rejection of Consequentialism: A Philosophical Investigation of the Considerations Underlying Rival Moral Conceptions* (Oxford: Clarendon Press, 1982).

SIDGWICK, HENRY, *The Methods of Ethics* (7th edn.) (London: Macmillan & Co., Ltd., 1907).

SLOTE, MICHAEL, *Common-sense Morality and Consequentialism* (London: Routledge & Kegan Paul, 1985).

WILLIAMS, BERNARD, *Ethics and the Limits of Philosophy* (London: Fontana Press, 1985).

Collections and Anthologies

DWORKIN, RONALD, *Taking Rights Seriously* (Harvard University Press, 1977).

FREY, R. G. (ed.), *Utility and Rights* (University of Minnesota Press, 1984).

MACKIE, J. L., *Persons and Values* (Oxford: Clarendon Press, 1985).

SEN, A. and B. WILLIAMS (eds.), *Utilitarianism and Beyond* (Cambridge University Press, 1982).

SMART, J. J. C. and B. WILLIAMS, *Utilitarianism: For and Against* (Cambridge University Press, 1973).

STEINBOCK, BONNIE, *Killing and Letting Die* (Englewood Cliffs, New Jersey: Prentice-Hall, 1980).

Articles

ADAMS, ROBERT, 'Motive Utilitarianism', *Journal of Philosophy* 73 (1976), 467–81.

ANSCOMBE, G. E. M., 'Modern Moral Philosophy', *Philosophy* 33 (1958), 1–19. Reprinted in Judith J. Thomson and Gerald Dworkin, eds., *Ethics* (New York: Harper and Row, 1968), pp. 186–210.

—— *Mr Truman's Degree* (privately printed).

BALES, R. EUGENE, 'Act-utilitarianism: Account of Right-making Characteristics or Decision-making Procedure?', *American Philosophical Quarterly* 8 (1971), 257–65.

BENNETT, JONATHAN, ' "Whatever the Consequences" ', *Analysis* 26 (1966), 83–102. Reprinted in *Killing and Letting Die*, ed. Bonnie Steinbock, pp. 109–27.

BRINK, DAVID O., 'Utilitarian Morality and the Personal Point of View', *Journal of Philosophy* 83 (1986), 417–38.

CONEE, EARL, 'On Seeking a Rationale', *Philosophy and Phenomenological Research* 45 (1985), 601–9.

DARWALL, STEPHEN L., 'Agent-centred Restrictions from the Inside Out', *Philosophical Studies* 50 (1986), 291–319.

DAVIS, NANCY, 'Utilitarianism and Responsibility', *Ratio* 22 (1980), 15–35.

—— 'The Priority of Avoiding Harm', in *Killing and Letting Die*, ed. Bonnie Steinbock, pp. 173–214.

FEINBERG, JOEL, 'The Nature and Value of Rights', *Journal of Value Inquiry* 4 (1970), 243–57.

FOOT, PHILIPPA, 'The Problem of Abortion and the Doctrine of the Double Effect', *Oxford Review* 5 (1967), 5–15. Reprinted in Philippa Foot, *Virtues and Vices* (Berkeley: University of California Press, 1978), pp. 19–32.

—— 'Morality, Action, and Outcome', in *Morality and Objectivity: A Tribute to J. L. Mackie*, ed. Ted Honderich (London: Routledge and Kegan Paul, 1985), pp. 23–38.

GRIFFIN, JAMES, 'Are There Incommensurable Values?', *Philosophy and Public Affairs* 7 (1977), 39–59.

—— 'Modern Utilitarianism', *Revue internationale de philosophie* 141 (1982).

HARRIS, JOHN, 'Williams on Negative Responsibility and Integrity', *Philosophical Quarterly* 24 (1974), 265–73.

—— 'The Survival Lottery', *Philosophy* 50 (1975), 81–7.

HART, H. L. A., 'Between Utility and Rights', *Columbia Law Review* 79 (1979), 828–46.

KAGAN, SHELLY, 'Does Consequentialism Demand Too Much?', *Philosophy and Public Affairs* 13 (1984), 239–54.

KAMM, FRANCES MYRNA, 'Killing and Letting Die: Methodological and Substantive Issues', *Pacific Philosophical Quarterly* 64 (1983), 297–312.

—— 'Supererogation and Obligation', *Journal of Philosophy* 82 (1985), 118–38.

LYONS, DAVID, 'Rights, Claimants, and Beneficiaries', *American Philosophical Quarterly* 6 (1969), 173–85.

—— 'Human Rights and the General Welfare', *Philosophy and Public Affairs* 6 (1977), 113–29.

MORILLO, CAROLYN, 'Doing, Refraining, and the Strenuousness of Morality', *American Philosophical Quarterly* 14 (1977), 29–39.

NAGEL, THOMAS, 'Libertarianism Without Foundations', *Yale Law Journal* 85 (1975), 136–49.

—— 'Subjective and Objective', in Thomas Nagel, *Mortal Questions* (Cambridge University Press, 1979), pp. 196–213.

—— 'The Limits of Objectivity', in *The Tanner Lectures on Human Values*, I, ed. S. McMurrin (University of Utah Press and Cambridge University Press, 1980), pp. 77–139.

PARFIT, DEREK, 'Later Selves and Moral Principles', in *Philosophy and Personal Relations*, ed. Alan Montefiore (London: Routledge and Kegan Paul, 1973), pp. 137–69.

—— 'Innumerate Ethics', *Philosophy and Public Affairs* 7 (1978), 285–301.

—— 'Prudence, Morality, and the Prisoner's Dilemma', *Proceedings of the British Academy* 65 (1979), 539–64.

PIPER, ADRIAN M. S., 'Utility, Publicity, and Manipulation', *Ethics* 88 (1978), 189–206.

—— 'A Distinction without a Difference', *Midwest Studies in Philosophy* 7: *Social and Political Philosophy* (University of Minnesota Press, 1982), 403–35.

RAWLS, JOHN, 'Kantian Constructivism in Moral Theory: The Dewey Lectures 1980', *Journal of Philosophy* 77 (1980), 515–72.

—— 'Social Unity and Primary Goods', in *Utilitarianism and Beyond*, ed. Sen and Williams, pp. 159–85.

RAZ, JOSEPH, 'Permissions and Supererogation', *American Philosophical Quarterly* 12 (1975), 161–8.

SCANLON, T. M., 'Preference and Urgency', *Journal of Philosophy* 72 (1975), 655–69.

—— 'Contractualism and Utilitarianism', in *Utilitarianism and Beyond*, ed. Sen and Williams, pp. 103–28.

SEN, AMARTYA, 'Utilitarianism and Welfarism', *Journal of Philosophy* 76 (1979), 463–89.

—— 'Well-being, Agency and Freedom: The Dewey Lectures 1984', *Journal of Philosophy* 82 (1985), 169–221.

SINGER, PETER, 'Famine, Affluence, and Morality', *Philosophy and Public Affairs* 1 (1972), 229–43.

SMART, J. J. C., 'An Outline of a System of Utilitarian Ethics' in J. J. C. Smart and Bernard Williams, *Utilitarianism: For and Against*, pp. 3–74.

TAUREK, JOHN, 'Should the Numbers Count?', *Philosophy and Public Affairs* 6 (1977), 293–316.

THOMSON, JUDITH, 'Killing, Letting Die, and the Trolley Problem', *The Monist* 59 (1976), 204–17.

—— 'Self-defence and Rights', The Lindley Lecture (University of Kansas, 1976).

WILLIAMS, BERNARD, 'Persons, Character and Morality', in Bernard Williams, *Moral Luck* (Cambridge University Press, 1981), pp. 1–19.

—— 'Utilitarianism and Moral Self-indulgence', in Bernard Williams, *Moral Luck*, pp. 40–53.

WOLF, SUSAN, 'Moral Saints', *Journal of Philosophy* 79 (1982), 419–39.

INDEX OF NAMES

Made in the USA
Middletown, DE
09 January 2015